WORK AND MIGRATION: CASE STUDI
THE WORLD

I0061569

WORK AND MIGRATION: CASE STUDIES FROM AROUND THE WORLD

Editor

Fethiye Tilbe and Elli Heikkilä

TRANSNATIONAL PRESS LONDON

2021

MIGRATION SERIES: 37

Work and Migration: Case Studies from around the World

Edited by Fethiye Tilbe and Elli Heikkilä

Copyright © 2021 Transnational Press London

First Published in 2021 by TRANSNATIONAL PRESS LONDON in the United Kingdom, 13 Stamford Place, Sale, M33 3BT, UK.
www.tplondon.com

Transnational Press London® and the logo and its affiliated brands are registered trademarks.

Requests for permission to reproduce material from this work should be sent to: sales@tplondon.com

Paperback
ISBN: 978-1-80135-089-1
Digital
ISBN: 978-1-80135-090-7

Cover Design: Nihal Yazgan
Cover Photo by Marliese Streefland on Unsplash.com

Transnational Press London Ltd. is a company registered in England and Wales No. 8771684.

CONTENTS

INTRODUCTION

Elli Heikkilä and Fethiye Tilbe

The present conditions of transnational migration are nothing short of alarming. We witness human rights violations at multiple stages of the migration process. The dramatic face of migration, beyond its reflection in the media, is not only in migration routes, but also in the post-migration process. Migrant employment, changes in labour markets, remittance transfers to home countries and migrants' integration are among the most discussed and important issues in the post-migration process. In addition to the main discussion topics centred on labour markets, we see that other most discussed issues related to the post-migration process, such as migrant integration, remittance transfers to source countries, often intersect with employment, labour markets and the work experience of migrants. The increasing emphasis on the phenomenon of migrant employment caused by this intersection brings with increasing interest. In this context, our book presents case studies of different groups of migrants from different countries by focusing on labour markets and the employment of migrants, which are the intersection point of the multifaceted nature of the migration phenomenon. This book, which includes the experiences of specific groups like qualified, unskilled, and female migrants, makes reference to a wide range of discussion topics such as migrant integration, remittance transfers, relations established and maintained with home countries, legal and institutional arrangements and policy making processes in the host countries, through the concepts of employment and work.

The migration literature is full of analyses on labour migration. However, the majority of them focuses on macroeconomic analyses such as the relationship between migration and development and the impact of remittances on the economies and households from the perspective of home countries and the impact of migrants on labour markets and the economies from the perspective of the host country. Studies focusing on the daily working experiences of migrants, their economic integration, the challenges and barriers they face entering the labour market, and discrimination experiences still find a limited place in the literature. However, migrants who seek well-being and a safe life by escaping from any type of conflict, such as economic or political, may face different types of conflicts in the host countries. The most likely conflict is one based on income and employment. In addition to their struggle for existence and recognition, being stuck in the bottom layer of the labour market is, in most cases one of the biggest obstacles in the integration process of migrants. This also means that the expected return is not achieved in both economies of the host and home countries.

This book takes an approach that listens to the voices of different migrant groups in different countries, based mostly on qualitative research. The purpose of this edited book is to look at work and migration from multiple viewpoints and illuminate challenges faced by immigrants in the labour markets around the

1

world. The chapters highlight immigrants' experiences both theoretically and empirically in the contributions. The following paragraphs briefly present the structure of the book and different chapters, mentioning some of the essential themes addressed.

Representing the Nordic country, in Finland the labour market participation of immigrants can be faced with challenges. In Chapter 2, written by Elli Heikkilä, immigrants' employment situation is assessed by multiple variables including primary activity, ethnic groups and occupations, and also pointed out challenges and barriers to successful economic integration. The research findings indicate that primary and secondary labour markets exist in Finland. Among immigrants, there are those who get so-called better "Finnish" jobs and those recruited for jobs that require little or no training. The immigrants who have been most successful in finding work are usually highly educated and come from other Western countries, while those who have not succeeded so well are often immigrants with a refugee background. Employers can act as so-called gatekeepers: they often point, for example, to migrants' lack of ability to speak and comprehend the national languages, Finnish or Swedish, as a significant constraint, but also positive experiences of recruitment of people with an immigrant background were described.

Chapter 3, by Basem Mahmud, studies the place attachment that Syrian refugee-workers maintain toward Istanbul, Turkey. The new-life hope in a place approach, and its instrumental (legal status and material satisfaction) and affective elements (empathic emotions and dignity-recognition), allows understanding of the refugees' and asylum seekers' sense of place and, therefore, their integration in the new place. In Istanbul, the main challenge comes from the instrumental elements: extreme exploitation at work and uncertain legal status with limitations. Furthermore, the affective side is mostly unsatisfied. This is because of the high level of discrimination, stereotypes, and ignorance of the refugee's culture from the country of origin. However, it is sometimes satisfied due to the increased number of Syrian refugees in the city that facilitate finding work in a more familiar atmosphere.

Syrians in Turkey is also in the focus of Chapter 4. Olgu Karan's research is dealing with Syrian refugee entrepreneurship and differentiated integration in the districts of Hatay, Turkey. The research illustrates those demographic, socio-economic and socio-cultural factors within the districts of Hatay province that led to differentiated entry possibilities, barriers, and strategies for Syrian refugees in small business ownership. The ability to overcome difficulties in small business ownership is dependent on the volume and quality of social capital. Moreover, spatial peculiarities of the districts influence Syrians' tendency to remain in Turkey or return to Syria.

Chapter 5 is analysing successful stories of women who managed to break through the glass ceiling. More closely, Adi Binhas and Hana Himi study the coping strategies and experiences of Israeli women of Ethiopian origin while studying for advanced degrees, and describe the elements of success and the unique barriers they face. The authors identified that inner strengths and high personal abilities enabled Israeli women of Ethiopian origin to deal with the challenges they faced. They were confident, knew how to adapt to changing situations, and were strongly ambitious to achieve their goals. They are role models for their environment, and especially for women from unique groups who have ambitions to advance in academia.

In next three chapters, skilled migrants are analysed around the world. In Chapter 6, Harika Suklun focuses on work lives of skilled female immigrants in the United States. The research illustrates female participants' professional life in the home countries, as well as in the host country. People view the world in different ways, thus cultural conflicts can occur in the working life. Because of the cultural gaps between their home countries and the United States, skilled immigrant women encountered adjustment difficulties concerning dissimilar workplace conflicts in the host country. To prevent intercultural conflicts, as the author points out in this chapter, organizations should provide a harmonized work environment where employees should value all aspects of other cultures. Organizations should understand the context of multiculturalism to keep a strong place in the competitive phenomenon of globalization.

Due to its stable economy, South Africa has attracted millions of skilled immigrants from neighbouring countries and beyond. In Chapter 7, Sikanyiso Masuku and Sizo Nkala explore South Africa's immigrant-driven labour market and they look into the experiences of skilled immigrant workers. The research focuses on four critical-skill occupations: health professions, teaching, engineering, and academia/research. The analysis highlights that skilled immigrants have minimal trust relationships with both capital and the state, facing among other challenges institutional closure, bureaucratic red tapes, and a cumbersome visa regime.

Renan Gadoni Canaan, in Chapter 8, describes the landscape of demographic, human capital, and occupational characteristics of immigrants in Science, Technology, Engineering and Mathematics (STEM) occupations in Brazil. Moreover, he assesses the key factors that determine earnings by immigrants in STEM occupations, disclosing intersectionalities affecting pay discrimination. Immigrants in these occupations in Brazil have higher average earnings compared to their Brazilian counterparts, which is because a greater percentage of immigrants work in managerial occupations. There is no evidence of discrimination regarding earnings between foreigners and natives in STEM occupations in Brazil. Immigrants, however, just like native-born Brazilians, face a historical system of discrimination based on racial and gender hierarchies in the workforce.

In Chapter 9, Eddy Bruno Esien analyses the implication of contractual obligation, individual autonomy, and sanction under targeting benefits to understand young third-country immigrants' transition from social welfare to work in Austria, Finland, and Czech Republic. Despite similarities in the conditional redistributive policy process, the institutional framework in Austria is dissimilar to those of Finland and Czech Republic, being based on the individual basis, and in the latter countries on the units of households. This research confirms previous findings and contributes to our understanding that targeting social benefits generates ethical issues, creates inequalities and/or stigma, and divisiveness in the regulatory redistributive governance.

Agricultural workers are an important migrant group in the global level. In Chapter 10, Parkpoom Kuanvinit explores the interpersonal relationship between Israeli employers and Thai agricultural migrant workers. More closely, he analyses the association of relationships between Israeli employers and Thai workers toward the vulnerability of rights abuse and psychological distress among Thai workers. Further, he studies the roles of social contacts, as well as conflict management approaches applied among Israeli employers and Thai workers toward the qualities of relationships between these two groups. The results depict the direct and indirect associations between the positive relationships and low degree of right abuse, as well as psychological distress. The positive social contact and cooperative conflict management approach also have correlations with the positive relationship.

There are also "unseen" sacrifices that migrants experience when moving to work abroad. Prakash Arunasalam and Thirunaukarasu Subramaniam, in Chapter 11, focus on this the "unseen" in migration and remittances with the case of South Asian migrant workers in Cameron Highlands, Malaysia. Five dimensions of sacrifices are identified by the authors in the study: financial sacrifice, sacrifice of family relations, sacrifice of life comfort, sacrifice of daily consumption and sacrifice of social relations. On the one hand, the main purpose of the sacrifices made by South Asian migrant workers is to maximize the remittances made to their home countries. On the other hand, they want to ensure that the debt taken to migrate settled, assets bought and money saved.

As editors for the book, Work and Migration: Case Studies from Around the World, we want to express our thanks to the chapter authors for their many-sided and valuable contributions.

Elli Heikkilä & Fethiye Tilbe

LABOUR MARKET PARTICIPATION OF IMMIGRANTS AND CHALLENGES IN FINLAND

Elli Heikkilä

Introduction

The Finnish population is aging, and this is becoming a serious problem in other developed countries as well. According to Population Reference Bureau (2020), Finland is among the top three countries with the oldest population in the world: first one is Japan, next Italy, and Finland already in the third position. The working-age population is decreasing, i.e. there are more 60–64 year olds exiting the labour market than 20–24 year olds entering it (Heikkilä, 2017). The "Labour 2025" report of Ministry of Labour (Työministeriö, 2007) suggests employing more elderly, unemployed and disabled persons as well as immigrants. The immigrant labour reserve consists of foreigners living in Finland, naturalised immigrants and new potential immigrants.

According to Ministry of Finance (Stenborg et al., 2021), measures to increase the amount of annual immigration and employment are important in Finland in order to improve the problems of matching the labour market and, on the other hand, would respond to the growing demand for labour. In order for immigration to respond to the projected decline in the labour force, net immigration should increase significantly from the current annual level of around 18,000 and the share of immigrants in the labour force should increase. The employment of non-labour immigrants should be upgraded by improving the employability of immigrants.

As there will be higher demand for immigrant labour in Finland, it is necessary to analyse what is immigrants' situation in the contemporary labour markets in the country. The purpose of this article is thus to analyse labour market participation of immigrants and assess the existing challenges to achieving successful economic integration in Finland. It analyses current labour market participation rates of immigrants with respect to different background variables, such as primary activity, occupational groups, gender, education and dropouts, age at time of arrival in Finland and ethnic background. Comparisons are also made to the Finnish-origin population. This article also highlights the challenges and barriers that can affect immigrant economic integration from the points of view of immigrants and employers. Finally, it discusses the future need for immigrant labour in an ageing Finland.

The study data consists of official statistics from Statistics Finland and quantitative data from the special longitudinal, register-based CAGE project, purchased from Statistics Finland. As research methods, it has been used basic statistical methods including tables and graphics drawn from the statistical data.

Next, this article highlights the theoretical approach to immigrants and labour markets from different selective angles. An overview of immigrants and their primary activity by multiple background factors, and occupations in Finland is conducted by wide statistical analysis. After this section, challenges and barriers hindering successful economic integration of immigrants are brought out. In the final section, the conclusion and discussion are drawn together.

Theoretical approach to immigrants and labour markets

In the following, the theoretical approach to immigrants and labour markets is presented. It highlights a set of factors affecting labour market participation as well as a set of barriers hindering immigrants from successfully entering the labour markets.

Migration as a phenomenon involves always a transfer of human capital from one place to another. According to human capital theory (Chiswick, 1978), at least part of human capital, including language skills, knowledge of customs and contact networks, is always tied to a particular country. For this reason, immigrants can, at the beginning, presumably be less employable and earn less than the native population in similar situations or those who have lived in the country for a long time as Hämäläinen et al. (2005) point out. When their skills, mastery of the language and familiarity with the labour markets improve, immigrants' social status will likely improve as well, allowing them to take higher productivity jobs.

Labour markets into which immigrants will enter are not homogenous. Dual labour market theory (Massey et al., 1993) splits labour markets into two non-competing blocks: primary and secondary. Employees in the capital-intensive primary sector find steady employment, requiring a certain level of education, while jobs in the more labour-oriented secondary sector are uncertain and require little training. Jobs in the latter category can easily be suspended, especially during an economic recession when the withdrawal of wages causes unemployment. Minorities, including immigrants, are more concentrated in the secondary rather than the primary labour markets.

Immigrants ethnic background can affect how smooth or struggling the entry and staying in the labour market can be. Cultural theories (Spence, 1974; Ryding Zink, 2001) describe an immigrant's success in the labour market in terms of whether his or her ethnic background is evaluated in a positive or a negative way. A positive evaluation would be inspired by theories of diversity management, i.e. that a multicultural workforce contributes both directly and indirectly to the success of a company. A negative evaluation is often evoked by ethnocentrism, i.e. the upgrading of natives' merits at the expense of foreign qualifications, which can lead to incidents of discrimination.

Further on according to labelling theory (Bustamante, 2002), there is a tendency among certain employers to label a person from a different culture as "deviant". In the labour market, a recruiter can be drawn to those immigrants who have cultural proximity to the native culture. Those immigrants who come from more distant cultures face difficulties in finding a job, and thus they are more vulnerable than those with cultural proximity (see Vourc'h et al., 1999;

Wrench, 1999; Heikkilä, 2005).

Employers' role as gatekeepers to the labour market can be seen by following theories. Theories on discrimination (Ryding Zink, 2001) make a distinction between statistical and preference discrimination. The former occurs when an employer is unaware or unsure of the immigrant's productivity and how to evaluate it. Not showing an interest in other cultures or underestimating the qualifications achieved in other cultural settings is likely to lead to the occurrence of statistical discrimination. Also, when feeling uncertain about the value of foreign qualifications, many recruiters are hesitant to employ immigrants. Recruiters might be unable to see an immigrant's hidden competence resources and may thus act as the biggest obstacle to his or her successful-employment. Instead, similarities in culture and values might become the main criteria of selection in the recruitment process.

According to Ryding Zink (2001), preference discrimination results from employers preferring a certain ethnic background at the expense of the others. Critics argue that a certain "ethnic ranking" exists in the labour market. Thus, existing attitudes cause employers to initially prefer to employ natives, followed by certain nationalities rather than others in relation to their reputation in the labour market. The ranking seems connected with general ideas about the culture of different nationalities. As a result of ethnic ranking, many well-educated immigrants are relegated to positions far below their level of education. Ethnic identity influences an immigrant's chances of finding a job, in particular a position corresponding to his or her qualifications. Discrimination can also be classified either as direct discrimination, which involves less favourable treatment on the grounds of colour, race, nationality or ethnic or national origin, or indirect discrimination, which may still result in a sense of victimisation (see Carter, 2003).

The entry to the labour market is not guaranteeing the participation for good. Labour market participation can be thus permanent or temporary by nature, i.e. persons may exit or enter the labour market at different times. The theory of transitional labour markets (Schmid & Gazier, 2002) draws attention to the fact that all labour market flows are interactive and can move in both directions: from education to job, and vice versa, from unemployment to job and back to unemployment, or from employment to retirement, and vice versa, which is nowadays a more common phenomenon in, for example, Finland. Kannisto (2020) points out that retired persons can contribute to the economy when re-entering the workforce. Transitions can lead to labour market inclusion or exclusion (Heikkilä, 2006; Krutova et al., 2016), and these processes can be repetitive in a person's life. For example, a study by Lyytinen and Toom (2019) found that the pathway of youth with a refugee background from education to the labour market has not been a linear one, but rather included several phases of education, work traineeships, unemployment and employment.

Next, it is revealed by empirical analysis how immigrants' primary activity including employment and unemployment differ from each other by ethnic groups.

7

Immigrants and their primary activity

This section describes immigrants' primary activity in Finland based on multiple variables. This analysis provides deeper knowledge regarding what kinds of factors can account for the differences in inclusion (both in primary and secondary labour markets) and exclusion in the Finnish labour markets. It shows also how wide labour reserves are nowadays and for the future, i.e. the share of those who are outside of labour markets including children under 15 years old, students, retired and others outside labour.

Primary activity by citizenship of global region

This study found notable differences in the primary activity among immigrants by citizenship of global region in Finland in 2018. Table 1 shows that, when focusing on primary activity and citizenship, as of 2018 most immigrants in Finland are from Europe (57%) and Asia (29%). Australia, Europe and North and South America had the highest shares of those employed and the lowest shares of those unemployed in the primary activity category. Only a quarter of African citizens were employed at the time, and their share of unemployed persons was somewhat higher than for citizens from other global regions. African citizens also have the most children under 15 years of age, which shows a younger population structure. The share of students is almost the same for Africans and Asians. Pensioners are more common among Europeans, but the share is, nonetheless, quite small. More than one fifth of Australians, North and South Americans, Africans and Asians fall into the category of others outside the labour force. This primary activity includes, for example, women working as homemakers.

Table 1. Primary activity of immigrants by citizenship of global region in Finland in 2018 (%) (Data: Statistics Finland)

Global region	Employed	Unemployed	0-14 years old	Students	Pensioners	Others outside labour	Total abs.	%
Citizenship:								
Europe (excluding Finland)	46.4	9.0	14.2	7.4	7.6	15.4	147,203	100
Africa	26.4	13.1	21.0	16.6	1.6	21.3	22,969	100
North and South America	42.5	10.8	6.3	11.3	4.3	24.8	8,154	100
Asia	33.6	11.3	17.0	15.8	1.8	20.5	75,625	100
Australia	48.0	7.0	6.0	6.1	7.9	25.0	671	100

Primary activity by citizenship of top 15 countries

Remarkable differences can be detected in the primary activity of those in the fifteen largest immigrant groups by country of citizenship in Finland in 2018 (Table 2). Over half of all Britons, Estonians and Polish persons were employed, followed by an employment rate of 40 percent or above for those from Ukraine, India, Vietnam, Thailand, China and Sweden. Unemployment was the highest among Iraqis, of whom almost every fifth person searching for a job was unemployed. Afghans, Somalis, Turks, Thais and Syrians had the next highest shares of unemployed persons by primary activity. The table clearly shows that many unemployed persons come from so-called refugee background countries. Children at the time accounted for approximately 40 percent of all Syrians immigrants, whereas the share was around a quarter of all Somalis and Iraqis. Afghans, Vietnamese and Somalis at the time had the highest shares of students, over a fifth of their population. Swedes had the highest share of retired people, many of whom could be persons who emigrated from Finland to Sweden especially during the 1960s and 1970s and after retirement had chosen to return to Finland as Swedish citizens. At least a fifth of next population groups were also at the time others outside the labour force: Chinese, Somalis, Indians, Iraqis, Turks, Syrians and Afghans.

Table 2. Primary activity of immigrants from the top 15 countries by citizenship in Finland in 2018 (%) (Data: Statistics Finland)

Citizenship	Employed	Unemployed	0-14 years old	Students	Pensioners	Others outside labour	Total abs.	%
Estonia	52.9	6.7	18.5	6.0		4.8	11.1	51,456	100
Russia	32.3	13.9	11.6	11.5	13.0	17.7	28,747	100
Iraq	12.5	18.6	25.4	18.9	2.5	22.1	13,078	100
China	41.5	5.7	12.6	12.3	1.0	26.9	9,230	100
Sweden	41.3	7.3	7.1	3.8	25.6	14.9	7,996	100
Thailand	44.5	14.4	7.1	13.2	1.4	19.4	7,632	100
Somalia	11.7	14.5	27.6	20.6	2.7	22.9	6,448	100
Afghanistan	13.1	14.6	20.7	28.5	2.5	20.6	6,198	100
Syria	5.2	14.2	40.2	18.2	0.6	21.6	6,016	100
Vietnam	44.6	6.8	9.4	22.3	1.9	15.0	5,941	100
India	44.8	6.3	18.7	7.0	0.9	22.3	5,730	100
Turkey	37.0	14.5	14.5	10.0	2.0	22.0	4,794	100
Great-Britain	53.9	8.9	4.5	5.3	7.5	19.9	4,619	100
Ukraine	48.5	8.1	15.2	8.8	3.8	15.6	4,593	100
Poland	50.3	6.6	15.6	5.7	2.9	18.9	4,410	100
All foreign citizens	40.5	10.1	15.5	10.8	5.2	17.7	257,572	100
Finnish citizens	43.2	4.4	16.0	6.9	26.9	2.6	5,260,7	10

Primary activity by foreign language

The data revealed the following results when assessing primary activity by foreign language, i.e. by foreign mother tongue, in Finland in 2018. One fifth of the immigrants are Russian speakers (20%), followed by Estonian speakers (13%). The highest shares of employed immigrants are found among those whose mother tongue is Estonian, English or Russian. Estonians often easily master the Finnish language, which positively affects their employability in the Finnish labour markets. As a comparison, the overall share of employed persons is lower for Finnish-language speakers than for Estonian-language speakers since the share of pensioners is quite high in the Finnish population. Somali and Arabic speakers in Finland have the lowest share of those employed. The highest shares of unemployed persons are found among Arabic, Russian and Somali language groups. Approximately one third of Somali and Arabic speakers are children under 15 years of age. Hence, the percentage of those who are students is quite high among Somali and Arabic speakers. Others outside labour force are most often those with English, Arabic and Somali as their mother tongue.

Table 3. Primary activity of immigrants by foreign language in Finland in 2018 (%) (Data: Statistics Finland)

Language	Employed	Unemployed	0-14 years old	Students	Pensioners	Others outside labour	Total abs.	%
Finnish	43.2	4.4	15.6	6.8	27.5	2.5	4,835,778	100
Russian	42.7	11.6	15.6	9.8	9.3	11.0	79,225	100
Estonin	54.8	6.5	17.1	6.0	5.1	10.5	49,691	100
Arabic	18.3	15.0	29.6	16.3	3.6	17.2	29,462	100
Somali	19.7	11.0	34.7	17.2	2.8	14.4	20,944	100
English	44.0	7.0	16.7	9.3	5.4	17.6	20,713	100

Primary activity by age at time of arrival

The special statistical analysis of the primary activity of immigrants derives from the CAGE project "Coming of Age in Exile – Health and Socio-Economic Inequities in Young Refugees in the Nordic Welfare Societies", funded by NordForsk, which used longitudinal register-based data purchased from Statistics Finland. Personal data was obtained from the Population Register Centre (VRK) from those born between 1971 and 1999 and had immigrated to Finland as minors, have lived in Finland permanently 1990–2015 and whose country of birth was a so-called refugee country. Personal data was also received from VRK from others born abroad in 1971–1999 and who immigrated to Finland as minors as well as native-born comparative data. Register data of Statistics Finland were combined with VRK's data dealing with studies and degrees, primary activity, occupation and employment from 1990 to 2015.

Persons with immigrant background had a minimum of ten years of residence in Finland at the end of the study follow-up period in 2015. All persons were living in Finland in 2015. The subjects in the CAGE study moved to Finland as children between 0 and 17 years of age, meaning that they have been socialised into two cultures: their parental culture of origin as well as the Finnish culture.

Figure 1 shows primary activity of refugees and other migrants in 2015 based on their age at the time of arrival in Finland. It is evident that those who arrived as young children (under seven years of age) have successfully learnt the Finnish and/or Swedish language, the official languages of Finland, since they entered into the Finnish school system at such an early stage. Similarly, a higher percentage of them also pursued further studies, as refugees and other migrants account for approximately one third of students. Refugees and other migrants who arrived in Finland at 7–14 or 15–17 years of age have participated more actively in the labour market and not continued with their studies. Also, their unemployment rate is higher compared to those who arrived at under seven years of age. Higher rates of employment do not, however, reveal much about the type of occupation of such persons, i.e. whether they had jobs in the primary or secondary labour markets.

Dunlavy et al. (2020) note that the CAGE education research reveals patterns of educational performance by age of arrival, with better outcomes being observed among children who migrated at younger ages (relative to older ages) and among the native-born children of migrants (relative to migrants). Socialisation processes at school and within the broader community at large often prove more challenging at older ages, and the need to start "with a clean slate" in a new country and learn a new language may be particularly disruptive for older children's social and emotional development. In addition, children who arrive at younger ages spend more time in the educational systems of the destination country, entailing greater opportunities for adaptation and the development of necessary skills.

Figure 1. Primary activity of refugees and other migrants by age at time of arrival in Finland and their situation in 2015, with the 1st generation born in 1971–1999 (%) (Data: CAGE project).

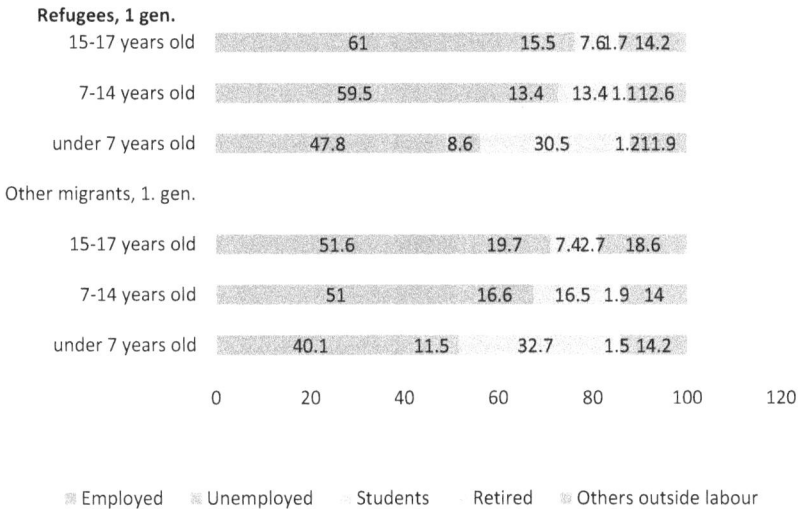

Refugees, 1 gen.

	Employed	Unemployed	Students	Retired	Others outside labour
15-17 years old	61	15.5	7.6	1.7	14.2
7-14 years old	59.5	13.4	13.4	1.1	12.6
under 7 years old	47.8	8.6	30.5	1.2	11.9

Other migrants, 1. gen.

	Employed	Unemployed	Students	Retired	Others outside labour
15-17 years old	51.6	19.7	7.4	2.7	18.6
7-14 years old	51	16.6	16.5	1.9	14
under 7 years old	40.1	11.5	32.7	1.5	14.2

Primary activity by education

Figure 2 shows refugees' primary activity and level of education in Finland in 2015. Most refugees with higher education were employed at the time, with only a small number being unemployed. While 75 percent of highly educated persons with a refugee background were economically active in the labour markets at the time, only 54 percent with secondary education were employed at the time. Unemployment was more common among those with a secondary education (17%) compared to higher educated refugees (8%). Some persons with a secondary education had chosen to continue with their studies (14%), while many more with just a primary education (34%) had chosen to keep studying. Only a small number of persons with primary education had found employment, while every tenth was unemployed. The primary education group included considerable amount of persons who fell into the category of others outside the labour force, whereas the primary activity is unknown for roughly a fifth of them.

11

This analysis shows that the higher the level of education, the better one's employment prospects within the Finnish labour markets are.

Figure 2. Refugees' primary activity and education in Finland in 2015 (%) (Data: CAGE project).

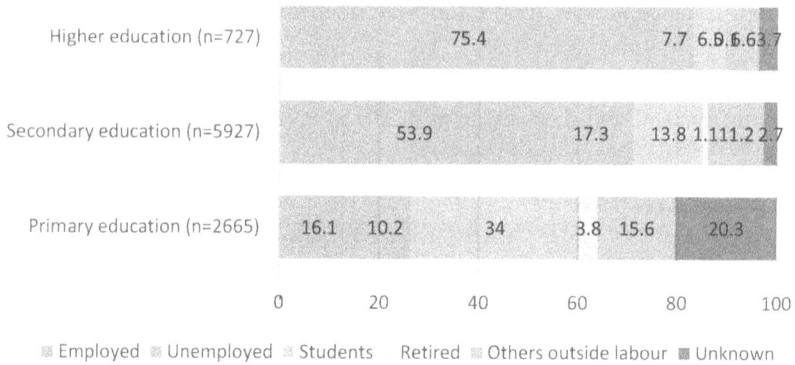

Higher education (n=727)	75.4			7.7	6.9 6.6 3.7	
Secondary education (n=5927)	53.9		17.3	13.8 1.1 11.2 2.7		
Primary education (n=2665)	16.1	10.2	34	3.8	15.6	20.3

0   20   40   60   80   100

▨ Employed ▨ Unemployed ▨ Students   Retired ▨ Others outside labour ▨ Unknown

Primary activity of those who dropped out of upper secondary education

Figure 3 shows the primary activity of those who had chosen not to complete their upper secondary education studies in Finland in 2015. While most such refugees, other migrants and Finns were employed at the time, knowledge is lacking regarding the type of work in which they are involved. More than one fourth of refugees and other migrants were unemployed at the time, while more than one fifth of them remained others outside the labour market. According to OECD (2020), young people, who were not in school, did not have a job and were not enrolled in a training programme (so-called NEETs: not in education, employment or training), fell into the category of others outside labour force. While several persons had started to study once again after dropping out of school, the percentage was quite low. In fact, NEETs as marginalised young people constitute a special group, and targeted actions and good practices have been initiated to encourage them to continue with their studies and to find employment in Finland. This problem also concerns native youth. Remaining outside the labour force and being excluded from the society at a young age are not fulfilling or healthy ways to live one's life. Additionally, the share of retired persons is high among first-generation refugees, many of whom are young and could still actively participate in the labour markets for quite some time.

In the following section, it is analysed occupations of employed immigrants and comparison are made to the natives. This empirical analysis shows which kinds of occupations actually are those in which immigrants have been recruited in Finland.

Figure 3. Primary activity of refugees, other migrants and Finns who dropped out of upper secondary education in Finland in 2015 (%) (Data: CAGE project).

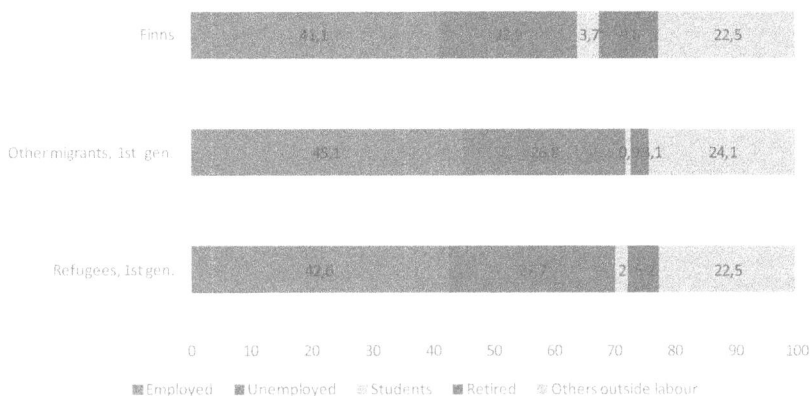

Immigrants and their occupations

A total of 162,201 persons with foreign origins were employed in Finland in 2018, although they only accounted for 7 percent of all employed persons. When analysing immigrants by occupational groups, differences emerge in terms of the jobs done by foreign-origin workers and those done by Finnish-origin workers. All persons with at least one parent born in Finland are considered to be of Finnish background. Persons with both parents or the only known parent having been born abroad are considered to be of foreign origin (Statistics Finland, 2020).

Comparing the distribution of foreign-origin men and Finnish-origin men by occupation group in Finland in 2018 we can see prominent difference related to elementary occupations: 13 percent of foreign-origin men were employed in that sector, whereas only 5 percent of Finnish-origin men had such jobs (Figure 4). Correspondingly, foreign-origin men were under-represented as technicians and associate professionals (8% vs. 15%). The differences were not so huge in occupation groups that typically employ the most foreign- and Finnish-origin men, i.e. as craft and related trade workers, professionals and service and sales workers.

Foreign-origin men were most often employed by the detailed occupational groups as building and related trade workers, but excluding electricians, personal service workers, drivers and mobile plant operators, as well as cleaners and helpers, in Finland in 2018 (Table 4). Especially work as cleaners and helpers is often classified as an entry-level job in the secondary labour market. However, it is important to note that many jobs included among the top 15 detailed occupational groups belong to the primary labour market, i.e. professionals and associate professionals in different occupational groups. This is a sign of a successful match between the type of work and education. The top 15

13

occupational groups account for three fourths (73%) of all occupational groups primarily employing foreign-origin men, the same share as for Finnish-origin men.

Figure 4. Employed Finnish-origin men (n=1,100,413) and foreign-origin men (n=90,963) by occupational group in 2018 (Data: Statistics Finland).

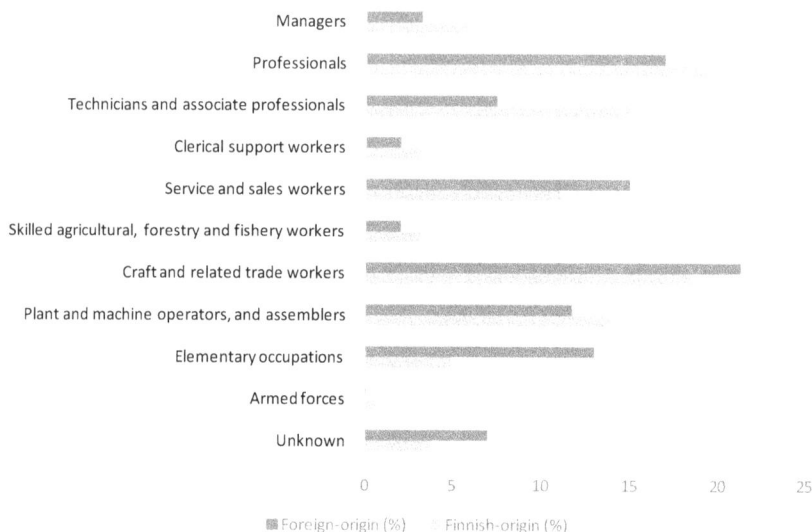

When comparing the top 15 detailed occupational groups in 2018 in terms of the numbers of foreign-origin and Finnish-origin men with jobs, a much larger percentage of foreign men work as building and related trade workers, excluding electricians (13% vs. 7%). Additionally, in relative terms foreign-origin men are more often employed as personal service workers than Finnish-origin men (9% vs. 4%). With respect to different professionals and associate professionals, the shares are slightly higher for Finnish-origin men than for foreign-origin men, but the differences are only a couple of percentage points. For example, 6 percent of Finnish-origin men were employed as science and engineering professionals compared to 4 percent of foreign-origin men. The share is slightly higher for foreign-origin men than for Finnish-origin men (5% vs. 4%) in the information and communications technology sector. This sector already attracted foreign men, in the early 2000s, for example from India, who chose to move as labour immigrants to work for the Nokia Company.

A number of detailed occupational groups are also not among the top 15 employers of foreign-origin men but still rank on the list of those employing tens of thousands of Finnish-origin men: work as business and administration professionals (number 10th on the list), as production and specialised services managers (13th), and as electrical and electronic trade workers (14th). Three occupational groups that tend to predominantly hire foreign-origin men but that are not on top 15 list for Finnish-origin men involve work as cleaners and helpers (number 4 on the list), as market-oriented skilled agricultural workers (14th) and as personal care workers (15th).

Table 4. Top 15 detailed occupational groups employing foreign-origin persons by number and their share in relation to all employed foreign-origin men and women in Finland in 2018 (Data: Statistics Finland)

Men		
Detailed occupational group	Employed	%
Building and related trade workers, excluding electricians	12,157	13.4
Personal service workers	8,056	8.9
Drivers and mobile plant operators	6,451	7.1
Cleaners and helpers	5,467	6.0
Metal, machinery and related trade workers	5,071	5.6
Information and communications technology professionals	4,337	4.8
Science and engineering professionals	3,863	4.2
Labourers in mining, construction, manufacturing and transport	3,835	4.2
Sales workers	3,259	3.6
Teaching professionals	3,031	3.3
Stationary plant and machine operators	2,591	2.8
Business and administration associate professionals	2,191	2.4
Science and engineering associate professionals	2,164	2.4
Market-oriented skilled agricultural workers	1,743	1.9
Personal care workers	1,723	1.9
Total top 15	65,939	72.5
Detailed occupational groups total	90,963	100
Women		
Detailed occupational group	Employed	%
Cleaners and helpers	11,700	16.6
Personal care workers	9,773	13.7
Personal service workers	6,088	8.5
Sales workers	6,087	8.5
Teaching professionals	3,808	5.3
Business and administration associate professionals	3,238	4.5
Health associate professionals	2,549	3.6
Stationary plant and machine operators	2,126	3.0
Food preparation assistants	1,766	2.5
Legal, social and cultural professionals	1,662	2.3
Science and engineering professionals	1,625	2.3
Health professionals	1,622	2.3
Business and administration professionals	1,583	2.2
General and keyboard clerks	1,370	1.9
Legal, social, cultural and related associate professionals	1,249	1.8
Total top 15	56,246	79.0
Detailed occupational groups total	71,238	100

When looking at female employment patterns, the share of those working as service and sales workers was the highest for both foreign-origin and Finnish-origin women in 2018 (Figure 5). This occupational group clearly had a higher share of females than males. The statistics show that Finnish women more commonly work as professionals, technicians and associate professionals than foreign-origin women. Foreign women tend more often to be employed in elementary occupations: the share was three times higher for them (21%) than for Finnish women (7%) and foreign males (6%). A strong male majority can be

15

detected among craft and related trade workers as well as among plant and machine operators and assemblers.

It is interesting to note, however, that when looking at the total number of employed professionals and of elementary occupations in absolute terms, i.e. the sum of males and females, the difference was small for all foreign-origin workers: 26,854 persons were working as professionals and 26,587 persons in elementary occupations in Finland in 2018. For Finnish-origin workers, the situation is noticeably different, i.e. in 2018 the total number of employed professionals was 456,937 persons, with 128,496 persons being employed in elementary occupations. At the time, it was thus 3.5 times more common for Finns to work as professionals than in elementary occupation. Foreign-origin workers typically work as professionals just as much as in elementary jobs. This means that foreign-origin workers find jobs much more often from the secondary labour market compared to Finnish-origin workers. In Finland, however, foreign-origin workers can be found in a wide range of occupations both in the primary and secondary sectors of the labour market, from elementary jobs to jobs requiring higher education.

Figure 5. Employed Finnish-origin women (n=1,111,054) and foreign-origin women (n=71,238) by occupational group in 2018 (Data: Statistics Finland).

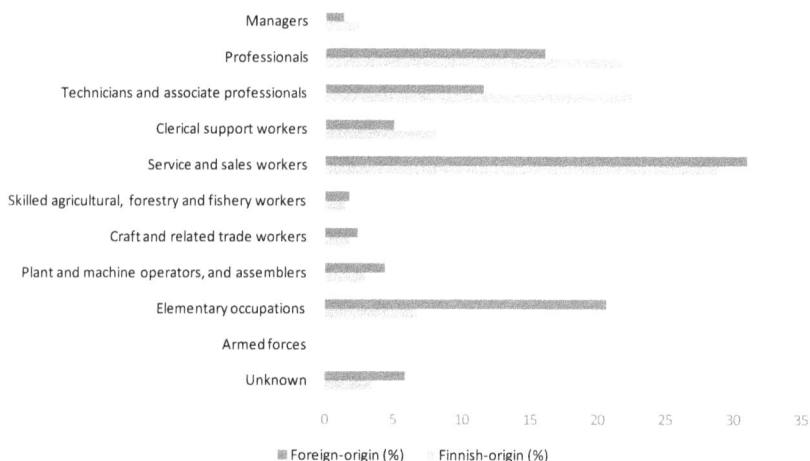

In Finland, foreign-origin women were most often employed in the top 15 detailed occupational groups as cleaners and helpers, personal care workers, personal service workers and sales workers in 2018 (Table 4). Work as cleaners and helpers is described as a so-called entry level job in the secondary labour market. Four times as many foreign-origin women (17%) as Finnish-origin women (4%) work as cleaners and helpers. A number of foreign-origin women, however, have been working in occupational groups classified as professional and associate professional. This means that these types of jobs require higher education in Finland and a demand for them continues to exist in the labour market.

It is striking that though foreign-origin women have found employment as health professionals and health associate professionals, neither foreign-origin men nor Finnish-origin men have sought such jobs (none of which fall in the top 15 for men). Health care and social care are economic sectors dominated by women. A much greater percentage of Finnish-origin women work as health associate professionals (9%) than do foreign-origin women (4%). The health care sector is one sector that will require more workers in the future as the population ages. These occupations are highly regulated, and it will require more effort to ensure that foreign qualifications match the standards set for Finnish qualifications (see Kyhä, 2011).

In general, foreign-origin women and Finnish-origin women can for the most part be found in the same occupational groups, but in different ranking order on the top 15 list. The only exceptions include food preparation assistants, an occupational group ranking 9th for foreign-origin women but not for Finnish-origin women, and customer service clerks, an occupational group ranking 12th for Finnish-origin women, but not for foreign-origin women.

When comparing the gender-based analysis of occupational groups by foreign origin, it is clear that certain occupational groups have an excess of male workers, such as craft and related trade workers, a category that includes construction workers. The list of detailed occupational groups reveals that the most important positions for males include work in building and related trade sector, excluding electricians. It is quite common for Finnish construction sites to hire many workers originally from foreign countries. In the ground transport sector, immigrant men work often as bus drivers, especially in the large urban centres of southern Finland. Foreign-origin women more often than foreign males find jobs as service and sales workers and are employed in elementary occupations. Both men and women typically find jobs as personal service workers which include restaurant workers. Personal care workers, clearly a more common job for females, include those working in health services and as health care assistants.

Table 5 presents a case study of the top 15 detailed occupational groups of employed Britons and Iraqis in Finland in 2018. The comparison is important because Great Britain is a western European country and the migrants are in the country voluntarily, whereas Iraqis came to Finland as refugees especially in recent years. For example, during the so-called Migration Crisis years of 2015–2016, two-thirds of refugees who came to Finland were Iraqis. The occupational groups occupied by Britons and Iraqis differ a great deal from each other in the example cases. Ten of the top 15 occupational groups for Britons include work as professionals or associate professionals and managers, i.e. professions that require higher education and belong to the primary sector. Iraqi workers were not employed in seven of these ten occupational groups. Fourteen percent of Britons work as teaching professionals, followed by information and communications technology professionals (7%) and personal service workers (7%). In fact, more Britons (14%) work as teaching professionals than do Finnish-origin workers (6%). Such jobs may include, for example, work as English language teaching, where Britons can use their mother tongue and ethnic-specific skills in their work. Jaakkola (2000) found that 71 percent of

Britons and 62 percent of persons from the United States worked in the teaching field, mainly as language teachers or as translators.

Table 5. Top 15 detailed occupational groups of employed Britons and Iraqis by number and share in relation to all employed Britons and Iraqis in Finland in 2018 (Data: Statistics Finland)

Great Britain		
Occupational group	**Employed**	**%**
Teaching professionals	344	14.1
Information and communications technology professionals	180	7.4
Personal service workers	159	6.6
Science and engineering professionals	157	6.5
Business and administration professionals	150	6.2
Legal, social and cultural professionals	115	4.8
Building and related trade workers, excluding electricians	99	4.1
Business and administration associate professionals	88	3.6
Personal care workers	88	3.6
Legal, social, cultural and related associate professionals	69	2.9
Science and engineering associate professionals	62	2.6
Sales workers	59	2.4
Production and specialised services managers	55	2.3
Administrative and commercial managers	53	2.2
Metal, machinery and related trade workers	50	2.1
Total	**1,728**	**71.4**
Occupational groups total	**2,419**	**100**
Iraq		
Occupational group	**Employed**	**%**
Personal service workers	660	16.2
Sales workers	353	8.7
Cleaners and helpers	293	7.3
Personal care workers	271	6.7
Drivers and mobile plant operators	253	6.3
Metal, machinery and related trade workers	234	5.8
Legal, social and cultural professionals	231	5.7
Food preparation assistants	193	4.8
Building and related trade workers, excluding electricians	180	4.5
Labourers in mining, construction, manufacturing and transport	142	3.5
Legal, social, cultural and related associate professionals	81	2.0
Health professionals	69	1.7
Assemblers	68	1.7
Business and administration associate professionals	67	1.7
Stationary plant and machine operators	63	1.6
Total	**3,158**	**78.2**
Occupational groups total	**4,040**	**100**

The majority of Iraqis, in contrast, have found jobs as personal service workers (16%), followed by sales workers (9%) and cleaners and helpers (7%). The share of personal service workers (16%) is much higher for Iraqis than for Britons (7%) and Finnish-origin workers (5%). At the time, Iraqi workers could be found in seven occupational groups that did not include any British workers at all: cleaners and helpers, drivers and mobile plant operators, food preparation assistants, labourers in mining, construction, manufacturing and transport, health professionals, assemblers and stationary plant and machine operators. Most of such jobs are secondary sector jobs, and one includes professional jobs, i.e. health professionals which include for example work as medical doctors and nursing professionals.

Next, the occupational groups of employed refugees are analysed by education based on available data from 2014 (Figure 6). It is interesting to focus on the educational background of employed persons in each occupational group. The share of persons with a secondary education is high in almost all occupation groups, except for those that require mostly higher education. Those jobs primarily include professionals and technicians and associate professionals. Also, slightly more than a fifth of refugees with higher education work as managers. Managers may include those persons who started their own business. They are thus managers in their own enterprise, meaning that refugees with all educational backgrounds can also be found in this category.

There are also signs of mismatch in work and education since one fifth of higher educated refugees are employed as clerical support workers. Smaller percentages of higher educated refugees also work as service and sales workers, as craft and related trade workers, in elementary occupations, as plant and machine operators, and as assemblers. This phenomenon can be classified as brain waste (see OECD, 2018), a situation existing when educational background and type of work do not match. The challenges and barriers that result in this kind of situation are discussed next in this article.

Figure 6. Occupational groups of employed refugees by education in Finland in 2014 (%) (Data: CAGE project).

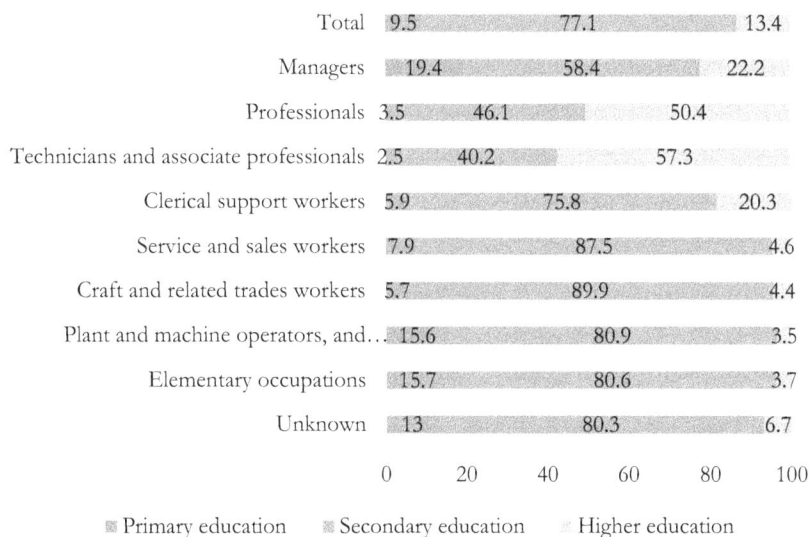

	Primary education	Secondary education	Higher education
Total	9.5	77.1	13.4
Managers	19.4	58.4	22.2
Professionals	3.5	46.1	50.4
Technicians and associate professionals	2.5	40.2	57.3
Clerical support workers	5.9	75.8	20.3
Service and sales workers	7.9	87.5	4.6
Craft and related trades workers	5.7	89.9	4.4
Plant and machine operators, and...	15.6	80.9	3.5
Elementary occupations	15.7	80.6	3.7
Unknown	13	80.3	6.7

Empirical analyses of primary activity and labour market participation of immigrants highlight that there exist remarkable differences by ethnic groups in the success of economic integration. What kind of challenges and barriers can explain these differences is illuminated in the next section.

Challenges and barriers to successful economic integration

The CAGE employment policy report by Gauffin and Lyytinen (2017) has highlighted that the integration of, for example, young refugees in the Nordic countries takes place in a policy environment characterised by a general transition "from welfare to workfare". This means that financial self-sufficiency is seen as the core dimension of successful integration and that other indicators of societal involvement are seen as subordinate to labour market participation. This perspective is relevant also for other background factors of immigrants in different age groups.

Both in Finland and in other industrialised countries, however, it is more difficult for immigrants to find work than for the native population. The result is that the former often have much higher unemployment rates than the latter (see Heikkilä, 2017). According to Gauffin and Lyytinen (2017), pre-migration factors, including demographics, education and skills, country of origin, reason for migration and health, will make the immigrants more or less prepared to find employment.

Transferability of human capital depends on the similarities and differences between the origin and destination countries. Language skills, the education system, the cultural environment and social climate in the country of origin, as well as state of the economy and general employment rates, are all important in this respect (Tassinopoulos & Werner, 1999; Gauffin & Lyytinen, 2017). Lens et al. (2018) emphasise that migrants arriving in a new country lack country-specific human capital (work experience, language proficiency and recognition of their home country credentials) and social capital. This tends to result in higher risks of unemployment and lower occupational status and earnings compared to native-born persons.

There are differences in the circumstances and motives of immigrants arriving in Finland. Labour immigrants often have an advantage in the labour market since they can already apply from abroad for jobs suitable to their educational background and economic status. Non-labour migrants are those persons who immigrate for other reasons: marriage migration, to study, return migration and as refugees.

Dunlavy and Gauffin (2020) express that refugee immigrants in particular face greater labour market disadvantages given the forced nature and potentially difficult circumstances of their migration, which can have lasting effects on their mental and physical health, both necessary for employment. Refugee-background immigrants are, thus, in the most vulnerable position and their unemployment rate is the highest (see Heikkilä, 2017). According to Smith Jervelund at al. (2020), labour market demands regarding educational qualifications, together with experiences of discrimination and racism, might partly explain why refugees from Somalia and Iraq were found in the course of the CAGE project to have special disadvantages compared to the majority populations throughout the Nordic countries. The importance of education may also be reflected in the fact that completing upper secondary education leads to a smaller gap in employment among the refugees in all Nordic countries.

The employment rate is highest for those with a higher education level. Some, however, still experience unemployment and difficulties in entering the Finnish labour market even though they have certificates from higher educational institutions. According to Forsander (2003), most employers tend to devalue education received abroad, especially in countries considered less important in the global hierarchy. This devaluation by employers can be the result of mistrust (see Ferm, 2017). Employers know the content of education received in Finland, but they have difficulty in evaluating the content of foreign degrees because the content of education and degrees differ to a significant extent between countries around the world (Kyhä, 2011).

Learning and having a command of the Finnish or Swedish language is one of the key factors for successfully entering the labour market in Finland. International companies may have English or another language as the working language, and thus skill in one of Finland's official languages is not always necessary in working life. Larja and Sutela (2015), though, have found that proficiency in Finnish is taken as a sign of reliability by employers.

Discrimination reportedly occurs indirectly when employers demand excessive language competence, even though performance of the job tasks may in practice not require full command of the language (see Aaltonen et al., 2009). A study by Heikkilä and Pikkarainen (2008) found that some immigrants have the opinion that if their Finnish language skills were better, the likelihood of their staying in Finland would grow. Even if they enjoy their current work and social life, they are nonetheless disturbed by the communication gap caused by imperfect language skills. Likewise, CAGE qualitative labour market research by Lyytinen and Toom (2019) has highlighted the extent to which talented workers from abroad are not hired by employers because of a lack of sufficient Finnish skills:

> *One must know Finnish in order to be able to work in Finland. So, we have a lot of these people who are highly educated. There are lawyers, doctors. People from any field, graduated coders from the IT field. But they do not get a job because they do not know Finnish. (Cleaning firm)*

According to Flatau et al. (1995), employees in the capital-intensive primary sector note that steady employment requires a certain level of education, whereas jobs in the labour-oriented secondary sector are uncertain and require little training. Immigrants may be sorted into secondary labour markets because of prejudice arising from "socioeconomic distance", which is increased by differences in racial origin, religion, education and sociocultural factors.

Dualism exists in the labour markets, but so too does an ethno-stratification of jobs which is pointed out by Ouali and Rea (1999). Within the secondary labour market, some employment sectors hire more foreign workers than native workers and others in which certain ethnic groups are overrepresented and natives not found. It has been noted that a process of hierarchisation exists with respect to occupational integration on the basis of an immigrant's nationality, an issue that applies especially between workers from Western countries and those from the so-called Third World countries. For the latter, the main problem has not so much to do with achieving stability in employment, but rather in first getting a job. The same hierarchical structuring has been noticed in the research of Edvardsson et al. (2007) of all Nordic countries as well: higher employment participation rates exist among native and other Nordic and Western immigrants compared to non-Western immigrants. Non-Western immigrants do, however, achieve increased labour market participation rates after several years of living in the Nordic countries, but their employment rates are still far below those of natives.

Elementary occupations, which include cleaners and helpers, labourers in mining, construction, manufacturing and transport, and food preparation assistants, are generally considered so-called "foot-in-the-door" occupations, by which immigrants gain access to the job market (see Forsander, 2002). Such occupations are also known as "3D" jobs – dirty, dangerous and degrading (Kofman, 2003). Immigrants are sometimes ready to take a job that does not correspond to their level of education, constituting brain waste and over-education, just to take the first step in the labour market, and thereby, to begin the integration process into society. Kosonen et al. (2019) express that short-term and unskilled work can, however, help with the transition to more meaningful work, especially in the early stages of immigration. Such work helps an immigrant ultimately master the language and culture and learn the working skills needed in the new country.

It is important to ensure that, for example, short-term and part-time work do not hinder the recruitment of immigrant workers to skilled jobs or lead to incentive traps, wherein the recruitment process does not lead to better income. According to Flatau et al. (1995), underemployment, which is also one type of brain waste, is also a phenomenon that exists in the labour markets. This means that even when a person has work, her or his employment is not optimal or is inadequate in some specified way, for example in terms of working hours. Further, occupational mismatch represents an important source of skill underutilisation.

Involuntary part-time work has become more common in Finland as Kuivalainen (2020) points out. According to her, such jobs are in low-wage sectors, with zero-hour contracts. Additionally, the number of self-employed workers (sole proprietorships, freelancers and so forth) has clearly increased. The risk of poverty for self-employed workers is higher than for wage earners. Dunlavy and Gauffin (2020) highlight that in general insecure labour markets have made it increasingly difficult for immigrants to obtain secure and well-paid jobs, and this in turn has increased the segregation of immigrants into less desirable low-wage and precarious positions. Sutela's (2015) research shows that immigrants are employed more often in part-time and fixed-term jobs than the native population.

According to Pehkonen (2017), social networks have an essential role in how an immigrant enters and advances in the labour markets. Social networks, though, can potentially play a dual role in the occupational attainment process. On the one hand, they serve as a crucial resource opportunity structure in providing employment opportunities for immigrants, while on the other they operate as constraining factors by channelling such persons into low-prestige sectors of the labour market. In the Finnish labour market, so-called hidden working places also exist as Kesä (2016) points out. Finding these types of vacancies means having active contacts with employers, since the positions are not advertised in the papers (see Työministeriö, 2004). The networks are useful because they give persons the possibility to find such hidden working places. Social capital is thus crucial in gaining access to labour markets for both immigrants and natives in Finland.

Jaakkola's (2000) research revealed that according to employment authorities, prejudices among employers are the major barriers to the recruitment of immigrants. The prejudices are caused by fear, language problems and different customs, whereas their attitudes are not affected by religion, colour of skin or the need for supervision. The employment authorities highlighted the fact that immigrants are recruited for their professional know-how. Their recruitment is facilitated by language skills and cultural factors (Eronen et al., 2014).

Employers can thus act as so-called gatekeepers. Lyytinen and Toom (2019) research shows that they consistently point to migrants' lack of ability to speak and comprehend the national language as a significant constraint. Other barriers are a lack of work experience, an inability to check and/or recognise foreign qualifications, and cultural factors, such as needing set times for prayer and wearing a hijab (see Ministry of Business, Innovation and Employment, 2013). Recruiters can also feel closer to those immigrants who have cultural proximity to the native culture (see Heikkilä, 2005). Those immigrants who come from more distant cultures face difficulties in finding a job. According to Lyytinen and Toom (2019), employers who have already recruited immigrant-origin workers are generally ready to recruit more of them, i.e. the threshold for further recruitment is lowered after having first-hand experiences with immigrants in the labour markets. This is in line with so-called contact theory (Allport, 1954), i.e. the more different groups come into contact with each other, the more they learn from each other. Negative attitudes and prejudices can change into positive ones and facilitate cooperation.

Some research (Sjöblom-Immala, 2006; Lyytinen & Toom, 2019) have shown that firms which have recruited immigrants have reported good experiences. The advantages they have mentioned include their employees' diligence, high level of motivation, honesty, politeness, flexibility, commitment and strong work ethic. Two firms interviewed as part of CAGE qualitative labour market research of Lyytinen and Toom (2019) emphasised the experiences this way:

Their willingness to work and how they, well let's just say that a person can do miracles when there is enough will, and I have seen what one tiny step or some guidance in the right direction can do ... how far it can carry [someone]. (Interpretation firm)

We actually have one slogan only, and that is that "we hire the best ones". That does not sort out the nationalities or anything. (Industry)

Vorobeva (2019) stresses that one phenomenon affecting the labour markets is that of forced entrepreneurship. According to her, a migrant entrepreneur is pushed to, rather than pulled into, self-employment due to labour market discrimination, dissatisfaction with working conditions, non-recognition of professional value, immobility or a lack of relevant skills. As cultural outsiders, migrant entrepreneurs often lack cultural knowledge of the local social system and have troubles in navigating their way through the complex legal frameworks. It is believed that consultants with a migrant background could provide more migrant-tailored business advice in the future.

Next, in the last section of this article, conclusion and discussion are drawn and in the end there is discussion of the future need for immigrant labour in an ageing Finland.

Conclusion and discussion

The sphere of employment is central to the discussion of inclusion and exclusion, i.e. in wider terms of possible vulnerability of immigrants since it is through work that people earn money and gain status and job satisfaction. Employment can be said to be a crucial part of integration into the wider society (see Carter, 2003). The CAGE employment policy report by Gauffin and Lyytinen (2017) has highlighted that the integration of, for example, young refugees in the Nordic countries takes place in a policy environment characterised by a general transition "from welfare to workfare". This means that financial self-sufficiency is seen as the core dimension of successful integration and that other indicators of societal involvement are seen as subordinate to labour market participation.

In this study, primary activity of immigrants were analysed by multiple background factors. When analysing by citizenship of global region, Australia, Europe and North and South America had the highest shares of those employed. Only a quarter of African citizens were employed at the time, and their share of unemployed persons was somewhat higher than for citizens from other global regions. In primary activity by citizenship of top 15 countries, over half of all Britons, Estonians and Polish persons were employed. Unemployment was the highest among Iraqis, of whom almost every fifth person searching for a job was unemployed. Data concerning primary by foreign language, i.e. foreign mother tongue, revealed that the highest shares of employed immigrants were found among those whose mother tongue was Estonian, English or Russian. Estonians often easily master the Finnish language, which positively affects their employability in the Finnish labour markets. Somali and Arabic speakers in Finland had the lowest share of those employed.

Age at the time of arrival by CAGE project data plays an important role for immigrants in primary activity. It is evident that those who arrived as young children (under seven years of age) have successfully learnt the Finnish and/or Swedish language, the official languages of Finland, since they entered into the

Finnish school system at such an early stage. Similarly, a higher percentage of them also pursued further studies, as refugees and other migrants account for approximately one third of students. Refugees and other migrants who arrived in Finland at 7–14 or 15–17 years of age have participated more actively in the labour market and not continued with their studies. Higher rates of employment do not, however, reveal much about the type of occupation of such persons. Primary activity by education showed that the higher the level of education, the better one's employment prospects within the Finnish labour markets were. Primary activity of those refugees, other migrants and Finns, who had chosen not to complete their upper secondary education studies in Finland, were employed at the time. Knowledge is lacking regarding the type of work in which they are involved. More than one fourth of refugees and other migrants were unemployed at the time, while more than one fifth of them remained others outside the labour market.

The research findings of employment show that primary and secondary labour markets, in accordance with the Dual Labour Market Theory (Massey et al., 1993), exist in Finland. In the former, human capital is fully utilised, whereas this might not be the case with secondary labour markets, i.e. work and education do not always correspond. Among immigrants, there are those who get so-called better "Finnish" jobs and those who are recruited for jobs that require little or no training. The immigrants who have been most successful in finding work are usually highly educated Westerners, while those who have not succeeded are usually refugee-background immigrants. Resources are also wasted if the immigrant has a good education level but gets employed only in the elementary occupation, for example, as cleaners and helpers. These jobs are often classified as entry level jobs in the secondary labour market.

The occupational structure showed some gendered differentiation with respect to the labour market, as is the case also for Finnish-origin workers. It is striking that the share of foreign-origin workers in elementary occupations was much higher than for those of Finnish origin. Also, when comparing occupations between Britons and Iraqi origins, the Britons were employed especially as professionals, but the Iraqis more often worked in the occupations of secondary labour market.

Education and acquired human capital are essential for employment, and it is clear that higher education guarantees employment. The transfer of immigrant's human capital by Human Capital Theory (Chiswick, 1978) has thus succeeded from the origin country to the host country. The CAGE analysis also showed that highly educated refugees and other migrants were employed especially in the primary labour market, as were the Finns as a reference group. Some persons, however, experienced mismatch, working in the secondary labour market and overeducated for their professions indicating brain waste.

Immigrants seeking to enter the labour market face many kinds of challenges and barriers as this article has expressed. According to Lens et al. (2018), immigrants arriving in a new country lack country-specific human capital (work experience, language proficiency and recognition of their home country credentials) and social capital. This tends to result in higher risks of unemployment and lower occupational status and earnings compared to native-born persons. In Finland, learning and having a command of the Finnish or Swedish language is one of the key factors for successfully entering the labour market.

There exists also discrimination which can occur also indirectly when employers demand for example excessive language competence, even though performance of the job tasks may in practice not require full command of the language (see Aaltonen et al., 2009). Also prejudices among employers are significant barriers to the recruitment of immigrants as well as an inability to recognise foreign qualifications (Jaakkola, 2000; Lyytinen & Toom, 2019). Dunlavy and Gauffin (2020) express that refugee immigrants in particular face greater labour market disadvantages given the forced nature and potentially difficult circumstances of their migration, which can have lasting effects on their mental and physical health, both necessary for employment.

Discussion: the future need for immigrant labour in an ageing Finland

Finland will need immigrants to compensate for the mounting labour deficit due to the large number of the so-called baby boomers retiring. Many of them have already been leaving the workforce. As a result, the share of elderly people is growing in the population age structure. The demographic dependency ratio has in the long run switched from a higher child dependency ratio to a higher elderly dependency ratio in Finland. In terms of the population age structure, the share of persons aged 20–44 is clearly greater among foreign citizens than among Finnish citizens. Immigrants are thus at a favourable age with respect to finding work and forming families (see Heikkilä, 2017).

Finland needs immigrants for a variety of sectors, and it must compete for them with other ageing societies. There is a need for immigrants with different educational backgrounds: professionals to work as experts and less-educated persons to fill less-demanding positions. Likewise, with respect to the welfare sector in an ageing society, more labour will be needed in, for example, the areas of health care and social care.

It is thus important that immigrants find employment and remain in Finland as employees, tax payers, consumers and even as employers themselves. The benefits that immigrants bring to the host country cannot be measured only in monetary terms. The amount of knowledge, experience and international contacts, i.e. cultural and social capital, they possess are a valuable asset to any country.

Acknowledgements

I express my acknowledgements to Adjunct Professor Maili Malin, who is working as Senior Researcher at the Migration Institute of Finland. She has produced graphics for "Coming of Age in Exile (CAGE) – Health and Socio-

Economic Inequities in Young Refugees in the Nordic Welfare Societies" based on the project's register data. The CAGE project was funded by NordForsk.

References

Aaltonen, M., Joronen, M., & Villa, S. (2009). *Syrjintä työelämässä: pilottitutkimus työsuojelupiirien aineistosta.* Sisäasiainministeriön julkaisu 43. Helsinki: Sisäasiainministeriö.

Allport, G. W. (1954). *The nature of prejudice.* Cambridge, MA: Addison-Wesley Blackwell.

Bustamante, J. A. (2002). Immigrants' Vulnerability as Subjects of Human Rights. *International Migration Review, 36*(2), 333–354.

Carter, J. (2003). *Ethnicity, Exclusion and the Workplace.* Palgrave, Macmillan.

Chiswick, B. R. (1978). The Effect of Americanization on the Earnings of Foreign-born Men. *Journal of Political Economy, 86*(51), 897–921.

Dunlavy, A., de Montgomery C. J., Lorentzen T., Malin M., & Hjern A. (2020). *Equity in Education? A comparative analysis of educational outcomes among refugee children in the Nordic countries.* CAGE Project Report 1. https://cage.ku.dk/publications/dokumenter/ Equity_in_education__CAGE_report_2020.pdf

Dunlavy, A., & Gauffin, K. (2020). Labour Market Outcomes among Refugee Youth in the Nordic Countries: A Quantitative Comparative Overview. In S. Smith Jervelund, A. Krasnik, & A-K. Rosenkrantz de Lasson (Eds.), *Coming of Age in Exile. Health and Socio-Economic Inequalities in Young Refugees in the Nordic Welfare Societies* (pp. 50–56). Copenhagen: University of Copenhagen, Department of Public Health.

Edvardsson, I. R., Heikkilä, E., Johansson, M., Johannesson, H., Rauhut, D., Dall Schmidt, T., Stambøl, L. S., & Wilkman, S. (2007). *Demographic Changes, Labour Migration and EU-Enlargement: Relevance for the Nordic Regions.* Nordregio, Nordic Research Programme 2005–2008. Report: 2. https://www.diva-portal.org/smash/get/diva2:700425/FULLTEXT01.pdf

Eronen, A., Härmälä, V., Jauhiainen, S., Karikallio, H., Karinen, R., Kosunen, A., Laamanen, J-P., & Lahtinen, M. (2014). *Maahanmuuttajien työllistyminen: Taustatekijät, työnhaku ja työvoimapalvelut.* Työ- ja elinkeinoministeriön julkaisuja, Työ ja yrittäyys 6/2014. Helsinki: Työ- ja elinkeinoministeriö.

Ferm, N. (2017). *Unused talent.* Työelämä 2020 -blogi, Ilmiöitä työstä. Työ- ja elinkeinoministeriö.

Flatau, P., Petridis, R., & Wood, G. (1995). *Immigrants and Invisible Underemployment.* Melbourne: Bureau of Immigration, Multicultural and Population Research.

Forsander, A. (2002). *Luottamuksen ehdot: Maahanmuuttajat 1990-luvun suomalaisilla työmarkkinoilla.* Väestöntutkimuslaitoksen julkaisusarja D 39/2002. Helsinki: Väestöliitto, Väestöntutkimuslaitos.

Forsander, A. (2003). Insiders or Outsiders Within?: Immigrants in the Finnish Labour Market. *Yearbook of Population Research in Finland, 39*(2003), 55–72.

Gauffin, K., & Lyytinen E. (2017). *Working for Integration: A Comparative Analysis of Policies Impacting Labour Market Access among Young Refugees in the Nordic Countries.* CAGE Policy Report 1. https://cage.ku.dk/publications/dokumenter/CAGE_Policy_Report_1. pdf

Hämäläinen, K., Kangasharju, A., Pekkala, S., & Sarvimäki M. (2005). Maahanmuuttajien taloudellinen asema Suomessa. *Talous & Yhteiskunta,* (1), 33–39.

Heikkilä, E. (2005). Mobile vulnerabilities: perspectives on the vulnerabilities of immigrants in the Finnish labour market. *Population, Space and Place, 11*(6), 485–497.

Heikkilä, E. (2006). Regional development and labour market dynamics in Finland. *Nordia Geographical Publications, 34*(4), 13–27.

Heikkilä, E. (2017). Immigrants in the Finnish labour market and future needs in an ageing society. In E. Heikkilä (Ed.), *Immigrants and the labour markets. Experiences from abroad and*

Finland (pp. 131–160). Publications 17. Turku: Migration Institute of Finland. https://siirtolaisuusinstituutti.fi/wp-content/uploads/2020/04/elli-heikkila_immigrants-and-the-labour-markets-book.pdf

Heikkilä, E., & Pikkarainen, M. (2008). *Väestön ja työvoiman kansainvälistyminen nyt ja tulevaisuudessa.* Siirtolaisuustutkimuksia A 30. Turku: Siirtolaisuusinstituutti. https://siirtolaisuusinstituutti.fi/wp-content/uploads/2020/04/elli-heikkila-ja-maria-pikkarainen-vaeston-ja-tyovoiman-kansainvalistyminen-nyt-ja-tulevaisuudessa.pdf

Jaakkola, T. (2000) *Maahanmuuttajat ja etniset vähemmistöt työhönotossa ja työelämässä.* Työpoliittinen tutkimus 218. Helsinki: Työministeriö.

Kannisto, J. (2020). *Eläkkeellä ja työssä. Tilasto eläkeläisten työnteosta vuosina 2007–2019.* Eläketurvakeskuksen tilastoja 14/2020.

Kesä, M. (2016). *Missä ovat piilotyöpaikat ja miten niihin pääsee töihin?* Sitra Blogi. http://www.sitra.fi/blogi/missa-ovat-piilotyopaikat-ja-miten-niihin-paasee-toihin/

Kofman, E. (2003). Women Migrants and Refugees in the European Union. Conference on Economic and Social Aspects of Migration. The European Commission and the OECD.

Kosonen, R., Saari, E., Aaltonen, S., Heponiemi, T., Jauhiainen, S., Kankaanpää, R., Palander, J., Pöllänen, P., Steel, T., & Yijälä, A. (2019). *Maahanmuuttaja osalliseksi ja työhön.* Policy Brief 14.3.2019. Helsinki: Suomen Akatemia.

Krutova, O., Lipiäinen, L., & Koistinen, P. (2016). Patterns of Integration: A Longitudinal View of the Labour Market Attachment of Immigrants in Finland. *Nordic Journal of Migration Research, 6*(2), 102–114.

Kuivalainen, S. (2020). *Kun palkka ei riitä.* Turun Sanomat, January 31, 2.

Kyhä, H. (2011). *Koulutetut maahanmuuttajat työmarkkinoilla: Tutkimus korkeakoulututkinnon suorittaneiden maahanmuuttajien työllistymisestä ja työurien alusta Suomessa.* Turun yliopiston julkaisuja C 321. Turku: Turun yliopisto.

Larja, L., & Sutela, H. (2015). Työllisyys: Ulkomaalaistaustaisten miesten työllisyysaste lähes samalla tasolla kuin suomalaistaustaisella – naisilla enemmän vaikeuksia työllistyä. In T. Nieminen, H. Sutela, & U. Hannula, (Eds.), *Ulkomaista syntyperää olevien työ ja hyvinvointi Suomessa 2014* (pp. 71–82). Helsinki, Tilastokeskus.

Lens, D., Marx, I., & Vujic, S. (2018). *Is Quick Formal Access to the Labour Market Enough? Refugees' Labour Market Integration in Belgium.* Discussion Paper Series 11905. Bonn, Germany: Institute of Labour Economics, IZA.

Lyytinen, E., & Toom, N. (2019). *Two-way labour market integration? Perspectives on youth with a refugee background and employers in Finland.* CAGE 3B project report. https://cage.ku.dk/publications/dokumenter/Two-way_labour_market_integration_-_CAGE_report_2019.pdf

Massey, D. S., Arango, J., Hugo, G., Kouaouci, A., Pellegrino, A., & Taylor E. J. (1993). Theories of International Migration: A Review and Appraisal. *Population and Development Review, 19*(3), 431–466.

Ministry of Business, Innovation and Employment, MBIE (2013). *Employers' Role and Influence in Migration: A Literature Review.* Wellington: Ministry of Business, Innovation and Employment.

OECD (2018). *Working together. Skills and Labour Market Integration of Immigrants and their Children in Finland.* Paris: OECD Publishing.

OECD (2020). Education at a Glance 2020: OECD Indicators. Paris: OECD Publishing. https://doi.org/10.1787/69096873-en.

Ouali, N., & Rea, A. (1999). Young Migrants in the Belgian Labour Market: Integration, Discrimination and Exclusion. In J. Wrench, A. Rea & N. Ouali (Eds.), *Migrants, Ethnic Minorities and the Labour Market: Integration and Exclusion in Europe* (pp. 21–34). London: Macmillan/University of Warwick, Centre for Research in Ethnic Relations.

Pehkonen, A. (2017). The role of social networks in diverse work communities. In E.

Heikkilä (Ed.), *Immigrants and the labour markets. Experiences from abroad and Finland* (pp. 177–194). Publications 17. Turku: Migration Institute of Finland. https://siirtolaisuusinstituutti.fi/wp-content/uploads/2020/04/elli-heikkila_immigrants-and-the-labour-markets-book.pdf

Population Reference Bureau (2020). *Countries with the Oldest Populations in the World.* https://www.prb.org/countries-with-the-oldest-populations/

Ryding Zink, C. (2001). *Where You Come From Decides Where You Are Heading – a Qualitative Study of Well-Educated Immigrants Entering the Labour Market in Sweden.* Working Paper Series 7. Uppsala: Uppsala Universitet, Sociologiska institutionen,.

Schmid, G., & Gazier, B. (2002). *The Dynamics of Full Employment. Social Integration through Transitional Labour Markets.* Camberley: Edward Elgar Publishing.

Sjöblom-Immala, H. (2006). *Maahanmuuttajat Turussa yrittäjinä ja palkansaajina.* Työpoliittiinen tutkimus 318. Helsinki: Työministeriö.

Smith Jervelund, S., Krasnik, A., & Rosenkrantz de Lasson, A-K. (2020). Synthesis of the Labour Market Studies. In S. Smith Jervelund, A. Krasnik, & A-K. Rosenkrantz de Lasson (Eds.), *Coming of Age in Exile. Health and Socio-Economic Inequalities in Young Refugees in the Nordic Welfare Societies* (pp. 62–63). Copenhagen: University of Copenhagen, Department of Public Health.

Spence, M. A. (1974). *Market Signaling: Informational Transfer in Hiring and Related Screening Processes.* Harvard Economic Studies 143. Harvard: Harvard University Press.

Statistics Finland (2020). Population. www.stat.fi

Stenborg, M., Ahola, I., Palmén, O. & Pääkkönen, J. (2021). *Talouskasvun edellytykset tulevaisuudessa: Lähtökohdat, suunnat ja ratkaisut.* Valtiovarainministeriön julkaisuja 2021:6. Helsinki: Valtiovarainministeriö.

Sutela, H. (2015). Ulkomaalaistaustaiset työelämässä: Ulkomaalaistaustaisten työsuhteet usein määrä- tai osa-aikaisia – ammattirakenne selittää suuren osan eroista. In T. Nieminen, H. Sutela & U. Hannula (Eds.), *Ulkomaista syntyperää olevien työ ja hyvinvointi Suomessa 2014* (pp. 83–110). Helsinki: Tilastokeskus, Terveyden ja hyvinvoinnin laitos ja Työterveyslaitos.

Tassinopoulos, A., & Werner, H. (1999). *To Move or Not to Move – Migration of Labour in the European Union.* IAB Labour Market Research Topics 35.

Työministeriö (2004). *Kätevät ja pätevät: Esimerkkejä työhallinnon toteuttamista ESR-hankkeista.* Työministeriö.http://www.rakennerahastot.fi/vanhat_sivut/rakennerahastot/tiedos tot/esr_julkaisut_2000_2006/muut_julkaisut/01_katevat_ja_patevat-julkaisu.pdf

Työministeriö (2007). *Työvoima 2025. Täystyöllisyys, korkea tuottavuus ja hyvät työpaikat hyvinvoinnin perustana työikäisen väestön vähentyessä.* Työpoliittinen tutkimus 325. Helsinki: Työministeriö.

Vorobeva, E. (2019). *Black African Entrepreneurs in Finland: Structural Barriers.* Master's Thesis. Turku: The University of Turku, Baltic Sea Region Studies.

Vourc'h, F., De Rudder, V., & Tripier, M. (1999). Foreigners and Immigrants in the French Labour Market: Structural Inequality and Discrimination. In J. Wrench, A. Rea & N. Ouali (Eds.), *Migrants, Ethnic Minorities and the Labour Market. Integration and Exclusion in Europe* (pp. 72–92). University of Warwick, Centre for Research in Ethnic Relations. London: Macmillan Press Ltd.

Wrench, J. (1999). Employers and anti-Discrimination Measures in Europe: Good Practice and Bad Faith. In J. Wrench, A. Rea & N. Ouali (Eds.), *Migrants, Ethnic Minorities and the Labour Market. Integration and Exclusion in Europe* (pp. 229–251). University of Warwick, Centre for Research in Ethnic Relations. London: Macmillan Press Ltd.

FORCED MIGRANT'S SENSE OF PLACE: THE CASE OF SYRIAN REFUGEE-WORKERS IN ISTANBUL, TURKEY[1]

Basem Mahmud

Introduction

The issue of the integration of migrants has long been at the heart of public debates taking place in the societies of the Global North. Many of the refugees who move to these societies start their journey by first entering (often illegally) a neighboring country in the Global South, after which they tend to move to another country with better conditions. A good example is the case of those refugees who go to Indonesia and then to Australia or those who go to Turkey or Libya to arrive at a European country. This leads to more negotiations and collaborations among the states of the Global North and Global South. However, in these negotiations, the voices and lives of refugees are not considered; in the best cases, their rights and interests are acknowledged only "nominally". This is because Global North states seek to stop the flow at any cost.

In contrast, the Global South states (mostly governed by authoritarian regimes) are interested in acquiring funds or other political benefits (see Sørensen et al., 2017). Furthermore, research about refugees is almost always done with a structural approach that does not consider refugees' and asylum seekers' subjectivities. Moreover, there is little research on forced migrants in the Global South because of power relations in academic production; Global North institutions dominate the field and its interests and agenda.[2] Therefore, more research is needed about refugees' integration into societies of the Global South based on their perspectives.

This research studies refugee integration in one city of the Global South (Istanbul) by focusing on refugees' sense of place. It is divided into four parts; first, it reviews the available literature and explains the grounded theory developed in my previous research conducted among Syrian refugees and asylum seekers in Berlin. The second describes the methodology used in the present research. The third, which is the largest part, presents the findings.

[1] This paper is based on research funded by the European Union's Horizon, 2020 research and innovation program, Marie Sklodowska-Curie Actions, under Grant 841144 (Project FMGESI).
[2] A recent research study about *publishing in Refugee Survey Quarterly (RSQ) journal, the* researchers concluded the following: "Although 85% of the world's 79.5 million forced migrants reside in the Global South, almost all of the authors of articles in the RSQ over the past 10 years (89%) were affiliated to Global North institutions. This can have implications for the content of the research, with only 27% of the articles focused on forced displacement in the Global South, a figure which might change significantly if the journal had more articles by Global South authors" (McNally et al., 2020).

Background and state of the art

Since the 1980s, many Western companies have relocated to developing countries in search of more favorable conditions of production (i.e., increased and accelerated production at lower costs). In addition to technology and the reduced cost of transportation, inequality, and differing levels of development among countries have enabled these firms to operate on a transnational level. Industrial relocation clearly has had an effect on migration movements, reorganizing the place(s) where these firms are located and thus where workers searching for better opportunities move with the expectation of finding better jobs. On the other hand, countries compete to attract more foreign investment and situate their national economy globally, providing "legal security to investment, guaranteeing profits without social-labor conflicts" (Soriano Miras, 2019). Many researchers have analyzed the impact of this process on workers' situations (see Benería & Santiago, 2001; Chand, 2012). Some have analyzed this impact by focusing on the lives of migrant workers, who found themselves in a precarious situation when "frustrated expectations re-emerge and therefore external migration appears as a way out."(Soriano Miras, 2019). Other studies have tried to show another side; that the impact on the economy is very limited or even positive. To do this, they show how the formal economy is not affected, or sometimes positively affected (Akgündüz et al., 2018; Del Carpio & Wagner, 2015; Fakih & Ibrahim, 2015). Another route is to analyze the contributions of highly-skilled or educated refugee entrepreneurs (Bizri, 2017; Psoinos, 2007; Sayre et al., 2016; Wauters & Lambrecht, 2006). The result is that the situation of the refugee-worker in the global economy remains neglected. Therefore, their integration into these societies should be addressed differently from their countrymen who have greater access to facilities due to their social, cultural, or economic capital.

To assess the extent of integration we must first be clear on what integration requires. In the literature, there are different definitions of integration which generally revolve around the following dimensions: access to employment, housing, education, and health; social connection with various groups, language and cultural knowledge, safety and stability, rights and citizenship (Ager & Strang, 2008). Based on these dimensions, we can determine four domains; (1) Structural (related to the relationships with the state institutions), (2) Social (about social relations), (3) Cultural (language and cultural knowledge), and (4) Psychological; concerning emotional bonds with the new place and a feeling of inclusion in it (see Toruńczyk-Ruiz & Brunarska, 2020). Most research about integration in forced migration focuses on the first three domains. That is because when researchers study refugees' emotions, they do it based on therapeutic or pathologic approaches (cf Albrecht, 2016). Furthermore, social scientists tend to focus on social relations, while neglecting the spatial dimension. Kely and Chick (2007) found that the meanings attached to place (in the context of leisure activities) were based on memory, experience, and social relations. The physical attributes of the place were less significant: "Informants' perceptions of place and associated meanings were for the most part driven by what they did in the setting and with whom" (Kyle & Chick, 2007, p. 215). However, the relevance of this physical attribution may differ depending on the context, as another study shows: researchers compared both tourists' and locals' relations with the place and found that the local's sense of place is primarily shaped by aspects of everyday life (occupation, property, and most importantly, social relationships), and strongly associated with memories of childhood and youth. The tourist's sense of the place, however, is primarily shaped by the aesthetics and characteristics of the place experienced in their leisure-activity context (Kianicka et al., 2006). Therefore, the question arises, *how do refugees and asylum seekers construct their sense of place?*

Sense of place or place-attachment could be described as "the affective link that people establish with specific settings, where they tend to remain and where they feel comfortable and safe" (Hernández et al., 2007, p. 310). Therefore, this affective link is crucial for their well-being and behavior, affecting their practices of belonging and homemaking (Adams et al., 2018; Corcoran, 2002; Stedman, 2002). Moreover, although many researchers found that sense of place is essential for integration (Du & Li, 2010; Lin et al., 2020; Qian et al., 2011), little research has been done to understand it in the context of forced migration. When research considers place-attachment, they do so on a smaller scale (e.g. a neighborhood). Exploring refugees' place-attachment to their host city might be a better scale to consider social integration (Lin et al., 2020).

Consequently, I argue that understanding forced migrant´s sense of place will not only fill a gap in the literature about the affective dimension of integration, but it also could be the most appropriate way to understand the situation of refugees as they move from one place to another until arriving at a final destination. Therefore, the question is, *how do they decide to move or stay in a particular place, and what kind of relationships do they maintain with these places?*

Many researchers (mostly geographers) distinguish between place and "placelessness" or "non-place", in the words of Marc Augé. For Augé, place can be defined as relational, historical, or concerned with identity. Spaces that cannot be described with these terms are non-places (Augé, 1995, pp. 77–78). By this definition, a bus station, square, port, or street are non-places. However, during my Ph.D. research (Funded by the German Academic Exchange Service – DAAD), I found that all of these "non-places" may become places from the forced migrant's perspective. In my research, I used constructivist grounded theory to develop a theory based on the empirical data that I produced.[3] This theory explains the interaction between emotions and belonging (understood as feeling at home) in forced migration: The hope of starting a new life in a place and its elements (dignity/recognition, empathic emotions, legal status, and material satisfaction) determine refugees and asylum seekers' relationship with the place; non-places are those in which refugees and asylum seekers do not find any of these elements. When a place provides them only with the affective elements (dignity-recognition and empathic emotions), I describe this relationship as temporary in the sense that they cannot remain in the place for a

---

[3] I conducted 33 semi-structured in-depth interviews with 22 men and 11 women between 2015–2017. All of them are Syrian refugees and asylum seekers who live in Berlin who fled Syria after the uprising around March, 15th 2011.

long time. When the place provides them only with the instrumental elements (material satisfaction and legal status), I describe this relationship as rational-conditional. Feeling at home in a specific place emerges only when they find both the affective and instrumental elements in a given place. Once they are in such a place, the role of further emotions – social reciprocity, durable safety, and gratitude – become very significant in enhancing practices of home-building and subjective well-being; another two concepts which are indispensable for feeling at home. Therefore, while the tourist's relationship with a place is based on its physical attractiveness and the activities undertaken there, and the local's relationship with the place is based on memory, I argue that the forced migrant's relationship with the place is constructed based on the hope that s/he perceives, as Figure 1 demonstrates. Based on this idea and focusing on the case of the Syrian refugee workers in the textile industry in Istanbul, I will examine the relationship that refugees in a Global South society (Istanbul) maintain with the places where they live and work.

Figure 1. Forced migrant's relationship with a place.

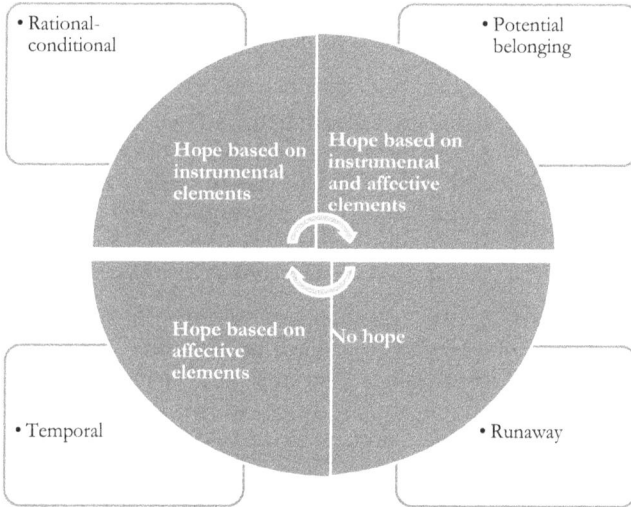

Despite some periods of crisis (Yendi & Çetin, 2012), since the 1980s Turkey's exportation has increased, making it one of the most important export countries (Ertugrul & Selcuk, 2001); its clothing industry significantly increased its exports from 777 million dollars in 1980 to 9.9 billion dollars in 1999 (Garrido Sotomayor, 2017). Among the world's textile-exporting countries, Turkey ranks eighth, and third among those supplying to Europe (Alkaya & Demirer, 2014). Most of the companies have been located in Istanbul, Izmir, Bursa, Denizli, Gaziantep, and Kahramanmarash (Marco Lau et al., 2012). Indeed, Istanbul became one of the most important destinations for migrants searching for work in the new economic system since 1950 (Guven, 2017). Its population grew significantly around the time it started to adopt proactive industrial relocation policies and later became one of the most important destinations for industrial relocation (OECD, 2008). In Istanbul, there is a significant amount of child labor and a weak social security system. The situation of the female workforce is even worse, and their participation in the total labor force is relatively low. Women in urban areas suffer from the under-participation trap; they are most likely to work in informal labor and housework (cooking, weaving, cleaning, childcare etc.) where the wage is very low. As a result, many of them stay at home. In addition, these women tend to invest less in girls' education, believing that girls' chances of participating in the labor market later in life are low. In this way, the cycle continues (Anderson, 2016, p. 15; Kabasakal et al., 2017, p. 229; Taymaz, 2010). As a whole, therefore, a high number of men and women of working age remain without coverage from the social security system (Günaydın, 2017). In a study aimed at evaluating the quality of workers' lives in a textile company in Turkey, which surveyed 87 workers, researchers found various negative indicators, especially the "Physical and Psychological", "Occupational Health" and "Organization, Motivation and Performance" (Koruca et al., 2011). Under these working conditions, refugees arrived with expectations of starting a new life after fleeing a war, many of whom leaving behind loved ones, who were either killed or detained.

Turkey currently hosts around 3.6 million displaced Syrians, of whom 98% live in urban areas (outside camps). By November 2019, 552,080 Syrians were registered in Istanbul (Directorate General of Migration Management, n.d.). Most of them work in the informal economy because of the restrictions on their access to the labor market.4 They have faced distinct challenges in Istanbul because of their specific status as a "guest" or a person with a "temporary protection residence permit." In addition to the difficult working conditions, this has also led to tensions with the local working-class (Europe Report N°248, 2018). Recent research about those who work in the textile industry shows that they often accept jobs with conditions which locals no longer accept, and are usually paid lower wages in comparison with locals (Kayaoglu, 2020). Therefore, studying their working conditions is essential to better planning for integration and understanding their decision to stay or move to another country.

Methodology

To understand the integration of the refugee workers in a Global South society, I analyzed data collected in Istanbul over the course of an ongoing project entitled *Refugees in the Global Economy: Situation, Role, and Implications: The case of Syrian refugee workers in the export industry in Istanbul.* This project aims to study the situation of refugee workers in the global economy and its implications for their everyday lives. It is a qualitative research based on semi-structured in-depth interviews. So far, I have conducted 60 interviews (12 women, 10 minors, and 38 men). All of them are Syrian refugee workers in the textile industry in Istanbul. Questions were open-ended, and broadly focused on their lives both in the place of work and outside it. This reflects the symbolic interactionist approach, which seeks to learn about participants' views concerning their own experiences. I tried

---

4 For example, the number of Syrians in a firm (working legally) cannot be more than 10% of the total number of native workforce. The number of Syrians with a work permit by April 2020, is only 34,573 (Kayaoglu, 2020).

to keep the interviews informal and conversational at all times, as Charmaz (2006, p. 29) suggests. Therefore, I did not even consult the guide until I felt that all of my questions had been answered. I then briefly reviewed the guide while notifying the interviewee that we had almost finished but that I needed to be sure that we had discussed all of the relevant points. Furthermore, I tried to make the questions "sufficiently general to cover a wide range of experiences and narrow enough to elicit and explore the participant's specific experience" (Charmaz & Belgrave, 2012, p. 351). One of the most important questions used to develop this research was the following: *do you think Istanbul could be the place where you say; here I will stay forever? Why? What would it need in order to become this place?* In order to protect the privacy of the participants, all names mentioned in this paper are pseudonyms.

Findings

During the data analysis, I coded and classified the data under the four categories or dimensions of the new-life hope in a place; legal status, material satisfaction, empathic emotions, and dignity recognition.

Legal status

Here I refer to the status that a person has in a specific country as defined by law. It is defined and categorized in terms of legal rights and duties which differ according to whether a person is a citizen, granted temporary protection, undocumented, an asylum seeker, refugee, visitors/or tourist. The legal status is based on the idea that rights are determined differently for different segments of the population living in the national territory. Thus, it is about the contractual relationship between the state and the inhabitants (Butenschøn, 2015). Obtaining legal status is crucial because people cannot engage in any of the activities necessary for starting a new life without it. The first step occurs when the forced migrant arrives and applies for asylum. The moment when their application is accepted is critical because it is vital for their entire future (see Bernhard & Young, 2009). However, Syrians in Turkey are not recognized as refugees; they are "guests" under temporary protection status. This status gives them limited access to fundamental rights (access to health and education and social services). Still, they have limited and conditional access to employment and freedom of movement within Turkey.[5] In 2018, Turkish authorities stopped registering most of the newly-arrived Syrian asylum seekers in Istanbul as well as in nine provinces on or near the Syrian border. This suspension of registration has given rise to several problems for refugees who need to move to another city other than the one in which they registered. Many of the Syrian minors lose their right to enroll in schools, thus pushing them to look for work. Since the Syrian refugees' legal status in Istanbul is weak, it directly affects the other instrumental element; the material satisfaction. Muhammed, who is working in the informal market,

---

[5] In order to travel to another province they need a "travel permit" (yol izin belgesi), and to work formally they need a work permit, to which there are enormous bureaucratic barriers. The result is that only 15,000 have obtained the permits needed for formal employment and about 750,000–950,000 Syrians work in the informal sector (International Crisis Group, 2018).

describes this situation. Even though his situation is extreme (he is without any kind of legal status in Turkey), the situation of other workers who obtained temporary protection status does not considerably differ. The difference lies in their abilities to move freely in the city without being persecuted and in their access to health and social services.

Muhammad: [there is] a great deal of exploitation of human effort, of the person's psyche, and great exploitation of children in general, and of women. I mean in terms of rights, we do not have even the simplest rights. Today as a refugee sitting in a certain place, my presence is illegal, I do not get the salary that I should for the work that I do, and I do not have any insurance, neither health nor material nor financial. Just this!

Material satisfaction

By material satisfaction, I refer to "housing and living conditions, with income's purchasing power, and with financial solvency" (Rojas, 2007). Refugee workers' salaries differ based on the kind of work they do, which is related to their experience. For example, an *ortacı* (runner – errand boy) who does not have a clearly-defined job task and is not allowed to learn a specific task in most cases, earns between 1,300–1,700 Turkish lira (around 140–185 euros) monthly. This is the work of most of the minors in this industry. Other workers who have more experience (usually as a tailor) earn between 2,000–4,000 Turkish lira (around 220–440 euros). These numbers are calculated based on an 11–12 hours of daily work. Due to a restrictive system of punishment, they may lose a significant portion of this amount; if they come late or are absent one hour, they sometimes lose the equivalent of a half-day of wages. To understand how this would affect material satisfaction, it would be useful to mention that Turkey's monthly minimum wage is 2,943 Turkish lira (around 325 euros), and to rent an apartment in a remote area in the city, one will need about 1000 Turkish lira including water and electricity (around 110 euros). The Syrians Barometer 2019 (Erdoğan, 2020) found that the area in which Syrians face most problems is "working conditions"; it ranked 1th out of 7 problems.[6] As becomes apparent in the words of Lina, the combination of low wages and long working-hours has a harsh effect on their subjective well-being in the place. In the case of families in which at least one minor is working, feelings of guilt were always present in the parents' narratives.

Me: Do you think that Istanbul could be the place where you live forever?

Lina: No.

Me: What would it need in order to become this place?

Lina: Comfort, psychological comfort, the most important thing is

---

[6] The order is as follows: (1) working conditions, (2) communication/language, (3) accommodation, (4) food, (5) discrimination, (6) health, (7) education. With the exception of communication, the main problems concern material satisfaction, followed by discrimination which has to do with dignity-recognition and empathic emotions.

psychological comfort, as our situation I mean frankly, I oppress my daughters, meaning that they know nothing about life, and they know nothing because they must work. I mean, it's my dream that my daughters study. I mean [...] my only wish is that my daughters complete their studies, and that they succeed in their studies and their lives, I mean. I want the place that makes my daughters feel comfortable with their studies, and that they do not lose their future. As for work, it means having security in the job that they do. This is not ... I mean, at any moment, we can go back to Syria, at any moment they can expel us, no one knows. I mean, this is not a future for me or for my children, even for us in Syria. I mean, we do not have these factories in our region, so you cannot say that they could go to work there. These factories are in Aleppo and Damascus, but we are from Aljazeera.

In this way, both of the instrumental elements of the new-life hope in Istanbul are weakened. Therefore, rational-conditional or the potential-belonging relationship with the city cannot stand among the refugee workers in the textile industry in Istanbul. In the following, I examine the affective elements.

Empathic emotions

Here I refer to empathic emotions such as empathy, tenderness, sympathy, compassion, and soft-heartedness as "other-oriented emotions elicited by and congruent with the perceived welfare of someone in need" (Lishner et al., 2011, p. 614). These emotions are evoked by putting oneself in the place of the other (cf. Shott, 1979). Empathic emotions are fundamental for the perception of justice in society (Hoffman, 1989) and are therefore essential for the individual's engagement with the environment in which they live, and thus for their well-being and adaption (Dalbert, 2009; Lerner, 1980; Lerner & Miller, 1978). Researchers argue that empathy could be used to improve intergroup relations (Batson & Ahmad, 2009).

Feeling welcome and safe are both essential for the forced migrant's well-being. People may feel partially safe as soon as they put their feet on a territory in which there is no longer the possibility of attack or threat from the very forces from which they fled. However, this is not enough to feel a durable safety and welcome; the perception of empathic emotions (among the other elements of the new-life hope) in the new place is essential. When these emotions do not exist, the initial feelings of safety in the place cannot persist, even if the forced migrant has obtained legal status and economic support.

The political discourse of the Turkish government and its open-door policy during the first years after the Syrian uprising positively affected the perception of empathic emotions among Syrians in Turkey. However, the situation changed later as Nimer and Içduygu explain; "the solidarity of society towards Syrian refugees slowly faded, especially as the government progressively took steps to provide social services, employment rights and citizenship, and the public perceived Syrians as competing for the same resources." (Içduygu & Nimer, 2020). In a survey (2016) conducted by Kemerburgaz University and the

University of Kent about the perception of Turks in Istanbul toward Syrian refugees, researchers found that 72% of respondents said that they feel uncomfortable encountering refugees, and about 75% said that they do not feel any sympathy towards the Syrians. It seems that the media plays an essential role in negatively representing Syrian refugees (see Onay-Coker, 2019). I found Salam's words to reflect the essentiality of the empathic emotions for the relationship with the place. In her description of why she will not leave Istanbul, she remarks that people in her neighborhood "like us", and she feels that her daughter (who lives in Syria) is close to her.

Salam: I do not want to leave Istanbul, especially Istanbul, I mean, because the first time I came here I went to many areas and I liked all of them, even an area like this. I mean, a very clean area and its people like us. Go to another country? Why? I do not want to. Here I feel that I am close to Damascus, and I feel my daughter is close to me. I have the hope that my daughter could come to visit me. That is, when I look at Europe I become afraid that I would return to starting again from zero (nothing). (Silence) I become afraid because when I came to Turkey I suffered so much, it was tiring just to reach this stage, even though I don't feel that I have really arrived … but I live in stability.

However, the absence of empathic emotions or even inimical orientation is reflected in most of the interviews I have conducted. Most participants complained about the lack or absence of any of these emotions as Razan's words show:

The rights of the worker. What does it mean? Unfortunately, here there are no rights especially if you are Syrian. It is well known that "Syrians go to work", unfortunately, our work generates problems between us and the Turks! My neighbor said because of you my son will lose his job? I said why because of us? What is our fault? You want to work and we want to work, even though we do not ask for insurance nor do we ask for anything more than work. We do not ask for a salary, we just want to pay our rent and pay our bills so that we do not depend on others. This is our request, nothing more.

Dignity – recognition

Here, I refer to human dignity and social dignity. The first is "the inherent and inalienable value that belongs to every human being simply by virtue of being human" (Jacobson, 2007, p. 294) while the second – which is related to the first – is about recognition and is thus reflected in behavior, social interactions, and perception. It is "experienced, bestowed, or earned through interaction in social settings" (Jacobson, 2007, p. 294).

Perception of dignity influences the forced migrant's well-being in the place and can take different forms. Dignity is based on four main themes (Khatib & Armenian, 2010); (1) Autonomy, which includes independence, control, the ability to make one's own decisions, and functional capacity. (2) Worthiness, which is about feeling important and valuable to others. (3) Self-respect, which means respect for oneself and others. (4) Self-esteem, which concerns all qualities that help to maintain self-respect such as the role of preservation, continuity of self, legacy, and so on. This perception is constructed based on interactions both inside and outside the workplace. As I explained previously, however, since refugee workers spend most of their time in the workplace, those interactions are central for their perceptions of dignity; discrimination in salary or treatment, stereotypes, ignorance of their culture that most of these refugees believe to be similar to the Turkish one, and mockery of their language or accent. All of this has a severe negative effect on their perceptions of dignity-recognition. Most of the refugees whom I met mention this. However, it is also related to hierarchy: attacks on *ortacı* are common and repeated, whereas, in the tailor's case, it is relatively less common (see Fadi's words).

> *Fadi: In the workshop where I used to work, I mean, they look at you as if you do not see anything in your life. I mean, there are some things like this, asking you questions, for example…*

> *Me: For example.*

> *Fadi: Football is my hobby. I go to play, so they ask you if you have this in Syria? Ahh, we are from another planet so you ask me this question? In many things, they will be surprised when they know that we have it in Syria, do you have this in Syria? Yes we do, but the war obligated us to come here.*

Discussion

The new-life hope in a place approach – and its instrumental (legal status and material satisfaction) and affective elements (empathic emotions and dignity-recognition) – allows understanding the refugees' and asylum seekers' sense of place and, therefore, their integration in the new place. In Istanbul, the main challenge comes from the instrumental elements; extreme exploitation at work and uncertain legal status with limitations. Furthermore, the affective side is mostly unsatisfied. This is because of the high level of discrimination, stereotypes, and ignorance of the refugee's culture from the country of origin. However, it is sometimes satisfied due to the increased number of Syrian refugees in the city that facilitate finding work in a more familiar atmosphere.

Consequently, in Istanbul, the runaway or temporary relationships with place are dominant. Therefore, policy planning for the integration of refugees in Istanbul should focus on allocating more resources toward providing them with the necessary instrumental elements. Regarding the affective elements, "a dramatic change of policy in Turkey is desperately needed, one that allows for Syrians to work and encourages new thinking regarding Syrian people not as a burden but as potential. This will not solve the problems faced by Syrians in Turkey, in Europe, or elsewhere, but it will surely be a good beginning" (Chemin, 2016, p. 72).

As mentioned earlier, Turkish authorities' cessation of registering the majority of newly-arrived Syrian asylum seekers in Istanbul and nine provinces on or near the Syrian border since 2018 has led to various severe problems. As a result, many Syrian minors do not have the right to enroll in schools and are pushed to look for work. All of this has severe consequences for their physical and psychological development and, of course, their future work-prospects. This issue has a special importance in the case of minor refugee workers who were either born in Turkey, or left Syria at a very young age. Further research is required on how these minors attempt to build a life in Istanbul and develop a relationship with Istanbul. Indeed, when asked about the city, they do not refer to it as other refugees normally would. They describe it locally – *this is my city* – even though the state does not recognize them as such.

Ensuring material satisfaction is a complicated issue because it requires a change at the level of the national economy and a reorganization of both the formal and informal work sectors. Toward this end, it would be useful to facilitate the work permit process, to facilitate refugees' movement among the different provinces while searching for a job, raising awareness among employers about procedures for applying for a work permit, and providing assistance in doing so. Most of them do not know how, and therefore prefer to avoid it. The findings suggest a clash between the idea of temporary protection and the development of a feeling of belonging. Integration policies need to be questioned in terms of this contradiction; *how could we invite people to be integrated while at the same time never ceasing to remind them that they will soon go back to their home?*

References

Adams, H., Ghanem, S., & Collins, M. (2018). *Same space, different places: How bonds to place affect well-being and social-cohesion in Syrian refugees and their Lebanese host communities*. British Academy & King's College London.

Ager, A., & Strang, A. (2008). Understanding integration: A conceptual framework. *Journal of Refugee Studies*, *21*(2), 166–191. https://doi.org/10.1093/jrs/fen016

Akgündüz, Y. E., Van Den Berg, M., & Hassink, W. (2018). The impact of the syrian refugee crisis on firm entry and performance in Turkey. *World Bank Economic Review*, *32*(1), 19–40. https://doi.org/10.1093/wber/lhx021

Albrecht, Y. (2016). Emotions in Motion: How feelings are considered in the scope of migration sociological studies. *Digithum*, *18*.

Alkaya, E., & Demirer, G. N. (2014). Sustainable textile production: A case study from a woven fabric manufacturing mill in Turkey. *Journal of Cleaner Production*, *65*, 595–603. https://doi.org/10.1016/j.jclepro.2013.07.008

Anderson, R. (2016). *Variations in Turkey's Female Labor Market: The Puzzling Role of Education*. Duke University Durham.

Augé, M. (1995). *Non-places*. Verso.

Batson, C. D., & Ahmad, N. Y. (2009). Using Empathy to Improve Intergroup Attitudes and Relations. *Social Issues and Policy Review*. https://doi.org/10.1111/j.1751-2409.2009.01013.x

Benería, L., & Santiago, L. E. (2001). The impact of industrial relocation on displaced workers: A case study of Cortland, New York. *Economic Development Quarterly*. https://doi.org/10.1177/089124240101500107

Bernhard, J. K., & Young, J. E. E. (2009). Gaining institutional permission: Researching precarious legal status in Canada. *Journal of Academic Ethics*. https://doi.org/10.1007/s10805-009-9097-9

Bizri, R. M. (2017). Refugee-entrepreneurship: a social capital perspective. *Entrepreneurship & Regional Development*, 1–22. https://doi.org/10.1080/08985626.2017.1364787

Butenschøn, N. (2015). Arab Citizen and the Arab State: The "Arab Spring" as a Critical Juncture in Contemporary Arab Politics. *Democracy and Security*, *11*(2), 111–128.

Chand, P. (2012). Implications of Industrial Relocation on Workers in Delhi. *Social Change*, *42*(1), 49–68.

Charmaz, K. (2006). *Constructing grounded theory: a practical guide through qualitative analysis* (Vol. 10). SAGE Publications Ltd. https://doi.org/10.1016/j.lisr.2007.11.003

Charmaz, K., & Belgrave, L. (2012). Qualitative interviewing and Grounded Theory analysis. In *The SAGE Handbook of Interview Research: The Complexity of the Craft* (pp. 347–366). https://doi.org/10.4135/9781452218403

Chemin, J. E. (2016). Guests-Hosts Relations in the Context of the Syrian Exodus: A Study of Turkish and Syrian Populations in Two Turkish Cities. *Middle East Journal of Refugee Studies*. https://doi.org/10.12738/mejrs.2016.1.2.0003

Corcoran, M. P. (2002). Place attachment and community sentiment in marginalised neighbourhoods: A European case study. *Canadian Journal of Urban Research*.

Dalbert, C. (2009). Belief in a just world. In *Handbook of individual differences in social behavior*.

Del Carpio, X. V., & Wagner, M. (2015). Impact of Syrian refugees on the Turkish labour market. In *Research working paper: Vol. WPS 7402* (Issue August). http://www-wds.worldbank.org/external/default/WDSContentServer/WDSP/IB/2016/02/09/090224b08415e3b5/3_0/Rendered/PDF/The0impact0of00Turkish0labor0market.pdf

Directorate General of Migration Management. (n.d.). *Geçici Koruma*. Retrieved November 27, 2020, from https://www.goc.gov.tr/gecici-koruma5638

Du, H., & Li, S. (2010). Migrants, urban villages, and community sentiments: a case of guangzhou, china. *Asian Geographer*. https://doi.org/10.1080/10225706.2010.9684155

Erdoğan, M. (2020). *Syrians Barometer 2019*. https://reliefweb.int/sites/reliefweb.int/files/resources/SB2019-ENG-04092020.pdf

Ertugrul, A., & Selcuk, F. (2001). A Brief Account of the Turkish Economy, 1980-200. *Russian and East European Finance and Trade*, *37*(6), 6–30.

Europe Report N°248. (2018). *Turkey's Syrian Refugees: Defusing Metropolitan Tensions*.

Fakih, A., & Ibrahim, M. (2015). The impact of Syrian refugees on the labor market in neighboring countries: empirical evidence from Jordan. *Defence and Peace Economics*, *2694*(June 2015), 1–23. https://doi.org/10.1080/10242694.2015.1055936

Garrido Sotomayor, V. (2017). *Approach to mango's supply chain in turkey*.

Günaydın, D. (2017). The Determinant of the Employment-Social Protection Relation in Turkey. In *Handbook of Research on Technology Adoption, Social Policy, and Global Integration* (pp. 1–19).

Guven, B. (2017). *Understanding Urban Change in Istanbul: From the Capital City to the City of Capital*. https://doi.org/10.17605/OSF.IO/NCV5Z

Hernández, B., Carmen Hidalgo, M., Salazar-Laplace, M. E., & Hess, S. (2007). Place attachment and place identity in natives and non-natives. *Journal of Environmental Psychology*. https://doi.org/10.1016/j.jenvp.2007.06.003

Hoffman, M. L. (1989). Empathic emotions and justice in society. *Social Justice Research*. https://doi.org/10.1007/BF01048080

Içduygu, A., & Nimer, M. (2020). The politics of return: exploring the future of Syrian refugees in Jordan, Lebanon and Turkey. *Third World Quarterly*. https://doi.org/10.1080/01436597.2019.1675503

International Crisis Group. (2018). Turkey's Syrian Refugees: Defusing Metropolitan Tensions. *Europe Report*.

Jacobson, N. (2007). Dignity and health: a review. *Social Science & Medicine (1982)*. https://doi.org/10.1016/j.socscimed.2006.08.039

Kabasakal, H., Karakaş, F., Maden, C., & Aycan, Z. (2017). Women in management in Turkey. In R. Burke & A. Richardsen (Eds.), *Women in Management Worldwide: Signs of Progress*. Routledge.

Kayaoglu, A. (2020). Labour market impact of syrian refugees in Turkey: The view of employers in informal textile sector in istanbul. *Migration Letters*. https://doi.org/10.33182/ML.V17I5.891

Khatib, R., & Armenian, H. (2010). Developing an Instrument for Measuring Human Dignity and Its Relationship to Health in Palestinian Refugees. *World Medical & Health Policy*. https://doi.org/10.2202/1948-4682.1077

Kianicka, S., Buchecker, M., Hunziker, M., & Müller-Böker, U. (2006). Locals' and Tourists' Sense of Place. *Mountain Research and Development*, *26*(1), 55–63. https://doi.org/10.1659/0276-4741(2006)026[0055:LATSOP]2.0.CO;2

Koruca, H. I., Stowasser, S., Ozdemir, G., Orhan, H., & Aydemir, E. (2011). Evaluation of working life quality for a textile company in turkey: A case study. *Gazi University Journal of Science*, *24*(1), 101–112.

Kyle, G., & Chick, G. (2007). The social construction of a sense of place. *Leisure Sciences*, *29*(3), 209–225. https://doi.org/10.1080/01490400701257922

Lerner, M. J. (1980). The Belief in a Just World. In *The Belief in a Just World. Perspectives in Social Psychology*.

Lerner, M. J., & Miller, D. T. (1978). Just world research and the attribution process: Looking back and ahead. *Psychological Bulletin*. https://doi.org/10.1037/0033-2909.85.5.1030

Lin, S., Wu, F., & Li, Z. (2020). Beyond neighbouring: Migrants' place attachment to their host cities in China. *Population, Space and Place*. https://doi.org/10.1002/psp.2374

Lishner, D. A., Batson, C. D., & Huss, E. (2011). Tenderness and sympathy: Distinct empathic emotions elicited by different forms of need. *Personality and Social Psychology Bulletin*. https://doi.org/10.1177/0146167211403157

Marco Lau, C., Suvankulov, F., & Filiz Karabag, S. (2012). *Determinants of firm competitiveness: case of the Turkish textile and apparel industry*.

McNally, R., Joel, M., & Rahim, N. (2020). *How global is the RSQ? A reflection on author affiliation and knowledge production in the global forced migration academic discourse*. Refugee Law Initiative. https://rli.blogs.sas.ac.uk/2020/11/12/how-global-is-the-rsq-a-reflection-on-author-affiliation-and-knowledge-production-in-the-global-forced-migration-academic-discourse/?fbclid=IwAR0VuIIPxpIfxLpDB-Zqvjp9qek2Qjz7hula_BlxnEUt14NkCXY7BO_PugY

OECD. (2008). *OECD Territorial Reviews OECD Territorial Reviews: Istanbul, Turkey 2008*.

Onay-Coker, D. (2019). The representation of Syrian refugees in Turkey: a critical discourse analysis of three newspapers. *Continuum*. https://doi.org/10.1080/103043 12.2019.1587740

Psoinos, M. (2007). Exploring highly educated refugees' potential as knowledge workers in contemporary Britain. *Equal Opportunities International*, *26*(8), 834–852. https://doi.org/10.1108/02610150710836163

Qian, J., Zhu, H., & Liu, Y. (2011). Investigating urban migrants' sense of place through a multi-scalar perspective. *Journal of Environmental Psychology*. https://doi.org/10.1016/j.jenvp.2011.01.002

Rojas, M. (2007). The complexity of wellbeing: A life-satisfaction conception and a domains-of-life approach. In *Wellbeing in Developing Countries: From Theory to Research*. https://doi.org/10.1017/CBO9780511488986.013

Sayre, N., Louise Mary, C., & Bruce, C. (2016). Labour mobility as part of the solution. *Forced Migration Review*, *52*, 31–32.

Shott, S. (1979). Emotion and Social Life: A Symbolic Interactionist Analysis. *American Journal of Sociology*, *84*(6), 1317–1334. https://doi.org/10.1086/226936

Sørensen, N. N., Kleist, N., Lucht, H., Holm, H., & Splidsboel, F. (2017). *Europe and the refugee situation: Human security implications*. https://www.econstor.eu/handle/10419/19 7639

Soriano Miras, R. M. (2019). A synthesis: The relationship between the global and the local in industrial relocation on the northern borders of Mexico and Morocco. In A. Trinidad Requena, R. Soriano-Miras, M. Solís, & K. Kopinak (Eds.), *Localized Global Economies on the Northern Borderlands of Mexico and Morocco*. Palgrave Macmillan, Cham. https://doi.org/https://doi.org/10.1007/978-3-319-96589-5_8

Stedman, R. C. (2002). Toward a social psychology of place: Predicting behavior from place-based cognitions, attitude, and identity. *Environment and Behavior*. https://doi.org/10.1177/0013916502034005001

Taymaz, E. (2010). *Growth, employment, skills and female labor force*. State Planning Organization & World Bank.

Toruńczyk-Ruiz, S., & Brunarska, Z. (2020). Through attachment to settlement: social and psychological determinants of migrants' intentions to stay. *Journal of Ethnic and Migration Studies*. https://doi.org/10.1080/1369183X.2018.1554429

University of Kent and İstanbul Kemerburgaz University. (2016). *Suriyelilere yönelik algı ve tutumlar araştırması ön değerlendirme raporu*.

Wauters, B., & Lambrecht, J. (2006). Refugee entrepreneurship in Belgium: Potential and practice. *International Entrepreneurship and Management Journal*, *2*(4), 509–525. https://doi.org/10.1007/s11365-006-0008-x

Yendi, R., & Çetin, S. (2012). The Turkish Economy and The Global Crisis. *International Business: Research, Teaching and Practice*, *6*(2), 45–58.

SYRIAN REFUGEE ENTREPRENEURSHIP AND DIFFERENTIATED INTEGRATION IN THE DISTRICTS OF HATAY, TURKEY

Olgu Karan

Introduction

The Syrian internal war that erupted in 2011 led millions of Syrians to leave their countries looking for refuge in Turkey. According to the figures provided by the Republic of Turkey's Ministry of Interior Directorate General of Migration Management, the number of Syrians under temporary protection with registered biometric data was 3,639,572 as of December 16, 2020 (Mülteciler Derneği, 2020). As Turkey hosts more than 3 million Syrians, the refugee integration policies regarding access to health, education, labor market, and citizenship are under intense public debate. Syrian entrepreneurs residing in specifically near border regions and big metropolitan cities like İstanbul are also known to have set up small shops in various sectors. According to the Union of Chambers and Commodity Exchanges of Turkey, 173 corporations and 8,038 limited companies operating with Syrian financial capital are found between January 2013 and April 2019 (TOBB, 2019). Accordingly, migrant entrepreneurship has been asserted to not only be able to foster migrant's self-reliance and integration into the host society, but also to be able to ease the social and cultural adaptation processes of migrants into their new environment (Rath & Swagerman, 2011). In this respect, analysing the dynamics, opportunities, and the difficulties within the field of migrant entrepreneurship is essential.

Turkey is not a homogeneous country within its regions in terms of demographic structure. Thus, strategies for integration, adaptation and daily life experiences of urban Syrian refugees living together with host society differ according to socio-economic, socio-cultural, and socio-spatial disparities. Accordingly, studies that neglect spatial differences, i.e., demographic characteristics of the space, and make over-generalisation would be misleading to understand the nexus between the space specific difficulties and the space specific strategies generated for economic survival as well as the field specific integration difficulties faced by Syrian refugees. Migrant survival strategies are differentiated by the characteristics of the region, neighbourhood, or even street. Because forms of capital generated by (would be) entrepreneurs within the field entrepreneurship are shaped and could only be understood in relation to the structure of the field, the power relations in the field and as well as the positions occupied by the actors in the field.

Literature review

While notable research studies on migrant/ethnic minority entrepreneurship on both sides of the Atlantic dates to early 1970s (see Light, 1972), this study aims to contribute to the emerging scholarship on migrant entrepreneurship in Turkey focusing on Syrian entrepreneurship. One of the influential approaches that dominate the migrant entrepreneurship literature is that agency-oriented studies. They are being developed to address the qualities, personal characteristics, cultures, motivations, strategies of migrants and the forms of capital they create in both source and destination countries (Altınay, 2008; Altınay & Altınay, 2006; Basu & Altınay, 2002; Basu 1998; Bizri, 2017; Hofstede, 1991; Katila & Wahlbeck, 2012; Kayalar & Yıldız, 2017; Mawson & Kasem, 2019; McEvoy & Hafeez, 2007; Obschonka & Hahn, 2018; Özkul & Dengiz, 2018; Shneikat & Alrawadieh, 2019; Srinivasan, 1995; Werbner, 1984, 1990). Although such studies are important and contribute to the recognition that refugees are not a homogeneous group and differ in terms of their qualities, and forms of capital they have, they ignore the socio-economic, socio-cultural, and demographic characteristics of the space where migrants are settled, the structure and functioning of the area.

Some scholars (Kloosterman, van der Leun & Rath 1999; Kloosterman & Rath, 2001, 2003; Rath, 2017) proposed a more nuanced mixed embeddedness approach to immigrant entrepreneurship that recognises the regulatory structures and market dynamics. The advantage of this multi-level mixed embeddedness approach lies in its focus on interplay between ethnic social networks and political, economic structures. As Rath (2017, p. 6) states, "it acknowledges the significance of immigrants' concrete embeddedness in social networks and conceives that their relations and transactions are embedded in wider economic and politico institutional structures." Even though the mixed embeddedness model stresses the importance of immigrant's agency, it fails to explore the agency dimension empirically (Karan, 2017; 2019; Tatlı et. al., 2014; Trupp, 2015. Economic actions of ethnic entrepreneurs are viewed as responses to larger structures beyond their influence without considering the entrepreneur's own sense of these structures. These structures viewed as an externality to ethnic entrepreneurs. Accordingly, their own sense of external structures, i.e., habitus, which brings agency and structure together, is neglected. Thus, the meanings, and definitions that people bring to their situation in the confrontation and negotiation between themselves and structures are not explored empirically (Tatlı et al. 2014, 59). However, potential entrepreneurs act according to the "feel for the game" (Bourdieu, 1990), a practical sense of entrepreneurial action, which could be successful, and meaningful survival strategy. Accordingly, Bourdieu's concept habitus could be utilised to fill this gap within ethnic minority entrepreneurship literature. The article argues that demographic, economic and socio-cultural differences within the districts of Hatay province led to differentiated entry possibilities, barriers, and strategies for Syrian refugees in small business ownership. This study aims to contribute to the emerging scholarship on Syrian Refugee entrepreneurship in Turkey by utilising Bourdieusian field theory.

Bourdieu's relational perspective

Rather than borrowing piecemeal from Bourdieu's work, Bourdieu's full theoretical account opens fresh and innovative possibilities for theoretical and empirical research. The research shows how Bourdieu's concepts such as field, habitus, and forms of capital are constitutively bound up within each other.

According to Bourdieu, a field may be seen as a relationally structured space of positions involving objective relationship between individual and institutional agents competing for the same stakes (Bourdieu, 1987). The concept of "the field" entails the contextual and institutional forces that define and govern the legitimate rules and resources of those who enter it. Fields are competitive areas of struggle for power/capital between the dominant group and the subordinate group (Swartz, 2002). Utilising the concept of field in small business research is fruitful for bringing in and operationalising the structural forces that are in play at social, institutional and organisational levels (Tatlı et al. 2014, p. 62–63).

Habitus refers to cognitive, internalised structures acquired through a relationship to a field that yields to a system of durable and transposable embodied dispositions (Bourdieu, 1977). It refers to actors relatively durable set of dispositions of judgement and practices acquired by an actor's early life experiences and modified (to a greater or lesser degree) in later life (Emirbayer & Johnson, 2008). The concept of habitus entails the subjective dimension of human agency (Tatlı et al., 2014 p. 63). Habitus mediates between structure and agency. It offers not only a powerful means of linking individual action and macro-structural processes within which future action is taken, but also links past fields and present fields through the individual actor moving from one field to another (Emirbayer & Johnson, 2008). Bourdieu's (1986) concept of forms of capital emphasises the conflicts and power relations in stratified societies where capitals are not distributed equally (Swartz, 1997, p. 74). Bourdieu (1986) defined four forms of capital: Economic capital refers to the resources that are immediately and directly transposable into money. Cultural capital exists in three subtype states, namely embodied, institutionalised and objectified. The embodied form of cultural capital refers to the "long standing dispositions of mind and body" such as someone's dialect or accent, while the objectified state addresses goods such as books, machines, dictionaries, and paintings. Finally, in its institutionalised form, educational credentials such as certificates and diplomas are sources of cultural capital. However, cultural capital also includes informal skills, and features transmitted through family, peer groups, and associations. Social capital places emphasis on the actor's social relations, which facilitate an actor's ability to fulfil his/her interests. Finally, symbolic capital refers to agents' political power, status and influence in society to achieve change in field-specific rules and policies. It is the amalgam of all other forms of capital (Özbilgin & Tatlı, 2005; Karataş-Özkan & Chell, 2015).

A Bourdieusian approach enables one to focus on the formation and reproduction of forms of capital. It is strategically generated and invested in a particular field to improve their relative positions in the class structure. Adjusting to the field of entrepreneurship requires investment and the transformation of forms of capital that are needed in small business ownership. As Bourdieu and Wacquant (1992, p. 101) put it, "Capital does not exist and function except in relation to a field." The formation and activation of social, cultural, and economic capital, rather than pre-existing, exists solely in relation to the field of entrepreneurship. A Bourdieusian approach enables researchers to focus on the formation and reproduction of concrete social network ties in a specific field. Moreover, forms of capital are not equally distributed among individuals and agents must transform one type of capital into another (Swartz, 1997, p. 74). To setup a business and to continue the activities of the workplace, they must be activated in the country of destination and transposed into one another. All these processes are problems of field studies that need to be examined.

Aim and methodology

This study aims to contribute to the emerging scholarship on Syrian refugee entrepreneurship in Turkey by utilising Bourdieusian field theory. The main research question of this chapter is as follows: How demographic and socio-cultural structures of different districts of Hatay province in Turkey impact on the experiences of Syrian refugee entrepreneurship? The research employs field observations and 34 in-depth interviews with 30 small business owners from Syrian refugees in various trades and 4 key persons from trade associations in the districts of Hatay province such as Samandağ, Defne, Antakya, Kırıkhan and Reyhanlı. Four of 34 interviewees were women and 30 were men. The interviews were held in July 2019.

Urban Syrian refugees in Hatay and entrepreneurial experiences in the districts of Defne, Samandağ, Reyhanlı, Kırıkhan and Antakya

In terms of migration and settlement location selection processes of urban refugees, peculiarities of urbanisation and the ways in which refugees are articulated to the urban space is an issue that should be emphasised (Karan et al., 2020). As of 16 December 2020, the number of Syrians under temporary protection with registered biometric data residing in urban areas was 3,580,667 that is 98.4% of all registered Syrians. Hatay constitutes the third most populate province with Syrian originated refugees after İstanbul and Gaziantep.

When we examine the ratio of the districts of Hatay to the total provincial population, it could be seen from the Table 1 (ATSO, 2020) below that the highest population is in Antakya (23.47%), İskenderun (15.43%) and Defne (9.32%), respectively. In addition, the population of Reyhanlı district is 98,534, while Syrians count 129,354 people. The number of Syrians exceed the number of Turkish citizens. The ratio of Syrian population to district population is 131.28%. Although Defne and Samandağ districts contain the third and fourth highest population with 151,017 and 121,109 people, respectively, the ratio of the Syrian population to the district population is 1.58% and 0.46%, respectively. Based on these data, it is intriguing to understand the reasons for Syrian uneven distribution within the province. Accordingly, how can we explain the Syrian concentration in Reyhanlı and the absence of the Syrian population in Defne and Samandağ?

Table 1. Population distribution in Hatay districts.

	Districts	District Population (2020)	Number of Syrian Resident Population Under Temporary Protection (2020)	Ratio of Syrian Population to District Population (%)
1	Reyhanlı	98,534	129,354	131.28
2	Kumlu	14,233	7,329	51.49
3	Kırıkhan	115,196	56,025	48.63
4	Yayladağı	35,460	15,233	42.96
5	Antakya	377,793	126,890	33.59
6	Belen	33,540	10,102	30.12
7	Altınözü	61,106	18,353	30.03
8	Erzin	41,368	7,450	18.01
9	İskenderun	248,335	38,642	15.56
10	Hassa	56,409	8,189	14.52
11	Payas	41,409	4,891	11.81
12	Dörtyol	123,891	11,056	8.92
13	Arsuz	90,456	2,482	2.74
14	Defne	151,017	2,379	1.58
15	Samandağ	121,109	561	0.46

It should be noted that there is no governmental settlement policy regulating the distribution of Syrians residing in Hatay province. Rather, socio-cultural, socio-economic, and socio-spatial features of the region determines the ethnic settlement features of the districts. During the field interviews, the dynamics of these spontaneous adaptation processes were tried to be discovered. Findings also show that location-specific urban and social dynamics can even differ from neighbourhood to neighbourhood.

As a result of our interviews with the authorities in the Chamber of Tradesmen and Craftsmen of Hatay's Defne and Samandağ districts, we have been informed that there are no registered or informal Syrian refugee small business owner in the districts. Residential patterns in the province are composed by the demographic peculiarities of the districts. The chamber officials stated that the civil war in Syria is based on the Sunni-Alevi originated sectarian conflicts, and that the actual situation in Syria and the population density of the Arab Alawites living in Defne and Samandağ districts caused Arab Alawis to look at Sunni refugees from Syria with prejudice and fear.

49

They also added to their expressions that Alevi massacres in Maraş, Çorum, and Sivas are still alive in the memories of the people living in Defne and Samandağ. Accordingly, people of these districts raise concerns over Syria's actual situation moving in to the districts. For this reason, there are no Syrian refugee small business owner in both districts. However, recently, it has been stated that Syrians who are employed as low-wage seasonal workers are employed daily and within this scope, Syrians come to the region and work as daily workers at certain periods even if they do not settle in the districts.

The fact that entrepreneurship is closed to Syrians in Defne and Samandağ districts does not make it possible to activate capital types in the field of entrepreneurship. Forms of capital are useless without fields. Therefore, to claim that Hatay provides a welcoming context for Syrian refugees and there are favorable conditions for Syrian entrepreneurship in the entire province of Hatay is a great generalisation and does not reflect the reality. Such generalisations neglect or overlook urban, social, and local discrepancies.

Reyhanlı district of Hatay stands out as an opposite case to the above districts in terms of Syrian population ratio. As can be seen in Table 1, the number of Syrians living in Reyhanlı district is higher than Turkish citizens. One of the reasons why Syrians prefer Reyhanlı district is that the Cilvegözü border gate located in the north of İdlib is in Reyhanlı. In this context, it is not coincidental that the place where the immigration movement from Syria first entered is again Reyhanlı. Another reason is that historically, most of the local population living in Reyhanlı has more trade and kinship relations with Syria compared to other districts of the province. Another reason is that in terms of socio-economic development between the 970 districts in Turkey, Reyhanlı is amongst the 711 (ATSO, 2020). That is living in Reyhanlı cost lower compared to other districts.

Based on the information obtained from the small business owner interviews held in Reyhanlı, it can be said that most of the customers of the business owners are Syrians. Considering that the local population living in Reyhanlı also knows Arabic, it is also possible for business owners to carry out their commercial activities without speaking Turkish.

One of my interviewees who runs a grocery store in Reyhanlı explained why he felt more comfortable in Reyhanlı instead of Antakya:

I am on good terms with neighbours. I also get along well with the Turks. Since most of the Turks speak Arabic, I have no problem. 90% of the people speak Arabic. It is even more spoken than in Antakya. That is why I get along easily.

When asked about the plans, business owners in Reyhanlı stated that they do not want to return to Syria, while business owners in Antakya and Kırıkhan would like to return if the situation in Syria improves. The reason for this request is that Syrians in Antakya and Kırıkhan districts stated that they felt like foreigners, while those living in Reyhanlı stated that they did not feel themselves foreign, excluded, and even felt at home. A Syrian business owner who owns a snack shop in Reyhanlı compared Reyhanlı with other districts with the phrase "everyone loves us here". A Syrian small business owner selling hookah products in Reyhanlı stated that he did not encounter racism in Reyhanlı as follows:

When I went to Kayseri (a province in central Anatolia) to get an identity card, I wanted to enter the timber business. They did not employ us because we were Syrian. However, I have never encountered such a thing in Reyhanlı.

During the interviews held in Kırıkhan, the interviewees stated that among other problems they faced when they first came to Turkey, they had difficulties in finding a house to rent. One of our interviewees stated that because of discrimination they could not rent three homes they liked as a tenant. In addition, it was emphasised that both home rents and business rents were increased due to being Syrian. In Kırıkhan, the overcharge of the rental fee paid by the clothing storeowner is expressed as such "I pay 8,000 TL per year. They overcharge me because I am Syrian. Normally, no-one would pay more than 4,000 TL".

Similarly, a jeweller business owner in Kırıkhan complains about the rental fees applied to Syrians as follows:

The annual rent of this place is 12,500 TL. When I first arrived, the rent was 3,500 TL. However, the owner sold the shop and the new owner doubled the rent. Every year, it increases 1,000 TL. I have been here for 5 years. Turks get higher rents from Syrians (meaning tenants).

It has been found that Syrian small business owners are having a barrier in Turkish language usage due to the population density of the Turkish-speaking group in Kırıkhan district. For example, if a barber would hire a worker to work in the workplace, he was thinking of "hiring a Turkish worker with the thought that he might attract customers". When this issue was asked to a grocery store in Reyhanlı, he stated, "He would prefer to hire a Syrian worker to make easier to communicate with customers as well as for himself".

A Syrian who runs a grocery store in Kırıkhan stated that he looks pessimistic about the future and that negative things are always written about Syrians. A cosmetics shop owner in Kırıkhan expressed his living conditions "Syria is my homeland and even I work much more here in Turkey, my income is much lower".

Just like in Kırıkhan, in Antakya district, Syrian entrepreneurs had difficulty in finding homes to shelter. Moreover, they told me that some customers did not want to buy goods from them because they are Syrians. When they used public transport, they were disturbed from the gaze of people from Turkey and stated that they felt themselves as aliens.

A Syrian who runs a grocery store in Antakya district Saraykent neighbourhood stated that they faced racist attitudes and expressed the racism he experienced as follows:

While a man was walking around with an empty bottled gas, I asked him if you were looking for a gas-bottle deliveryman. While I was going to help, the man asked me if I were Turkish. When I said I am Syrian, he said I would not get help from you and left. This went very hard. I felt like nothing at that moment.

On the other hand, it was observed that Turks and Syrians in Antakya were shopping from each other. The setting up shops side by side contributed to establish close relationship between Turkish and Syrian artisans. In many of the interviews I conducted in Antakya, Turkish shopkeepers became gatekeepers.

Unlike Reyhanlı district, most customers in Antakya district are not Syrians. Due to this difference, being able to deal with Turkish speaking customers in Antakya stands out as an important requirement of trade. Some Syrian business owners who are active in Antakya with the need to speak Turkish stated that they started learning Turkish, and some of them stated that they already know enough Turkish to manage their business. In cases where the knowledge of Turkish is insufficient, the business owners have Turkish-speaking children or the Turkish-speaking Turkish citizens rush to help. The need for cultural capital in the form of language usage has not been found as a necessity in Reyhanlı. The Table 2 summarises the major findings of this section.

Table 2. Local adaptation processes and social acceptance matrix of Syrian entrepreneurs in Hatay.

	Major Difficulties	Factors Facilitating Integration	Level of Social Acceptance	Future Expectation
Antakya	Discrimination and exclusion in the public space, Language barrier, Discrimination in housing	Arabic speaking intermediaries, Intermediaries, mutual trade relationships, Solidarity between small business owners	Social exclusion, Racism	Return tendency is high
Reyhanlı		No language barrier, Feeling at home, Lower cost of living, Kinship ties and mutual trade	High level of social acceptance	Expectation of Turkish citizenship, Permanent residency in Turkey
Kırıkhan	Discrimination in housing, High rent fees, Exploitation of Syrians	Children learn Turkish, Arabic speaking intermediaries	Social exclusion	Return tendency is high
Samandağ	Social segregation	N/A	Exclusionary	N/A
Defne	Social segregation	N/A	Exclusionary	N/A

Concluding remarks: differentiated integration

This article argued that demographic, economic and socio-cultural differences within the districts of Hatay province led to differentiated entry possibilities, barriers, and strategies for Syrian refugees in small business ownership. These differences change the local integration strategies of refugees. By utilising Bourdieu's (1987) field theory, it is revealed that Syrian refugee entrepreneurs' relational positions are differentiated by the peculiarities of the districts of Hatay. Spatial features of the districts impact their forms of capital, the difficulties they face and the spatial strategies for survival. It was seen that there are very different structures even in different quarters of the same district.

The research findings state that Syrian refugee entry in small business ownership in Defne and Samandağ is blocked. While Turkish citizens of Defne and Samandağ constitute the third and fourth populated districts of Hatay, Syrian population living in these regions are marginal as shown in the assessment table. Our key informants from chamber of artisans in Defne and Samandağ explained this fact as such: Defne and Samandağ regions are largely populated by Alevi's. These key informants believe that the negative experiences of Alevis, like massacres in Maraş, Çorum and Sivas, are still alive and these memories lead fear amongst Turkish Alevi's from Syrian Sunni population. They do not let Syrians to settle and set-up shops in Defne and Samandağ. Accordingly, it is not possible to claim that all the Hatay districts share the same culturally welcoming context. Accordingly, nuanced researchers should avoid regional generalisations.

In addition, Reyhanlı, border town with Syria, provides a contrary case with its established Arabic speaking majority and kinship as social capital. It provides a welcoming context, where the number of Syrian inhabitants exceed the number of Turkish citizens. Cultural capital of Turkish language usage in dealings with the customers is not a necessity and the tendency to stay business owners and remain in Turkey is higher than Kırıkhan and Antakya, while Syrian refugees in Kırıkhan and Antakya plan to turn back to Syria once ceasefire is in place. By the same token,

This study claims that Bourdieu's field theory provides a composite, multi-layered framework. It asserts that the dynamics of hardship faced by Syrian refugees and Syrian survival strategies can be fully understood by Bourdieu's theoretical concepts. The article adapts a Bourdieusian approach to explore the opportunities in understanding migrant labor markets and immigrants' interests and employability, particularly ethnic entrepreneurship. A Bourdieusian approach calls for an assessment of deeper political structures and the power relations that shape the current configuration of social and economic life.

Finally, the findings of this study suggest that not all Syrian shopkeepers possess these capitals equally. The ability to overcome difficulties in small business ownership is dependent on the volume and quality of social capital. Inequalities in the distribution of forms of capital in a particular moment in time could lead to different entrepreneurial strategies within the members of the Syrian community.

Acknowledgements

This study is supported by TÜBİTAK (1003) program within the scope of the project titled "A New Perspective on Adaptation and Adaptation Processes of Urban Refugees: Inclusive City Construction Purpose" (Project number 117K829).

References

Altınay, L. (2008). The Relationship between an Entrepreneurs Culture and the Entrepreneurial Behaviour of the Firm. *Journal of Small Business and Enterprise Development, 15*(1), 111–129.

Altınay, L., & Altınay, E. (2006). Determinants of Ethnic Minority Entrepreneurial Growth in the Catering Sector. *The Service Industries Journal, 6*(2), 203–221.

Antakya Ticaret ve Sanayi Odası (ATSO). (2020). İstatistiki Raporlar, Hatay İli Özel Teşvik Talep Analizi. Erişim tarihi 06 Nisan 2020. http://www.antakyatso.org.tr/dokumanlar/2020istatistiki/HATAY%20%c4%b0L%c4%b0%20%c3%96ZEL%20TE%c5%9eV%c4%b0K%20TALEP%20ANAL%c4%b0Z%c4%b0%20-%202020.pdf

Basu, A. (1998). An Exploration of Entrepreneurial Activity among Asian Small Businesses in Britain. *Small Business Economics, 10*, 313–326.

Basu, A., & Altınay, E. (2002). The Interaction Between Culture and Entrepreneurship in London's Immigrant Business. *International Small Business Journal, 20*, 371–394.

Bizri, R. M. (2017). Refugee-entrepreneurship: A Social Capital perspective. *Entrepreneurship and Regional Development, 29*(9/10), 847–868.

Bourdieu, P. (1986). The Forms of Capital. In J. G. Richardson (Ed.), *Handbook of Theory and Research for the Sociology of Education* (pp. 46–58). New York, NY: Greenwood.

Bourdieu, Pierre. (1977). *Outline of a Theory of Practice*. Cambridge: Cambridge University Press.

Bourdieu, P. (1987). What Makes a Social Class? On the Theoretical and Practical Existence of Groups. *Berkeley Journal of Sociology, 32*, 1–17.

Bourdieu, P. (1990). *The Logic of Practice*. Stanford, CA: Stanford University Press.

Bourdieu, P., & Wacquant, L. J. D. (1992). *An invitation to reflective sociology*. Cambridge, MA: Polity Press.

Emirbayer, M., & Johnson, V. (2008). Bourdieu and organizational analysis. *Theory and Society, 37*, 1–44.

Hofstede, G. (1991). *Cultures and Organizations: Software of the Mind*. London: McGraw-Hill.

Karan, O. (2017). *Economic Survival Strategies of Turkish Migrants in London*. London, UK: Transnational Press London.

Karan, O. (2019). Suriyeli Mültecilerin Esnaflaşmasını Anlamada Bourdieucu Yaklaşımın Olanakları. *İstanbul Üniversitesi Sosyoloji Dergisi, 39*(2), 249–276.

Karan, O., Çakır, B., & Kurtarır, E. (2020). Hatay'daki Suriyeli Mültecilerin Girişimcilik Alanındaki Deneyimleri ve Mekansal Faktörler. *Göç Dergisi, 7*(1), 77–94.

Karataş-Özkan, M., & Chell, E. (2015). Gender Inequalities in Academic Innovation and Enterprise: A Bourdieuian Analysis. *British Journal of Management, 26*(1), 109–125.

Katila, S., & Wahlbeck, Ö. (2012). The Role of (transnational) Social Capital in the Start-up Processes of Immigrant Businesses: The Case of Chinese and Turkish Restaurant Businesses in Finland. *International Small Business Journal, 30*(3), 294–309.

Kayalar, M., & Yıldız, S. (2017). Uluslararası Göç Sonrası Ortaya Çıkan Girişimcilik Türleri. *Süleyman Demirel Üniversitesi İktisadi ve İdari Bilimler Fakültesi Dergisi, 22*, 55–62

Kloosterman, R. C. (2010). Matching Opportunities with Resource: A Framework for Analysing (migrant) Entrepreneurship from Mixed Embeddedness Perspective. *Entrepreneurship and Regional Development, 22*(1), 25–45.

Kloosterman, R., & Rath, J. (2001). Immigrant Entrepreneurs in Advanced Economies: Mixed Embeddedness Further Explored. Special issue on immigrant entrepreneurship. *Journal of Ethnic and Migration Studies*, *27*(2), 189–202.

Kloosterman, R., & Rath, J. (2003). *Immigrant Entrepreneurs: Venturing Abroad in the Age of Globalization*. Oxford/New York: Berg.

Kloosterman, R., van der Leun, J., & Rath, J. (1999). Mixed Embeddedness, Migrant Entrepreneurship and Informal Economic Activities. *International Journal of Urban and Regional Research*, *23*(2), 253–267.

Light, I. (1972). *Ethnic Enterprise in America: Business and Welfare among Chinese, Japanese, and Blacks*. Berkeley: University of California Press

Mawson, S., & Kasem, L. (2019). Exploring the Entrepreneurial Intentions of Syrian Refugees in the UK. *International Journal of Entrepreneurial Behaviour & Research*, *25*(5), 1128–1146.

McEvoy, D., & Hafeez, K. (2009). Ethnic Enclaves or Middleman Minority? Regional patterns of Ethnic Minority Entrepreneurship in Britain. *International Journal of Business and Globalisation*, *3*(1), 94–110.

Mülteciler Derneği. (2020). Türkiye'deki Suriyeli Sayısı Aralık 2020. https://multeciler.org.tr/turkiyedeki-suriyelisayisi/?gclid=Cj0KCQiAlsv_BRDtARIsAHMGVSYEFHSEFsxweWykb_tMoO_D1rtDvMiz4nS6Dx8iyW_zUodwnibgZPwaAhcfEALw_wcB)

Obschonka, M., & Hahn, E. (2018). Personal Agency in Newly Arrived Refugees: The Role of personality, Entrepreneurial Cognitions and Intentions, and Career Adaptability. *Journal of Vocational Behavior*, *105*, 173–184.

Özbilgin, M., & Tatlı, A. (2005). Book Review Essay: Understanding Bourdieu's Contribution to Organisation and Management Studies. *Academy of Management Review*, *30*(4), 855–877.

Özkul, G., & Dengiz, S. (2018). Economic Contributions of Syrian Immigrants to the Hatay Province in the Context of Immigrant Entrepreneurship. *Mehmet Akif Ersoy University Journal of Social Sciences Institute*, *10*(26), 897–919.

Rath, J. (2017). *The Transformation of Ethnic Neighborhoods into Places of Leisure and Consumption*. Working Paper 144. University of San Diego, Center for Comparative Immigration Studies (CCIS), San Diego, CA.

Rath, J., & Swagerman, A. (2011). *Promoting Ethnic Entrepreneurship in European Cities*. Luxembourg: Publications Office of the European Union.

Sandercock L. (2000). When Strangers Become Neighbours: Managing Cities of Difference. *Planning Theory & Practice, 1*(1), 13–30.

Shneikat, B., & Alrawadieh, Z. (2019). Unravelling Refugee Entrepreneurship and Its Role in Integration: Empirical Evidence from the Hospitality Industry. *The Service Industries Journal*, *39*(9–10), 741–761.

Srinivasan, S. (1995). *The South Asian Petite Bourgeoisie in Britain*. Aldershot, UK: Avebury.

Swartz, D. (1997) *Culture and Power: The Sociology of Pierre Bourdieu*. Chicago: University of Chicago Press

Swartz, D. (2002). The Sociology of Habit: The Perspective of Pierre Bourdieu. *Occupational Therapy Journal of Research*, *22*(1), 61S–69S.

Tatlı, A., Vassilopoulou, J., & Özbilgin, M. F. (2014). A Bourdieuan Relational Perspective for Entrepreneurship Research. *Journal of Small Business Management*, *52*, 54–69.

Trupp, A. (2015). Agency, Social Capital, and Mixed Embeddedness among Akha Ethnic Minority Street Vendors in Thailand's Tourist Areas. *Sojourn: Journal of Social Issues in Southeast Asia*, *30*(3), 780–818.

Türkiye Odalar ve Borsalar Birliği, (TOBB). (2019). Kurulan/kapanan Şirket İstatistikleri. http://www.tobb.org.tr/BilgiErisimMudurlugu/Sayfalar/KurulanKapananSirketistatistikleri.php.

UNHCR. (1995). UNHCR's Policy and Practice Regarding Urban Refugees: A Discussion

Paper, Inspection and Evaluation Service. http://www.urban-refugees.org/wp-content/uploads/2015/08/Discussion-paper-on-urban-refugees-1995.pdf

Werbner, P. (1984). Business on Trust: Pakistani Entrepreneurship in the Manchester Garment Trade. In R. Ward & R. Jenkins (Eds.), *Ethnic Communities in Business: Strategies for Economic Survival* (pp. 1–19). Cambridge, MA: Cambridge University Press.

Werbner, P. (1990). Renewing an Industrial Past: British Pakistani Entrepreneurship in Manchester. *Migration*, 8, 17–41.

ETHIOPIAN-ISRAELI WOMEN IN ACADEMIA: A GENDER EQUALITY PLAN, IN THE FRAMEWORK OF THE CHANGE[1] PROJECT

Adi Binhas and Hana Himi

Introduction

The glass ceiling is a key concept in gender research, describing invisible barriers which inhibit the promotion of talented women to senior positions in various fields – industry, education, and others (Ansari, 2016; Basu, 2015). Andersen found that in innovative leadership biotechnology firms, the greater number of senior professional women who mentor young women weakened the glass ceiling effect. The issue at the heart of this study is the identification and definition of pivotal themes that create a glass ceiling for women in minority groups in Israel.

The study focused on exploring personal experiences and the kinds of unique barriers and challenges facing Israeli women of Ethiopian origin in academia. It analysed ten success stories of women who managed to break through the glass ceiling and progressed to high academic degrees despite being the children of immigrants, young women who had to deal with all the problems entailed in adapting to the host country's traits. That confrontation included socialization processes that were characterized, among others, by prejudice, economic straits, and the distinctive demands of the higher education system. We begin by describing the barriers facing unique groups; describe the particular characteristics of this group of women, using the term *coherence* and its three components; list the resources available to those women which helped them break down the barriers; and conclude with a discussion where we argue that the women's inner forces were significant for their success, despite the many barriers.

Most of the women we researched were born in Ethiopia, immigrated to Israel as children and studied in the Israeli education system. Few Ethiopian women in Israel have reached doctoral studies, which is a great challenge for women from immigrant families, who have to deal with immigration, and economic, cultural, and social challenges. This preliminary study is unique because this group has not yet been studied in Israel.

Theoretical background

The theoretical background is based on a description of the existing barriers which face unique groups at the entrance to academia, with specific reference to the challenges facing the immigrant population. We also present coherence as a

[1] This project has received funding from the European Union's Horizon 2020 research and innovation programme under grant agreement No 787177.
This article reflects only the authors' view. The European Commission is not responsible for any use that may be made of the information it contains. https://www.change-h2020.eu

resource which helps when individuals must deal with all the demands placed on them in situations of stress and crisis. The content world of coherence helps us explain how the women cope with the immigration process and integrating into a new society.

Barriers to immigrant women

To enter and integrate into a society, immigrants must acquire not only the language but also the society's culture, norms and values; they must structure social networks which can help them to progress. Immigrant women face unique challenges and are often channelled to specific jobs on the lowest rungs of the occupational hierarchy and do not access higher education (Boyd & Grieco, 2003). While there is substantial literature on women's empowerment, little reference is made to the integration of non-traditional women, or to demographic issues and power relations. In particular, there is a need to engage with academic development and integration into normative employment of immigrant women, who face dual challenges as women and immigrants (Hugo, 2000). Education is a crucial variable which can advance people into their place in deficient stratification, and change their status in society, especially in traditional societies. A study of women in Turkey showed that until the 1970s, women rarely left their homes, but about four decades later a significant change in women's status was discernible in terms of social hierarchy and their social, political, and religious status. Over that period they gained liberation and self-fulfilment (Gretty & Abadan-Unat, 2015). A study that looked at the identities of nineteen female and male Ethiopian-Israeli immigrants dealt with identity-related experiences, and described the processes associated with defining personal identity, their connection to ethnic and other identities, and their ways of coping and building themselves within a complex identity (Yakhnich, Getahune & Walsh, 2021).

Academic entry barriers

Admission threshold barrier

Admission thresholds to academic institutions are a significant barrier for unique populations, constituting a factor that impedes admission even if other barriers have been overcome. In the Israeli case, criticism of the psychometric entry tests has argued that they are culturally biased, and that to pass the tests the applicant requires 'western' know-how, unfamiliar to immigrants from non-western countries. The applicants' grades in matriculation exams and other academic selection methods are directly linked to their social, cultural, and economic background. Admission thresholds are adjusted to candidates from a medium-high socioeconomic background, who belong to the majority culture, and are familiar with the demands through other groups they belong to. For students from a low socioeconomic background, lacking an environment conversant with academic education, these requirements could lead to adjustment difficulties, reduced self-confidence, and fear of failure. They are often exposed to negative remarks about their prospects for fitting in, stereotypes, and racism, which damage their motivation and adjustment abilities (Griffin et al., 2012, Carter, Locks, & Winkle-Wagner, 2013).

Financial barriers

Lack of economic resources impacts on students' achievements and experience, as well as the percentage of students who will graduate. A weak economic background is one of the factors that prevents pursuit of academic studies or causes concerns and burdens during them. Worry about finances affects students' ability to complete their degree. Some also work, and must help support their families (Erisman & Looney, 2007).

Professional barriers unique to immigrant women

Regarding the constant tension between social expectations of women in general to fulfil the roles of housekeeper, wife, and mother, and the world of education and career, for immigrant women the tension between the two spheres is stronger. This is particularly true for immigrant women from patriarchal societies in which women are expected, and expect of themselves, to take a major part in running the home and looking after the family. Aspirations for education and employment clash with the expectations at home (Buchsbaum & Dagan, 2010). This part has presented the barriers to academic education among the study population and similar groups. The very admission to an academic institution is the initial barrier, followed by the unique challenges and barriers which these populations face – readiness for and knowledge about academic studies, financial barriers, and others. Women must deal with unique difficulties vis-à-vis societal or family expectations to marry and have children, which are typically postponed by academic studies. If they already have a family, they must cope with the disruption of the family equilibrium and the demand that they continue fulfilling their previous role within the family framework.

Antonovsky's sense of coherence (SOC) approach

The present study is based on the central concept of sense of coherence (SOC) within the salutogenic approach of Aaron Antonovsky (1987, 1993, 1994), which emphasizes the strengths of the individual. SOC has three key components: understandability, which refers to a general conception of the world as having an understandable sequence, so that individuals believe that the challenges they face are understandable; this experience is a basis for manageability, which refers to a manageable reality, wherein individuals perceive themselves as better able to cope with stressors and believe they can avail themselves of resources for coping, and thus have the motivation to cope; while experiencing significance. Antonovsky (1987, 1993, 1994) maintains that the intensity of SOC is an important factor in the movement towards health. These components are essentially close to concepts such as optimism, mental resilience, sense of efficacy, resourcefulness, and more. In Antonovsky's opinion, the extent to which individuals have such experiences is the result of their status in their social environment, a product of their culture, and above all, related to the type of work they engage in, their family structure, and other factors like gender, ethnic origin, genetics, and even coincidence. SOC reflects individuals' ability to understand events taking place in their lives, the extent of their preparedness to handle the expected pressures with the resources at their disposal, and their perception of life as meaningful. SOC already develops during childhood and adolescence. The social conditions, socioeconomic conditions, and social relationships that exist within the family, experiences and exposure to culture within the family, as well as gender, ethnicity, genetics, and more are all significant for the development of SOC (Antonovsky & Sourani, 1988). Antonovsky (1987) argues that individuals with a high SOC perceive events as less threatening, and therefore their level of anxiety is lower than that of individuals with a low SOC (Svavarsdottir, McCubbin, & Kane, 2000).

Case study: Israeli-Ethiopian women in academia

Integration of Israeli-Ethiopian women in higher education

Israeli women of Ethiopian origin encounter unique difficulties when integrating into higher education. The division of roles between women and men in Ethiopia was of the kind common in patriarchal societies, where the man holds the key position. With the emigration to Israel, the woman's position changed, and became more central and equal (Bostin, 2008). Despite the negative impact on the family structure, there have been positive changes in the status of Israeli-Ethiopian women. They are integrated in various public systems in a variety of roles – formal and informal education, the military, the media, and other fields of employment[2]. As regards academic studies, most Israeli-Ethiopians (men and women) study social sciences. Ethiopian women mostly train in social work; at the other end, very few study engineering, architecture, biology, maths, physics, statistics or computer science. The divide between women and men in these fields is common in general, but is more pronounced among Israeli-Ethiopian women (Fuchs & Friedman-Wilson, 2017).

Methodology

Research method

The research used the qualitative method and qualitative phenomenological research, in which the researcher tries to understand the interviewee's personal experience and interpretation of reality from her personal experience. Through the questions asked, researchers try to understand the interviewees' interpretation of reality and their feelings (Creswell, 2007). The present research is based on the subjective and reflective experience of Israeli-Ethiopian women who are studying for a PhD or already have a PhD. Our focus was on the opportunities which helped them succeed (in their opinion), and on the barriers and challenges they have confronted during their academic career. We assumed that, by drawing on the personal experience of these women who are also immigrants, we could identify means for encouraging similar future success by formulating suitable policy (for this group and perhaps similar ones). The research was aimed at deepening the understanding of the external barriers facing women from minority groups in academia – in our case, academic women of Ethiopian origin. Which tools could break those barriers, and which sources were contributory to their success? The interviewees were asked to describe their career development track, the barriers that stood in their path, and how they overcame them. The interview content formed the basis for a qualitative content analysis aimed at learning about their choices, coping style, and the resources they drew on, thanks to which they reached high academic achievements.

The study population

The study consisted of ten interviews, conducted with Israeli-Ethiopian women with a PhD or studying towards a doctorate in different fields (Table 1).

Table 1. Study population of Israeli-Ethiopian women.

Name	Number of children	Age on immigrating	Study field	Institution	Career
Tzippi	2	15	Social Sciences	University in Israel & abroad	Civil service
Sarit	2	16	Social Sciences	University in Israel	Management position in the civil service
Keren	3	7	Social Sciences	University in Israel	Management position in the civil service
Reut	2	10	Social Sciences	University in Israel	Academic & civil service career
Roni	3	6	Science	University in Israel	Civil service career
Soli	2	Born in Israel	Life Sciences	University in Israel	Civil service career
Ravit	0	6	Engineering	University in Israel	Academic & civil service career
Shir	0	Born in Israel	Social Sciences	University in Israel	Civil service career
Orit	2	5	Social Sciences	University in Israel	Academic career & management position in NGO
Batya	3	5	Social Sciences	University in Israel	Management role in the civil service

Data analysis

The research used a qualitative research method of semi-structured open interviews. The data analysis applied the coordinated phenomenological approach of Moustakas (1994). After conducting conversations with the interviewees, significant themes were identified and analysed. Through these themes, the research attempted to explain and understand the experiences and perceptions of women about the elements which contributed to their success.

Ten interviewees participated in the research. Meetings with them were held face-to-face in a university, café, or hospital (in the case of a doctor who works at a hospital). The interviewees lasted between one to two hours and were transcribed by the authors. Guiding questions were prepared in advance of the meetings, but the participants were allowed to freely describe their experiences and introduce other topics than those they were asked about. The aim was to obtain a picture of their academic experience and what it entailed in terms of the challenges, feelings, attitudes of the institute, the community and the family, and their perception of the process of academic progress.

Ethical issues and rights of the participants

The interviewees participated freely in the research. They were informed that they could decide not to answer some of the questions, and could halt the interview at any stage. Their details remain confidential. The broad context of the research was explained to the interviewees, and they were given a document containing all the details of the project. The entire research proposal was approved by the Ethics Committee of the institutional research authority, and the interviewees signed a consent document for the interview.

Findings – barriers and opportunities

The interviews made possible an in-depth exposure of the interviewees' world, as well as the characteristics of their prolonged and complex coping throughout their lives. The results of the interviews elicited findings about barriers which originated in the respondents' external environment – economic barriers, lack of instrumental resources, their home environment and lack of proper conditions for learning – as well as barriers connected to their intrapsychic and emotional worlds, due to their confronting racist attitudes prevalent in various people and officials in their external environment.

1. External barriers: economic barriers, challenges of socialization and prejudice

A. An external barrier – economic resources

All the interviewees described a complex array of coping with economic issues. While at university, it was hard for them to hold a job, nor could they help their parents and siblings. Sometimes they had to move far from home, which they cited as a significant external limitation and a contributory issue to the sense of guilt and pangs of conscience caused by not meeting responsibility towards their family. By choosing to pursue higher education and to live far from the family for years, they felt they had "abandoned" their families, and failed in their responsibility towards them. Reut, for example, mentioned that "when we started college, they emphasised that because of the psychological burden, we must also be sure to get enough rest, so we would be physically and mentally in equilibrium … it was clear that I'd always have to work while I was a student. Studying at night, after work, meant that I paid a high price in my achievements. I knew I could have done better if I didn't have to always work." The respondents indicated that their lack of funds made it difficult for them both in getting by daily life, due to the need to work intensively in parallel with studies, and also caused guilt feelings to develop because they were unable to help their family.

B. An external barrier – the challenge of socialization as daughters of immigrants

A prominent common denominator in all the interviews was the statement that the respondents always sensed some insecurity around their lack of knowledge and orientation in the Israeli experience, both regarding the history of the State of Israel and the culture in Israel in general. This included the two interviewees who were born in Israel. In their experience, they lacked the information necessary to fit in, which their parents could not give them. They felt that they had a constant gap in knowledge about cultural issues, and in the study framework it created a sense of alienation, delay, social barrier and lack of belonging to wider society. Some noted the dramatic consequences of their lack of information – they were not admitted to certain institutions because they were not proficient in the level of cultural content required in the admission conditions – such as the university psychometric tests. While the first external barrier described above clearly stems from an external economic resource, the second resource combines an interaction between the inner experience and the encounter with characteristics of the external sociocultural environment.

In our opinion, the individual's emotional and cognitive ability to deal with the range of demands required in an interpersonal encounter with a different cultural environment is actually an encounter which integrates interpretation from their inner world and external events, including external barriers. The more an individual's interpretation makes room for personal space, self-confidence, personal aspirations, meaning in life, and hope, while minimizing tagging messages which external society sometimes dismisses – the less significance and impact there is to the external barriers.

C. An external barrier – prejudice and racism

Coping with the characteristics of the third barrier seems to be the most complex and emotionally difficult because it is beyond the individual's control; it requires an encounter with content and messages which transmit labelling and rejection by the host society, which is almost impossible to change. The forces needed to deal with this barrier are thus more complex and harder to enlist. Eight out of the ten interviewees described situations in which they experienced a tagging, negative attitude towards their ethnic origin. When they achieved goals with excellence, reactions to them were typically of astonishment. Their outstanding achievements in high-school were a source of pride and in the process they were assigned – and accepted – a representative role as outstanding students in the schooling system.

They described a dual attitude towards that representative role: they became role-models for other schoolgirls, and alongside the sense of pride they also developed feelings of responsibility towards the community – their schoolmates of Ethiopian origin who failed to meet the challenges as they did. In every interview there was a clear expression of their own attitude, or the environment's, to their skin colour and its prominent presence in the space as part of their identity, and an issue they always confronted. From childhood, at school, and until now as mature women with academic and professional status, they encountered prejudice. The participants noted that, in many ways, they have adapted to those reactions.

Sometimes, it was precisely exposure to that prejudice which contributed to the development of ambition, with an increasing desire to prove themselves. For example, Ravit says:

"When we had to choose study-tracks in high school, it was clear to all my classmates that I would go to physics, but when the physics teacher asked who would enrol in it, I said I, and she replied – 'you shouldn't, you won't be able to pay for private tuition'. I was the top student, and I took physics with 5 credit-points [the most demanding] in physics, without private tuition."

Roni told us: *"I always wanted to study psychology, but I knew I couldn't learn what I wanted but rather what would help me progress in life. And I also wondered – who would want to go to an Ethiopian psychologist?"*

That kind of coping seems to be an emotional and cognitive challenge because it entails dealing with the deepest layers of the individual's personal attitudes, and the community's, towards their skin colour and ethnic origin. Their physically conspicuous presence cannot be concealed or changed, so dealing with this barrier necessitates the mobilising of inner forces as a strengthening resource in the face of that complexity.

Beyond everything described previously, the combination of the three barriers appears to create a complex scheme for dealing with what the environment demands from the individual. Those demands can generate an emotional and cognitive burden which requires the young women to enlist strengths and abilities. That complex confrontation leads to the questions underlying this study: how did they, each in their own way, cope with these barriers? How did they build self-confidence and ability as they confronted them, reaching the highest achievements at academic level? We believe it was possible to elucidate the map of internal resources and sense of coherence which helped them reach their achievements. The study's findings suggest that an in-depth analysis of the interviewees' theories has the effect of instilling actual content into the concept of coherence: we enlarge on this in the following section. They were able to cope thanks to their ability, each in their own way, to mobilize internal forces that helped them overcome the external barriers.

The inner forces: understandability, manageability and significance

Understandability

All the interviewees in the study clearly indicated that they understood the challenges which faced them. Their ability to cope more effectively with the tasks ahead of them was made possible by realistic conduct, initiative, and motivation to achieve their objectives. They also realized that their achievements were distinctive and that, in their own way, they had also won affirmative positive preference in the various systems.

Soli told us: "*I'm not happy that my position is one that's reserved for people of Ethiopian origin, but I understand that that situation I wouldn't have received this job. If Ethiopians were already holding senior positions, we wouldn't have needed these 'reserved' jobs.*"

This position stemmed from a realistic understanding of reality, an ability to organize towards it while taking advantage of the opportunity they have in their positions to be a mission of change. Keren, Reut and Batya described that they are active in various activities to promote the community, and Orit is a senior public official in which she is involved in promoting the status of women in Israel. As for their attitude towards home, family and community, they describe processes of change that have taken place over the years: as children they were ashamed of their characteristics, language and family, and over the years, having grown stronger, they returned to their roots and pride and respect for their defining characteristics. Their ability to observe the processes retrospectively is noticeable when analyzing the changes that took place in them in the way they formulated things and reacted to them differently. They express deep understanding of their past development, and recognition of the ability they have developed to appreciate the home they came from, as a result of their strengthening and increased self-confidence. For example, Orit says: "*When I was a schoolchild, I thought my parents were irrelevant, I wanted to be different from them, I didn't speak Amharic, I had no friends from Ethiopia, I never invited friends home. It took me years to reconnect with my language and roots.*"

Manageability

Antonovsky (1987, 1993, 1994) defined manageability as the capacity of an individual to manage reality, to be able to deal with stressors, to be motivated, and possess coping abilities. The contents of the interviews with all respondents clearly reveal their excellent management skills; they have good capacities for managing their choices, and correctly identify the characteristics of the reality in which they operate and manage it in a manner that advances them. This was true for them, right from the very start vis-à-vis public systems. Orit, for example, recalled her integration into the school, a few months after she immigrated to Israel:

"*When I started school, they put me in the recent immigrants' class … I didn't like the idea of it … the class of native-born kids looked much better, and the teacher seemed interesting. When I asked to switch to her class, they asked me in surprise 'Do you know Hebrew?' It gave me the push to improve my Hebrew so they could transfer me. And I was transferred, and since then was never in recent immigrant classes.*"

Roni shared an experience from high school: "*I was accepted for the top track and when I chose the one beneath it, the head-teacher summoned me for a talk. He was really disappointed, saying 'Until a student of Ethiopian origin is accepted for this track, I'm not giving up'. He took it hard.*" Despite their young age, already as high-school students, they were assertive in the face of managerial authorities. They knew how to stand up for themselves in front of officials and manage their choices according to their considerations, a quality that was highly contributory to building their future academic career. They developed a long-term academic career track that was packed with challenges and setbacks, simultaneously dealing with their community's attitude towards academic studies – considered not immediately profitable or useful as a step towards obtaining a secure job.

Significance

According to Antonovsky (1987, 1993, 1994), significance means the intention for a life of health. Significance has components such as optimism, mental resilience, perceived efficacy, and resourcefulness. People build up those qualities from their culture, family, and origin. In the life stories, by analysing the contents of the interviews, it becomes clear that the study participants were typified by inner forces and imbued meaning into the way they coped with the demands placed on them around migration and adapting to transitions in different areas of life. Coping itself was a meaningful experience for them, representing a meaningful process with a sense of control and self-structuring in accordance with the objectives they were striving for. The inner capacity to believe in their abilities throughout the process stemmed from a combination of variables, including traits of independence, motivation, activism, the ability to handle change and transitions, personal resilience and long-term vision, curiosity, having strong opinions, aspiration for meaningful action and the ability to cope with stress and uncertainty.

The external barriers described did not weaken them, and were actually a challenge for them. Over the years of their development they displayed strong coherence and patience to deal with lengthy processes, self-confidence, and the aspiration to succeed in academic careers and in general. In conclusion, the content analysis of the interviews clarified the dominant expressions of each component of coherence: understandability, manageability, and significance. The integration of all three is reflected in very strong coherence which when put to the test, resulted in exceptional achievements.

To summarize our findings: from the description of the many and varied barriers which women encounter, we identified that inner strengths and high personal abilities enabled them to deal with the challenges they faced. They were confident', knew how to adapt to changing situations, and were strongly ambitious to achieve their goals. They are role-models for their environment and especially for women from unique groups who have ambitions to advance in academia.

Discussion

Conforming with what is described in the research literature, the study participants, who are the daughters of immigrants from Ethiopia, also dealt with parents and an environment that did not provide support and familiarity with opportunities for starting an academic career, or the tools children must receive in order to foster academic skills (Griffin et al., 2012; O'Shea, 2016). Nor were there people in their close environment who would help them learn from their experience or were aware of the demands of the academic and bureaucratic system, as well as the options they might have in the academic context (Carter, Locks, & Winkle-Wagner, 2013).

As children of immigrants, they had to cope with life in families for whom economic survival was almost always on the agenda, and their family's financial hardships were also among their concerns for years ahead. Investing in academic studies was not always understood, for in the participants' homes it didn't seem to be a possible and realistic path to take (Erisman & Looney, 2007). In addition, they faced prejudice from their environment over the years – in their own community, at school, and among friends, teachers, and officials in the education systems. The women dealt with various barriers: the economic barrier, for example, was expressed to some extent by the barrier to receiving scholarships from foundations, and by having to work.

In that area, participants pointed out that because they grasped the circumstances, they organised towards and controlled it, worked diligently and took advantage of opportunities; they were able to find resources in the economic field. In contrast, the second and third barriers were characterized by a combination of coping with emotional and cognitive variables. The second barrier is focused on the interviewees' interpersonal capacity for dealing with what the socialization process involved, while the third barrier is almost impossible to break down because it is entirely rooted in the personal attitudes of the "other", and the more rigid their prejudices, the harder it is to change their attitudes and perceptions, if at all.

In the face of the second and third barriers, the participants' high levels of coherence (Antonovsky, 1987, 1993, 1994) helped them. Their ability to instil meaning into the long academic path they had started helped them understand the implications of their future achievements. They were able to manage, even when the immediate environment did not support and understand what was required of them, and even criticizes them (for example, regarding the fact that they were still unmarried at a relatively late age, that they lived far from home, and were often absent from family reunions due to school constraints and more).

The importance of the power of coherence is clear and noticeable, given that despite the environment's attitude, they understand the personal benefits likely to result from their choices. Thus, they can internally manage contradictions between the different worlds they live in, without plunging into dilemmas which the conflicts surface, and instead to grow. Participants knew how to rationally prioritize between major and minor issues, to show restraint and be flexible in places where they realise they can't influence every situation and every encounter (such as when facing prejudice). They harness their inner strengths to achieve personal and professional benefit. In terms of Antonovsky's approach (1987, 1993, 1994) one finds that the participants well understood the obstacles confronting them and drew on inner forces to deal with reality's challenges. They displayed creativity, flexibility, and the ability to understand complex situations; along the way they showed determination, self-confidence and perseverance, even in conditions of uncertainty and stress. Their drive, optimism, belief in their skills and mental resilience, helped them break the barriers. When they described the course of their lives, one identifies from an early age the desire for meaningful endeavours, curiosity, and understanding how to conduct themselves in complex situations, by planning the next stages (such as choosing a high-school track or the field of academic studies). The external barriers could have contained elements of threat, but activism and positive thinking helped deal with those barriers; in retrospect, they could identify the factors which weakened them, and were aware of the path they took, and returned there with renewed strength.

Our findings show that the participants understood that acquiring education is a long journey but education is a vital resource offering them a channel with which they can break through and successfully build a professional career. Along with the fact that academic education is based on personal achievements, the interviewees realized that they represent and demonstrate not only personal development but also that they represent the collective. Their ability to engage with that complexity, alongside the responsibility (or perhaps the burden it imposes) is reflected in the interviewees' narratives. It is evident that they underwent, and are still undergoing, processes of development and a constant internal discourse in the face of those issues. The participants were undeterred by hard work, a critical environment, and also "paying prices" in other arenas (economic, family, community).

Examining the external barriers versus the internal forces, it is discernible that their inner forces were resources through which they overcame objective and environmental constraints which were actually external barriers. In addition to the personal perception, that is, seeing themselves as subjects of a collective mission, there is another significant layer that is part of their personal and professional lives – they are role-models for others in their community. It is reflected in different ways, in their chosen fields, in research and in public and voluntary efforts. They indeed embody messages of change, control, and hope, and thus fulfil their mission by sending a message. They are an example for the whole community, and for unique communities generally, illustrating that personal and professional development is also possible for within a challenging environment, strewn with assorted external barriers.

It is clear that the respondents' coping process is a long and tough one, certainly accompanied by crisis and distress. But their ability to harness inner forces, to foster, establish a high sense of coherence, that integrates clear understanding of short- and long-term goals, and the significance of different goals thus advanced their manageability. And all this while recruiting flexibility and formulating the personal narrative in the face of reality in a way that identifies and articulates opportunities and hope. It is worth emphasizing that given the young age of all the interviewees on immigrating to Israel, and the very practical way they embarked on their external and inner journey, the achievements described are even more significant and impressive. This should be enlarged on in another article addressing the meaning of those processes, against the backdrop of traits of adolescence.

In conclusion, this article has illuminated the uniqueness of the personal journey that our respondents undertook that hones the significance of the struggle and challenge entailed in coping with the inner forces – and in terms of this research – coherence, alongside the external barriers of their cultural and social environment that is marked with prejudice and impedes the socialization processes.

Practical recommendations

The study offers practical recommendations to encourage more women from unique groups to pursue higher academic studies:

1. identifying outstanding female students in B.A. studies and providing them with information on options for further academic studies;

2. creating a mechanism which provides mentoring to women from unique groups in academia, to provide the guidance and information to which they have not been exposed;

3. providing financial support from the institute during studies;

4. offering joint meetings of students with doctoral graduates who can tell their story and show that different groups have representation in advanced degrees as well.

References

Anderson, D. R. (2005). The importance of mentoring programs to women's career advancement in biotechnology. *Journal of Career Development,* 32(1), 60–73.

Ansari, N. (2016). Respectable femininity: A significant panel of glass ceiling for career women. *Gender in Management,* 31(8), 528–541.

Antonovsky, A. (1987). *Unravelling the mystery of health.* San Francisco: Jossey-Bass.

Antonovsky, A. (1993). The structure and properties of the sense of coherence scale. *Social Science and Medicine, 36,* 725–733.

Antonovsky, A. (1994). The sense of coherence: An historical and future perspective. In H. I. McCubbin, E. A. Thompson, A. I. Thompson & J. E. Fromer (Eds.), *Sense of coherence and resiliency: Stress, coping, and health* (pp. 3–20). Madison, WI: University of Wisconsin.

Antonovsky, A., & Sourani, T. (1988). Family sense of coherence and family adaptation. *Journal of Marriage and the Family,* 50, 79–92.

Basu, S. (2015). Glass ceiling intact for women in academia. *Economic Times,* 1–19. https://journals.sagepub.com/doi/10.1177/0971890717700533

Bostin, A. (2008). Studies of immigration absorption: Society and Culture. Men from Ethiopia: Why do they have such a hard time? *Hed Ha'Ulpan Ha'Hadash, 94,* 56–64. (Hebrew)

Boyd, M., & Grieco, E. M. (2003). Women and migration: incorporating gender into international migration theory. http://www.migrationpolicy.org/article/women-and-migration-incorporating-gender-international-migration-theory

Buchsbaum, Y., & Dagan, M. (2010). *Women – Between age and employment.* Haifa: Mahut Center. (Hebrew)

Carter, D. F., Locks, A. M., & Winkle-Wagner, R. (2013). From when and where I enter: Theoretical and empirical considerations of minority students' transition to college. In M. B. Paulsen (Ed.), *Higher education: Handbook of theory and research* (pp. 931–949). New York, London: Springer Dordrecht Heidelberg.

Creswell, J. W. (2007). *Qualitative inquiry and research design: Choosing among five traditions.* Thousand Oaks, CA: SAGE.

Erisman, W., & Looney, S. (2007). *Opening the door to the American dream: Increasing higher education access and success for immigrants.* Washington: Institute for Higher Education Policy.

Fuchs, H., & Friedman-Wilson, T. (2017). *Trends in education and wages among Israeli-Ethiopians: A gender-related viewpoint.* Jerusalem: Taub Institute. (Hebrew)

Gretty, M., & Abadan-Unat, N. (Eds.) (2015). *Emancipation in Exile: Perspectives on the Empowerment of Migrant Women.* Istanbul: İstanbul Bilgi University Press.

Griffin, K., del Pilar, W., McIntosh, K., & Griffin, A. (2012). "Oh, of course I'm going to go to college": Understanding how habitus shapes the college choice process of black immigrant students. *Journal of Diversity in Higher Education, 5*(2), 96–111.

Moustakas, C. (1994). *Phenomenological research methods.* Thousand Oaks, CA: SAGE.

O'Shea, S. (2016). Avoiding the manufacture of 'sameness': First-in-family students, cultural capital and the higher education environment. *High Education, 72,* 59–78.

Svavarsdottir, E. K., McCubbin, M. A., & Kane, J. H. (2000). Well-being of parents of young children with asthma. *Research in Nursing & Health, 23,* 346–358.

Van Kaufman, Buchnik, T., Magdala, H., Guetta, E., & Shustak, N. (2016). *Mapping the needs and challenges of minority students at the Hebrew University in Jerusalem.* Jerusalem: Surveys and Assessment Unit. (Hebrew)

Williams, N. (2009). Education, gender, and migration in the context of social change. *Social science research,* 38(4), 883–896. https://doi.org/10.1016/j.ssresearch.2009.04.005

Yakhnich, L., Getahune, S., & Walsh, S. D. (2021). 'This identity is part of you, you cannot run away from it': Identity experiences among young Israelis of Ethiopian origin. *Journal of Ethnic and Migration Studies,* doi: 10.1080/1369183X.2020.1866514

WORK LIVES OF SKILLED FEMALE IMMIGRANTS IN THE UNITED STATES

Harika Suklun

Introduction

Immigration has become central in the public conversation especially in the United States. The most common topics are political controversy, struggling statistics, and the perceptions of the noteworthy interval to changing realities (Batalova, Blizzard, & Bolter, 2020). With the phenomena of globalization, international immigration keeps growing around the world. The market for skilled workers is becoming increasingly global, and in parallel to that, the new knowledge and ideas are becoming increasingly global in markets. Adserà and Pytliková (2015, p. 79) conclude that people in countries with a higher level of education migrate more than in other countries which might be the reason for the increased need for highly skilled migrants globally. Although skilled immigrants in the United States represent a smaller proportion of the workforce, in countries such as Australia, Canada, and the United Kingdom, immigrants have a vital role in advancing innovation and economic growth and providing domestic labor supply (National Academies of Sciences, Engineering, and Medicine, 2015). Some countries are receiving more immigrants than others, and the top immigrant-receiving countries are the United States, Germany, the United Kingdom, France, Canada, and Australia. According to Gonzalez-Barrera and Connor (2019, p. 4), the United States held 18 percent of the total number of immigrants in the world in 2017. In 2019 there were 13,590,000 Lawful Permanent Residents (also called Green Card holders) and, of the total number, 7,070,000 were females in the USA (Baker, 2020, p. 6).

Within the increasing number of immigrants in those countries, some common beliefs about immigrants grew during certain times. The most common misassumptions are: immigrants are a burden, reasons for crime increase, terrorism, and the increase in natives' unemployment. Although some misassumptions are changed, some of them are there still valid today. The reasons for those misassumptions might be considerable disruptions such as September 11 attacks and changes in immigration policies. For example, 46 percent of the surveyed people supported deporting unlawful immigrants (Gonzalez-Barrera & Connor, 2019, p. 11) in 2019 which is the time of Trump's administration. As president of the USA, he made statements on immigrants being reasons for increasing crimes, and those comments might be reasons for 63 percent of responders supported deportation who might be an enthusiast of the republic party (conservatives) who voted for Trump.

The USA is at the top of the highest immigrant-receiving country amongst other countries and, receiving more immigrants generates extra forces for interaction between people with different cultural backgrounds at workplaces and in daily lives. Although there are different types of immigrants, this study

71

focused on skilled female immigrants who are Lawful Permanent Residents or naturalized in the USA. In this study, a qualitative methodology is applied, and semi-structured interviews are conducted to understand skilled immigrant women's experiences about work lives. The method let participants describe their experiences and share their perspectives about being immigrants in the United States in detail. Participants explained the differences between their working life in the home country and the host country.

Immigration

Although the reasons for the earliest human migration are not fully understood yet, it is known that the first humans migrated from one place to another place. Some scientists argue that the development of language led people to make plans, solve problems, and organize effectively. As a result, better communication is followed by understanding each other, and it might lead to the desire and ability to migrate (Manning, 2020). Additionally, numbers of scientists argue that climate changes (climatic), depletion of natural resources (economic), competition, and war danger (political) caused migration among early humans. Additionally, by the new inventions, new places were discovered thus, increased and accelerated the migration. For example, the wheel invention created new transportation techniques that helped people move from one location to another, move faster and go farther easier than before. Migrations affected all aspects of human history, directly or indirectly, in conquest, resettlement, or slow cultural infiltration. For example, colonial immigration has led to the formation of countries such as Australia and America and the empowerment of skilled immigrants with a strong workforce those countries started ruling the world.

While industrialization and migration accelerated since the eighteenth century, it increased even more in the nineteenth century. According to Cohen and Sirkeci (2011), immigrants moved as new jobs and opportunities became available. When the industrial revolution emerged, migration movements started from one place to another places. Overpopulation, open agricultural areas, and rising industrial centers have initiated voluntary, incentive, and sometimes coercive migration. Besides, migration has been significantly eased by improved shipping techniques. According to the assessment of the International Organization for Migration (IOM) (2018), there were 244 million international migrants (3.3% of the world population) worldwide. Work remains the main reason for people migrating internationally. The report also projected that the global displacement reached a record level, and the number of refugees reached 22 million.

According to IOM and UN Migration (2020, p. 34), "male immigrant workers are more than female immigrant workers by 28 million in 2017, with 96 million males (58%) and 68 million females (42%), in a context where males comprised a higher number of international migrants of working age (127 million or 54%, compared with 107 million or 46% females)". However, recently female immigrants are increasing, and because of that, the immigration forms are changing. Because it seems most of the skilled immigrants are male, attention to skilled female immigrants is missing (Dumont et al., 2007). To prevent obstacles, and inequality practitioners, researchers and policymakers should pay much attention to skilled female immigrants.

Among the immigrants, female immigrants are thought to be more vulnerable than male immigrants. According to IOM (2020, as cited in Flahaux, 2017), female immigrants are vulnerable before, during, and after migration, for their shelter and security, psychological needs, and admittance to services and rights. On the other hand, migration, and even displacement, can also bring openings for female immigrants. Although female immigrants are on the rise gender-based policies are still behind the increase. The lack of policies would increase obstacles faced by female immigrants (IOM & UN Migration, 2020). Besides, barriers may affect female immigrants on labor market inclusion. For instance, in 2017, 73 percent of male immigrants were employed where only 54 percent of female immigrants were employed in Europe, and 40 percent of these female immigrants overqualified for their positions (IOM & UN Migration, 2020).

Policymakers should consider including mechanical obstacles and dissimilarities faced by female immigrants. With such policies dissimilarities economically and other policy areas could be advanced. The report discusses that making such policies can also protect female immigrants from experiencing vulnerable situations that may put them at heightened risk of violence, abuse, and exploitation (IOM & UN Migration, 2020). Another obstacle raised by the report is that immigrant women are responsible for taking care of children and the elderly, handling household assets, and responding to new challenges (IOM, 2020; as cited in Adepoju, 2016). Kenny and O'Donnell (2016) argue that some countries don't use a point system for immigrant acceptance and they suggest that policymakers should find other ways to give preference to female immigrants.

Many studies argue that most of the skilled female immigrants hold positions in female-dominated works such as education and health. According to IOM, 2020's report, such works are regulated by professional bodies within national welfare states. The report argues that there are reasons that might explain progress. One of the reasons is the literature on female migration has increasingly come to focus on their role in the domestic and caring sector, where the growth of labor in the household and residential homes has occurred across all types of European welfare regimes (as cited in Kilkey et al., 2010; Kofman, 2000).

Culture

Cultures do not come by birth opposite to that cultures are learned later on while living in a culture. Culture includes beliefs, languages, morality, arts, etc. in which based on the cultural norms that people live. At the same time, culture determines the knowledge, beliefs, ethics, and traditions of that society. Different fields of social sciences view cultures from different angles. For instance, cultural geography investigates how cultures are distributed, how identities are formed, how they perceive and develop their sense of place, how people gather knowledge and transmit, by location. Although the same aspects of cultural norms are applied at the domestic level, the culture still varies according to the regions, such as accents, behavior, clothing, etc. In addition to other contexts, sociology is a science that examines how cultures differentiate racial, ethnic, and class groups, the role of cultures in the emergence of inequalities and restrictions between groups, the formation, dissemination, acceptance, evaluation, and application of cultural meanings between groups (American Sociological Association, 2020). Due to the different points of view, there is no definitive solution to cultural conflicts. For example, "abortion" or "euthanasia" is considered natural in some cultures but false in other cultures. Therefore, lifestyles are no longer within the boundaries of national cultures and have gone beyond.

Understanding the values of a culture, adapting to and communicating in a new culture, immigrants must be able to speak and understand the native language of the host country. The use of communication skills required for adaptation to a new environment plays a vital role in adapting to the new culture. It is true that to integrate into a new culture, communication skills and knowledge is necessary. Conversely, the lack of communication skills and knowledge will inevitably slow or delay the integration process.

Furthermore, when people start to live in another culture, new acculturation takes place. The most studied forms of acculturation are assimilation, integration, discrimination, and marginalization (Berry & Hou, 2017). In the assimilation form of acculturation, while accepting the new cultural norms, the old culture is set aside. In the integration form, the old and new cultural norms are applied. In the discrimination form, the old cultural norms are kept, while the new cultural norms are rejected. In the marginalization form, the old and new cultural norms are abandoned. The marginalization form is often accepted by immigrants who had to leave their country by force. Although culture is a vital resource, this does not mean that everyone has access to everything. Some individuals or groups living in the same culture may not access all of the cultural resources, they need or desire. These include natural and social sources, education, housing, and health services, among others. Adapting and encouraging cultural diversity in the workplace environment is a must for businesses to be competitive globally.

Participants' life in the home country

"It is not in the stars to hold our destiny but in ourselves."
William Shakespeare

Stories of participants

Participants were recruited using social media, word to mouth, and contacted through emails. Participants' age ranged from 24 to 54, and years living in the host country were from 3 years to 45 years. In this study, 20 skilled immigrant women are interviewed by asking open-ended questions. Before starting interviews, participants signed consent forms. While recording conversations data collected by face-to-face personal interviews and participants living in other states, online tools are used. As the participants started to share the same experiences in the interviews, the interviews were ended because there was no new information to include in the study. From the records, transcripts are created and sent to each participant for their approval. To analyze data a phenomenological methodology was used. Women shared their experiences about working in their country (Figure 1) and working as an immigrant in the USA. Collected data was created verbatim without correction, except fillers words are omitted. For the protection of privacy, pseudo names are assigned to each participant.

Figure 1. Participants' home countries

(Map Source: https://geology.com/world/world-map.shtml).

Reasons to immigrate

Agate, a divorced single mother, was working as a bank teller, and she met her American boyfriend who was in the American military base in her country. After dating for a while, he turned to the USA. Later she followed him: "*I know it sounds crazy. I was young and took the risk to follow him. I don't think I would do it today*," she says. Later on, they got married, and after ten years, she was a single mother again. She remarried again and had another child, and they are together since then. She knew some English, but she was not fluent, and she blames the education system in her home country.

Amber dreamed about moving to the USA, and somehow she made it. Her English was at the beginner level. Amethyst immigrated to the USA with her ex-husband. Her ex-husband moved first to go to school and after a year, she moved to the USA. "*I was not happy in my country because of the many restrictions and felt like I didn't have any freedom. It was my dream to move out of my country but, never dreamed about coming to the USA. Moving to the USA was my ex-husband's dream,*" she says.

Diamond earned her Ph.D. in her home country and moved to the USA to complete her post-doctoral studies. She met her husband and stayed in the USA.

Similarly, Zircon moved to the USA to earn her master's degree, and later, she met her husband (from her country) and stayed. Turquoise also moved to the USA for her Ph.D. and met her husband (from her country). Ametrine, Ruby, and Diaspore moved to the USA to earn a Ph.D., and now they work as a faculty in a university. Emeralds also moved to the USA to study but never completed. Garnet, Sapphire, and Jade met their American husband in their home country and they moved to the USA with their husbands. Being medical doctors Opal and Pearl moved to the USA because of the needs of the host country. Unlike other participants, Iolite, Sunstone, Topaz, Moonstone, and Tanzanite moved to the USA because of political problems in their country. They are not refugees, but because pf the situation in their country, they wanted to leave. In sum, most of them followed their dreams.

Professional life

Agate has a baccalaureate degree in Economics and was working as a bank teller in her home country. According to her, working as a bank teller is a good job with a decent payment and respectful position in her home country. *"Well, it was like that when I was there, not sure if it is the same way now, lots of things changed within 20 years. In my country, you usually became friends with your coworkers you visit each other share problems, etc. I mean your professional life and social life get mixed over there. As far as my job I had good relationships with customers, no complaints,"* she says.

Amethyst has a high school diploma and was working for the government as a technician. "I started working at the age of 19, and I liked what I was doing, and it was a secure job, the salary was above the average, but I wasn't happy. I was lack of belonging to that society. I was different than most of them. Being a good employee, receiving awards and promotions was not enough for me because I was seeking a more meaningful life, work, etc.," she says.

Garnet was working as a brain surgeon in her home country *"almost everywhere, it takes a very long time to become a brain surgeon, you have to be a general surgeon about 5 years then you can be a brain surgeon,"* she says. Opal and Pearl are medical doctors in internal medicine, and they were practicing in their home countries. Both of them mention that being a medical doctor is a privilege in their home countries. *"Everybody respects you because of your profession they need us,"* says Opal. *"It is not easy to become a medical doctor, and we don't have enough doctors in my country, it is the reason for respect,"* says Pearl.

Ametrine, Diaspore, Ruby, and Zircon were students thus; they did not have work experiences when they were in their home countries. After completing her Ph.D., Diamond worked as a faculty for a while in her home country. *"As in most countries, faculties are highly respected in society. They know you make differences in people's life,"* she says. Turquoise was also working as a faculty and confirmed what Diamond said about being a faculty in her home country.

Emerald was working as a manager in government and had many responsibilities, with many subordinates *"when I asked something it had to done as soon as possible. I had the authority to hire and fire people, I learned how to work people, give orders, and motivate them,"* she explains. Iolite, Jade, Moonstone, and Tanzanite were managers too, but in the private sector. "*I had to work long hours and weekends too. I did not have time for fun. It was only Work! Work! Work!*", Jade says.

Sapphire studied English and was working as a teacher. "*I was a popular teacher in the school because they know learning English is important. Being a teacher is ok over there, you have a salary and you can support yourself but you cannot afford to buy a house or eat outside often, etc.,*" she says. Sunstone and Topaz were a small business owner and had employees. "*Because of the unstable economic situation in my country running a business is always risky. I was stressed all the time. You are worried about the salaries of your employees, payment of materials, etc. You are afraid of filing bankruptcy anytime,*" says Sunstone. Zircon was working as a computer programmer in a High Tech company. "*In my home country, you don't see many females in this field. In the beginning, I had a hard time to prove myself and I was working with males,*" she says

Participants' life in the host country

> *Go confidently in the direction of your dreams. Live the life you have imagined.*
> *Henry David Thoreau*

Professional life

Agate has been working as a branch manager at the bank. Since she is free of financial problems, she doesn't work from time to time, but later on, gets bored at home then, she goes back to work. "*I am good at what I do here and my superiors know it. I struggled a lot at the beginning but adjusted many things. It was so weird calling your managers by their first name. I had a hard time to start calling them by the first name because in my home country it is disrespectful. I found relationship with coworkers here is different too. Even in chitchatting, you cannot ask someone's age wow! What a big deal. They take it as discrimination here. Once I had problems with that. My own culture and the culture here is very different,*" she says. "*Before I became a branch manager I worked whatever I found to support myself and my boy. My husband expected me to work so I didn't have any chance. It was hard at the beginning but later didn't care,*" she says.

Amber has been working as a hotel manager, and she likes her job, but at the same time, her family comes first. "*I always pick a job which could not jeopardize my family responsibilities. This is how it is in my home country family comes first,*" she emphasizes. Amethyst held many different jobs after moving to the USA, and now she works for the government and teaches in a college as an adjunct faculty. "*I had to work on my English first, and it took about two years to be comfortable with it. I delivered newspapers, cleaned houses, worked as a babysitter, took care of an elderly woman, you name it,*" she says. *Always I dreamed about going to college because of my family's economic condition I could not over there. I started going to college and got divorced but it didn't stop me from reaching my goal and I got my Ph.D. While attending school I kept working*" she says. She mentions that the work environment and relationships with coworkers are different in the host country. Amethyst feels that women are not valued employees in organizations in the USA.

Ametrine and Diaspore work as faculty at a university, and they speak with an accent. She says: "*Sometimes my students do not understand me I see it from their face. They don't feel comfortable to ask me to repeat what I said in the class*". On the other hand, Diaspore doesn't feel the same. "*I teach my mother tongue here, and my students know how hard to learn other languages. When they don't understand the subject or me, they always ask me in the class and outside of the class. They are very motivated to learn,*" she says. Although Diamond has an accent, she doesn't have a problem with her accent; indeed her students find her accent cute. "*Time to time I realize that instead of what I say they pay attention to how I say*". Other than her students she complains about the administration especially, the department head and the dean. "*It is hard to convince them, they pretend listening, but they don't. I don't know if the problem is me being a female and an immigrant. I am sure I would advance my career faster in my home country,*" she says. Turquoise is also a faculty, and she has an accent too. "*Although people are used to our accent because there are many people from my home county, very seldom students complain about my accent. A couple of students went to the dean and told him that they cannot understand me. The dean said 'go ahead and get your Ph.D. so I can hire you' I am not sure it was a compliment or sarcasm,*" she says.

Emerald works for the government, and she is a division head. Even though she tries very hard to make her subordinates happy she feels that people are not comfortable around her. She thinks that the reason is her accent. "*I know I have a heavy accent, but I am a hard worker, and I am trying to be an example for them so they would work like me. I do every kind of task just to show them that we are equal, we are all human beings. I wouldn't do the same in my home country I would say 'this is your job you have to do it' but I cannot act like that here,*" she says.

Opal and Pearl are working as medical doctors. Both of them say that people respect them because of their profession. "*I know my patients don't understand me sometimes. I believe not only because of my accent but also the medical terminology that I have to use so they don't understand what I am saying. I am not a social person so I don't establish a relationship with my coworkers and subordinates like nurses etc.,*" she says. Unlike Opal, Pearl doesn't have problems with her patients. "*Even I have a heavy accent they don't care. I cannot say the same for my coworkers. When I talk they kept asking me "what did you say, what you mean etc. those questions bother me from time to time,*" she says. Garnet is working as a brain surgeon, and she has an accent too. While laughing "*you don't need to talk while operating they cannot hear you,*" she says. She had to work hard to be able to work as a brain surgeon in the USA "*even though I was practicing in my home country, and I was a successful brain surgeon, because of the system here they didn't accept my profession, so I had to take medical specialty test and worked for a while. It was wasting time*" she says.

Iolite, Moonstone, Tanzanite, and Jade work as managers in a large size company and all of them speak with an accent. "*You have to work harder than natives here because you have to prove yourself. Some employees look at me in a pity way but still, they have to take my orders. I might be a pity for them I am the boss here,*" she says. Moonstone believes that if she didn't speak with an accent the situation would be different. "*Your employees repeat after you even mimic what you said. This is uncomfortable but you don't want to take disciplinary action.*" Tanzanite complains about sex discrimination. "*You are a female plus an immigrant manager the guys don't like it and they don't take you seriously. Actually, it is not as bad as in home country but when you think that the USA is* the most developed country in the world you don't expect that it would be happening here too," she says. Jade says *"since you are an immigrant everybody thinks that you send money to oversea so you don't have money to spend for other stuff. They are prejudice about immigrants. Most of the people have no clue about other countries or international experiences they believe that USA is the best country in the world. Unfortunately, ignorance is common here"*. Jade has similar experiences: *"They just don't want to accept that you came from another country, speak with an accent and you give them orders. I feel like they are always looking to catch faults or mistakes that I would make. Sometimes they are sarcastic but don't pay attention I focus on my work and try to be good with it,"* she says.

Topaz and Sunstone are business owners, they have American employees, and their suppliers are mostly Americans. They do not complain about their employees but customers and suppliers. *"My employees are thankful because they need a job, and I provide it. Being thankful doesn't mean that they would do extra works. Money talks here,"* says Topaz. Sunstone talks about her customers. *"Customers are always right here, which I never understand. You have customers who you don't want to see again. They know it and you will have many rude customers. You have to learn to be patient and stay quiet, which not fair."* She feels suppliers treat them differently than the natives.

Sapphire is a branch manager for a bank. *"When people come for a loan they are surprised you can see from their face. Why? Do they believe that immigrants cannot be managers or they cannot hold money? Honestly, I haven't figured it out all those years. I don't know maybe it is related to the location. I have not witnessed big problems in my branch, only small conflicts that I could manage well,"* she says. Unlike others, Zircon does not have problems with what she is doing other than her accent. *"Because of the field, we speak the same languages we all know the terminology. For example, C+ is the same everywhere. When you are coding you may use another speaking language, but the process is the same. My problem is socializing with my coworker. I want to join them when they chitchat but we don't have the same background so when they speak about an event, I don't have anything to say. They are trying to be nice and feel like they have to say something. It makes uncomfortable all of us, so I stay away even I don't want to,"* she says.

Challenges

All of the participants feel the biggest challenge is their accent and the language. Some of them wish that they were not speaking an accent, but they know that it is impossible. On the other hand, some of them are proud of their accent because it ties to their identity. Although they are fluent in English, they have problems with idioms and some words that those problems made them embarrassed in some situations. They also mention those language problems cause some problems because people misunderstand them and got offended sometimes. Native speakers starting to talk slowly, right after hearing their accent makes them angry. They think that people are acting like they are stupid.

Relationship with coworkers and subordinates is another challenge for most of the participants. Having a different cultural background makes it hard for them to change cultural values, like calling superiors by their first name. Some of them are surprised that asking someone's age is forbidden in the host country. They also believe that most people are not sincere in the host county they are just trying to be nice. Most participants pointed out that native people beat around the bush all the time instead of coming to the point.

Most of the participants also mention that some Americans are prejudice about immigrants. *"Whatever they observed before, they think that all of the immigrants are the same,"* says one of the participants. *"Here people think that we lived in poor conditions like no water, etc., and the USA is the best place in the world,"* says another participant. According to the participants, prejudice levels change by location. In big cities, people have more knowledge about immigrants, and citizens are not prejudiced as in small towns. They point out that *"some people are ignorant, their knowledge about the world's geography is very low, and because of that people asked them ridiculous questions"*, "*even a kid would know better them,"* says one of the participants. When people asked them such questions, they didn't know what to say or what to do, and some of them wanted to laugh at them and tell them how ignorant they are.

Dealing with challenges

Although each participant developed their way of dealing with challenges, and interestingly, they act alike in some challenges. To deal with their accent during the conversation, they keep observing listeners' body language, especially the mimics. When the listeners look confused, they reword the sentence. Some of the vowels don't exist in their mother tongue, and because of that, they cannot pronounce some words correctly. Therefore the time to time, they spell out the words to make sure that listeners understand what they meant. Additionally, when native speakers make fun of their pronunciation, they ask them to say, a word from their language, especially a word, which they cannot correctly pronounce, so they just wanted to show them that it is not easy. All of the participants also mentioned that when people don't understand them, they started speaking slowly, and if it doesn't work, they spell out the words.

All participants think that they have to be hard-workers to prove themselves in the host country so people would pay more attention to their work other than other issues, such as accents. Some of the participants decide not to behave like in their own culture and try to behave or mimic them to receive respect. The same participants feel like they are a cultural attaché in the host country, and they feel that telling people about the culture in their home country is their responsibility. Additionally, they believe that they would break the prejudices about immigrants. Some of the participants learned not to object even they are right not to lose their job.

Conclusion

A diverse workforce reflects a changing world, marketplace, and diverse-work teams bring high value to organizations. Organizations with a culturally diverse workforce have many advantages, such as creativity, a broader perspective spectrum, and talents. Adserà and Pytliková (2015, p. 79) assert that skilled immigrants inclining to promote innovation and cross-cultural exchanges are crucial to *transforming the ethnic diversity of the workforce into the firm's competitive advantage.* People view the world in different ways, thus cultural conflicts are inevitable. Because of the cultural gaps between their home countries and the

United States, skilled immigrant women encountered adjustment difficulties concerning dissimilar workplace conflicts in the host country.

To prevent intercultural conflicts, organizations should provide a harmonized work environment where employees should value all aspects of other cultures. According to Farnsworth et al. (2019), *diversity management benefits links by creating a fair and safe environment where everyone has access to opportunities and challenges*. Because of changes in the workforce Kubiciel-Lodzińska and Maj (2020, p. 813) recommend that managers and immigrant workers gaining skills to create and manage diverse teams is crucial for organizations. Additionally, organizations should use all kinds of available management tools to educate not only immigrant workers but, everyone in the organization. All employees need to have training about diversity and its issues, including laws and regulations (Farnsworth et al., 2019). Consequently, diversity management would prevent possible legal issues and a hostile work environment, which would decrease motivation and production. Additionally, by providing such a work environment, the organizations would keep skilled immigrants in the organizations. Moreover, it would be better if organizations can support the immigrant employees for smooth transitions on adapting customs, and organizational culture, especially for the newcomers.

One of the participants says that for living in another country, people have to have thick skin to survive and stay compatible in the workforce. To cope with difficulties, immigrant women employed several strategies to handle workplace conflicts. To be successful in work they also had to adjust both verbal and nonverbal language usage, relationships with their coworkers, family life balances, the subordinate-superior hierarchy among others.

This study offers implications for immigrants and organizations, especially organizations with high diverse cultural employment body. Since the numbers of people with multicultural backgrounds in organizations are increasing, related issues will not dissipate soon. Therefore, organizations should understand the context of multiculturalism to keep a strong place in the competitive phenomenon of globalization.

References

Adepoju, A. (2016). *Migration Dynamics, Refugees and Internally Displaced Persons in Africa*. United Nations Academic Impact (UNAI), 20 September. https://academicimpact. un.org/content/migration-dynamicsrefugees-and-internally-displaced-persons-africa.

Adserà, A., & Pytliková, M. (2015). The Role of Language in Shaping International Migration. *The Economic Journal, 125*(586), F49–F81.

American Sociological Association. (2020). Culture. https://www.asanet.org/topics/ culture

Baker, B. (2020). *Estimates of the Lawful Permanent Resident Population in the United States and the Subpopulation Eligible to Naturalize: 2015–2019*. Homeland Security. https://www.dhs.gov/sites/default/files/publications/lpr_population_estimates_ja nuary_2015-2019.pdf

Batalova, J., Blizzard, B., & Bolter. J. (2021). Frequently Requested Statistics on Immigrants and Immigration in the United States. *Migration Information Source*, February 11, 2021. https://www.migrationpolicy.org/article/frequently-requested-statistics-immigrants-and-immigration-united-states-2020

Berry, J. W., & Hou, F. (2017). Acculturation, discrimination and wellbeing among second generation of immigrants in Canada, *Int. J. of Intercultural Relations*, *61*, 29–39.

Cohen, J., & Sirkeci, I. (2011). *Cultures of Migration*. Austin: University of Texas Press. http://www.jstor.org/stable/10.7560/726840

Culture. (2020). American Sociological Association. https://www.asanet.org/topics/culture

Dumont, J. C., Martin, J. P., & Spielvogel, G. (2007). *Women on the Move: the neglected gender dimension of the brain drain*. IZA DP 2090.

Farnsworth, D., Clark, J. L., Green, K., López, M., Wysocki, A., & Kepner, K. (2019). *Diversity in the Workplace: Benefits, Challenges, and the Required Managerial Tools*. University of Florida, IFAS Extension. https://edis.ifas.ufl.edu/pdffiles/HR/HR02200.pdf

Flahaux, M. L. (2017). The role of migration policy changes in Europe for return migration to Senegal. *International Migration Review, 51*(4), 868–892.

Flahaux, M. L. & de Haas, H. (2016). African migration: Trends, patterns, drivers. *Comparative Migration Studies, 4*(1), 1–25.

Gonzalez-Barrera, A., & Connor, P. (2019). *Around the World, More Say Immigrants Are Strength Than a Burden. Publics divided on immigrants' willingness to adopt host country's customs*. PEW Research Center.https://www.pewresearch.org/global/2019/03/14/around-the-world-more-say-immigrants-   are-a-strength-than-a-burden/

Hondagneu-Sotelo, P. (1999). Introduction: Gender and Contemporary U.S. Immigration. *American Behavioral Scientist, 42*(4), 565–576.

International Organization for Migration (IOM) & UN Migration (2020). *World Migration Report 2020*. https://publications.iom.int/system/files/pdf/wmr_2020.pdf

International Organization for Migration (IOM) & UN Migration (2018). *World Migration Report 2018*. https://www.iom.int/sites/default/files/country/docs/china/r5_world_migration_report_20   18_en.pdf

Kenny, C., & O'Donnell, M. (2016). *Why Increasing Female Migration from Gender-Unequal Countries Is a Win for Everyone*. https://www.cgdev.org/publication/why-increasing-female-immigration-flows-gender-unequal-countries-could-have-significant

Kilkey, M., Lutz, H. & Palenga-Möllenbeck, E. (2010). Introduction: Domestic and Care Work at the Intersection of Welfare, Gender and Migration Regimes: European Experiences. *Social Policy and Society 9*(3), 379–384.

Kofman, E, (2000). The invisibility of skilled female migrants and gender relations in studies of skilled migration in Europe. *Int. J. of Population Geography,* 6, 45–59.

Kubiciel-Lodzińska, S., & Maj, J. (2020). Experience in Employing Immigrants and the Perception of Benefits of a Diverse Workforce *European Research Studies Journal, XXIII*(1), 803–818.

Manning, P. (2020). Migration in World History. In E. Heikkilä (Ed.), *Mihin suuntaan Suomi kehittyy? Liikkuvuuden ja muuttoliikkeen dynamiikka. In Which Direction is Finland Evolving? The Dynamics of Mobility and Migration* (pp. 18–39). X Muuttoliikesymposium 2019. Julkaisuja 39. Turku: Siirtolaisuusinstituutti.

National Academies of Sciences, Engineering, and Medicine. (2015). Immigration Policy and the Search for Skilled Workers. https://www.nationalacademies.org/our-work/international-comparative-study-of-high-skilled-immigration-policy-and-the-global-competition-for-talent

United Nations Conference on Trade and Development (UNCTAD). (2018). *Economic Development in Africa Report 2018: Migration for Structural Transformation*. United Nations, New York. https://unctad.org/en/pages/PublicationWebflyer. aspx?publicationid=2118.

HUMAN CAPITAL DEVELOPMENT AND SKILLED IMMIGRANTS LABOUR MARKET EXPERIENCES IN SOUTH AFRICA: AN OVERVIEW

Sikanyiso Masuku and Sizo Nkala

Introduction

Boasting a significantly bigger economy than those of its regional neighbours, South Africa has become a preferred destination for millions of both skilled and unskilled migrants from the Southern African region and beyond, especially since 1994. Voluntary, skilled immigration and its overall benefits to the destination country (increases in employment, capital accumulation and income) are not phenomena exclusive to South Africa as they have increased globally since the 1960s (Facchini & Mayda, 2012). Voluntary immigration to South Africa during the Apartheid era was, however, fraught with many challenges, as the national policies on entry, residence, temporary migration, immigration (permanent residence), and even refugee status, were all racialized and premised on immigration control. Through racialized immigration, a two-gate system under the Aliens Registration Act No 26 of 1936 (enacted in 1939) made it possible to prevent black African immigrants from entering the country, thereby limiting those that did enter to the thriving mining and agricultural sectors (Handmaker & Parsley, 2001, p. 41). Meritocracy was thus not the principal basis upon which voluntary immigrants (skilled or otherwise) were admitted into the country.

The Apartheid government's neglect of and disregard for the education of black people meant that South Africa transitioned into the democratic era with a thin skills base (Maisonnave et al. 2016, p. 215). The initial attempts of dismantling racial discrimination within the South African labour market came in 1991 with a repeal of the Aliens Registration Act of 1936 and the introduction of the Aliens Control Act. These efforts ensured that a steady flow of adequately qualified immigrants, regardless of their race composition, entered the country, but the labour market disparities were already apparent. The 1998 National Enterprise Survey (NES) and the 1999 World Bank Survey (WBS) both revealed that 54% of firms within the manufacturing and service sector faced productivity constraints associated with a shortage of skills (Bhorat & Lundall, 2005). In further addressing these disparities, migration policies in South Africa were incorporated within the framework of (i) the Southern African Development Community (SADC) 1995 draft protocol and the 2003 Cooperation Agreement in the fields of Migratory Labour, (ii) the African Union (AU), and (iii) the New Economic Partnership for Development (NEPAD) (Crush & Tshitereke cited in Nyamnjoh 2006, p. 34; Kleinsmidt & Manicom, 2010, p. 164). It is within this system of regional and continental dynamics that a new calibre of regional immigrants emerged, inclusive of, but not confined to, long-distance traders, asylum-seekers, students, skilled professionals, entrepreneurs, etc. Immigration statistics show that 127,000 work and business permits were issued by South

Africa's Home Affairs department between 2011 and 2015 alone (an average of 25,400 per year).

While South Africa has since managed to attract a large number of skilled immigrants, our study shows that, for most of them, life in the country has been fraught with challenges. Foreign teachers and engineers are hired on temporary contracts with limited rights and poor remuneration. Healthcare professionals must face cumbersome bureaucratic procedures, and foreign academics are rarely promoted or hired for permanent positions, regardless of their qualifications. Our study also discovered that a rigid and chaotic visa regime and a government facing a political dilemma also contributed to making skilled immigrants' lives difficult in the country. Moreover, skilled immigrants are not distinguished from unskilled immigrants, who are said to be saturating the job market in South Africa and supplanting the locals (Sichone, 2008). Reitzes and Crawhall (1998, p. 23) argued that black immigrant workers (both skilled and unskilled) are often viewed as an under-class whose presence is necessary but unwelcome. This has soured relations between mostly black economic immigrants and the unemployed, historically disadvantaged black South African population. The first three sections of this chapter, on South Africa's skills problem, legislation and policy, and the socio-political climate, set out the context with which skilled immigrants have to contend. The following sections examine, in depth, the experiences of skilled immigrants by focusing on systematic marginalization, precarious careers and lack of secure residence. The final section draws an overall conclusion highlighting the major findings.

South Africa's skills problem

As South Africa's economy evolved, a low employment elasticity, emanating from an increasing demand for high-wage high-productivity jobs (at the expense of low-wage labour-intensive development), resulted in a significant demand for professions at skill level 8 (Nattrass & Seekings, 2019). However, the majority of black South Africans did not possess the required skills to fill the emerging vacancies. A 2018 report from Statistics South Africa revealed that 4.5 million (12%) out of a total of 38 million economically active South Africans have tertiary education. The National Economic Development and Labour Council (NEDLAC) (2019) stated that only 23.1% of South Africa's 16.3 million labour force are classifiable as highly skilled while the less skilled make up 76.9%. Furthermore, the Manpower Group's 2019 report on the global skills shortage recorded a 34% skills shortage in South Africa against a global average of 54%. Among the top 10 skills in short supply in the country are the skills of engineers, technicians, teachers, sales representatives, managers and executives, information technology, accounting and finance (Van Rensburg, 2020). This widespread skills gap is why South Africa needs to attract skilled immigrants to plug the gap, in order to grow its economy. Although the advantage of immigrant workers with skill cells (education and experience) has gradually become less pronounced as education and skill levels of the native-born population have increased, there is still a skills shortage in South Africa. This skills shortage is defined by the South African government in both relative and absolute terms, and is conceptualized by the corporate sector or industry primarily in relation to productivity (Daniels, 2007, p. 1).

Despite the above facts, however, South African national policy documents from 1994 until 2002 were silent on how industry's growing demands for scarce skills were to be addressed. While the National Development Plan (NDP) (2012) and the Department of Home Affairs' 2016 government gazettes all envisioned skilled immigration or brain gain as a means to economic growth, this would only be effective to the extent that there was harmony between employment policy and migration policy. One of us (see Masuku, 2018), has previously identified controlled forms of association within the South African labour market for forced migrants as emanating mostly from a spectrum of primary cultural factors. Skilled immigrants are more at risk from structural factors. Given how access to unskilled jobs is often contingent upon strong family and social networks (Masuku, 2018), unskilled immigrant workers (unlike their skilled counterparts) can thus survive very well within the shadow that informal and casual employment provides. The reduced agency of skilled immigrants, on the other hand, is discussed here as emanating not only from structural gaps but also from discords in the interpretation, adoption and implementation of policy. Limitations to a full positive impact of skilled immigration on the South African labour market, public finance and economic growth index (as guided by the 2018 ILO, OECD and Development Centre methodology) are discussed in the chapter. The next section looks at the legislation and policies designed to avert the skills problem in the country.

Legislative and policy context

As Segatti & Landau (2011, p. 67) noted "From 1994 to 2002 South Africa generally opposed the emigration and immigration of skilled labour…the government focused on stimulating employment for South African citizens". Mattes, Crush and Richmond (2000) argued that in the 1990s the South African government saw immigration as a problem to be controlled rather than as an opportunity to be harnessed. The 1994 Reconstruction and Development Program (RDP), the 1996 Growth, Employment and Redistribution (GEAR) policy, as well as the Accelerated and Shared Growth Initiative for South Africa (ASGISA) of 2005, were thus consequently mute on how the country could benefit from foreign professionals in the service of the country's economic development (Segatti & Landau, 2011, p. 31). While the 1997 Green Paper on International Migration did mention the importance of skilled labour, skilled migrants were to be admitted into the country according to government quotas (Department of Home Affairs, 1997). This was perhaps a reflection of the prevailing political climate which rendered the embracing of foreign workers unpopular considering the high rates of unemployment among black South Africans. It was through the Immigration Act of 2002 that the government explicitly addressed the issue of skilled migrant labour. Section 19(4) of the Immigration Act states that "an exceptional skills work permit may be issued by the Department [Home Affairs] to an individual of exceptional skills or qualifications". A Government Gazette issued in 2014 (DHET, 2014), listed the skills and qualifications that aspiring skilled migrants must possess if they are to be issued with critical skills work visas. The skills included those of agricultural engineers, architects, actuaries, auditors, information and communication technologists, engineers, health professionals, life and earth scientists, artisans, academics and researchers, among others.

At the domestic policy level, the South African government only recently began to address the issue of skilled migrant labour explicitly. The need to enable skilled labour immigration was mentioned in the NDP of 2012. While lamenting that little has been done to take advantage of the benefits of migration, the NDP of 2012 implored the government to not only ease the entry of skilled immigrants but also work to address their rights and vulnerabilities through countering xenophobia and introducing support programmes to regularise their residence (National Planning Commission, 2021, p. 107). In a bid to drive South Africa's immigration policy in a progressive direction, the government released the White Paper on International Migration ((Department of Home Affairs, 2017). The 2017 White Paper outlines eight strategic interventions to be made in changing the immigration policy. Some of the strategic interventions include the management of international migrants with skills and capital, and the management of the integration process for international migrants. The policy proposed the introduction of a points-based system, and the issuance of family-oriented long-term visas and residence visas for international students, to attract and retain international migrants with critical skills which would help meet South Africa's development objectives. The adoption of all these progressive immigration policies, both domestically and at a multilateral level, has helped to put South Africa in a better position to exploit the movement of skilled labour for its own economic development. However, as the proceeding sections will show, the change in attitudes on paper have not always resulted in a change in practice. Skilled immigrants still face a hostile labour market environment.

On the international front, South Africa has been party to various conventions, treaties and agreements which have shaped its migration policies, and greatly influenced the immigration of skilled labour. Such continental policy frameworks include the Abuja Treaty of 1991, the 2006 African Common Position on Migration and Development, and the 2015 AU Agenda 2063, all of which underscore the importance of the link between migration and Africa's economic integration. In 2012, African countries under the auspices of the AU agreed to form the African Continental Free Trade Area to further deepen the economic integration of the continent. One of the general objectives of the agreement was to "contribute to the movement of capital and natural persons" (African Union, 2012, p. 4). This called for the review of the parties' immigration policies to enhance the movement of people and goods across borders. Several protocols, such as the 1996 SADC Protocol on Free Trade, the 1997 Protocol on Education and Training and the 1998 Protocol on Tourism, have also been agreed on, with implications for the immigration regimes of SADC members. South Africa is also signatory to other regional agreements under the SADC and these have shaped South Africa's approach to immigration policies. An example is the Protocol on the Facilitation of Movement of Persons (SADC, 2005), in which the main thrust was to enable the free movement of capital, labour, goods and services, and of the people of the SADC region. The protocol also made provision for the visa-free 90-day visit to another state, the issuance of temporary or permanent residence, and working in the territory of another State. The agreement also highlighted the need to harmonise laws and immigration policies of the SADC member-states.

Anti-immigrant social and political climate

Although the adoption of progressive domestic legislation and international conventions has made the hiring of immigrants legal, it has done little to reduce the hostility and associated challenges that skilled immigrants face in South Africa. The position of skilled immigrants in the South African labour-market is made awkward and precarious by the widespread anti-immigrant sentiments among the native population and, not infrequently, these sentiments flare up into violent and deadly skirmishes. According to Xenowatch (2019), between 1994 and 2018 there were 529 incidents of xenophobic violence involving 309 deaths, 901 physical assaults, more than 100,000 displacements, 2193 shops looted and 257 threats to safety and property. A 2013 survey by Afrobarometer revealed that about 44% of South Africans did not assent to granting asylum to refugees, and 45% were of the view that foreigners should not be allowed to live in the country since they take jobs and benefits away from citizens (Mataure, 2013). Moreover, 67% indicated that they do not trust foreigners at all (*ibid*). Thus, since 1994 South Africa has been grappling with widespread anti-immigration sentiments with little attention to whether the immigrants concerned are skilled or unskilled. As a consequence, immigrants are often blamed for increasing job competition and devaluing the local labour market (Nyamnjoh 2006). Xenophobic violence has thus been triggered by the belief that foreigners perpetuate socio-economic challenges in the country, as well as crime. This belief exists despite foreigners constituting less than 3% of the population living in South Africa.

The anti-foreigner wave has invaded the South African social media space. The hashtag #PutSouthAfricansFirst has been trending on Twitter for the better part of 2020. The hashtag has been endorsed by prominent people in the entertainment, religious, business and political circles. Political parties with representation in parliament, such as the African Transformation Movement (ATM), have explicitly and actively aligned themselves with the right wing hashtag. The supporters of the hashtag are of the view that foreigners are taking up jobs, leaving the majority of South Africans unemployed. In addition to crime, foreigners are also blamed for putting the public service system under strain and crowding out South African citizens (Bezuidenhout, 2020). Possibly reflecting the position of the ruling party, the Minister of Finance Tito Mboweni echoed the same sentiments when he argued that in the new (post Covid-19) economy, businesses hiring foreigners instead of locals, would risk being excluded from accessing the much needed government financial assistance (Cohen, Naidoo & Mbatha, 2020).

In a high-profile case in 2010 that brought the problems of skilled immigrants to light, retired South African national rugby team player Tendai Mtawarira came under attack from parliamentarians who wanted him deported for violating his work permit by playing for the South African national team when he was not a citizen (Rees, 2010). In 2019, the Member of the Executive Council (MEC) for Health in South Africa's KwaZulu-Natal province also issued a directive to stop the hiring of all foreign doctors in the province. This was despite the declaration by the national Minister of Health that South Africa was short of 4,143 doctors (Timeslive, 2019). In the same year, the chair of the South African parliament's Higher Education and Portfolio Committee, Mohlopi Mapulane, called for the reduction of the proportion of foreign students and lecturers to below 10% of the staff and student population. The chair said this move would protect higher education institutions "as South African universities so that we protect the South African brand" (Govender, 2020). As recently as the 11th of December 2020, one of the opposition parties, the Inkatha Freedom Party (IFP), introduced the Employment Services Amendment Bill to limit the hiring of foreigners in low-skill occupations. While the bill is focused on low-skill occupations, there is no clear definition of such occupations. The bill requires the Minister of Labour to decide on the employment of foreign nationals in various sectors of the economy, and also requires the government to set numerical targets for the employment of foreigners in the identified sectors (Ndenze, 2020). Such attitudes by the political elite partly account for discord in the interpretation, adoption and implementation of policy regarding skilled immigration. These attitudes also rationalise this chapter's discussion of the sociologies and politics of participation or inclusion of skilled immigrants within the South African labour market. This approach was chosen in cognizance of the importance of effective contributions to the ongoing debate about the existential threats and opportunities confronting the NDP's clarion call for the attraction and retention of critically skilled international migrants (National Development Plan, 2012, p. 107).

Experiences of skilled migrants in South Africa

While the policies say all the right things, the practice and behaviour of South African officials, politicians and citizens are decidedly conservative. This section takes a detailed look at some of the challenges faced by immigrants, including systematic marginalization, precarious careers and the lack of secure residence.

Brain waste; systemic marginalization

The failure to expedite the employment process of foreign health professionals exacerbates the acute shortage of staff, particularly in rural areas. The Human Resources for Health Strategy shows that the shortfall of health workers within the primary healthcare sector will have reached 87,000 by 2025 (Cleary & Low, 2020). Despite this, the Mercury Newspaper (5 June 2020) wrote about foreign nursing students who completed their nursing degree at the top of their class at the University of KwaZulu-Natal (Comins, 2020). However, due to their foreign status they could not be placed for a year of community service in a South African hospital, which is a requirement for registering with the South

African Nursing Council (SANC). Furthermore, SANC requires foreign qualified nurses to write an exam before they can register. While this is designed to protect the integrity of the health sector, this constitutes a bureaucratic red tape within the SANC that adversely hinders the employment of much needed, well-qualified foreign nurses if implemented inefficiently (Bateman, 2012). Similarly, despite a shortage of medical doctors in South Africa, with a persistent ratio of less than one doctor per 1,000 population between 1996 (0.59) and 2016 (0.8) (George et al., 2019), foreign trained immigrant physicians also face bureaucratic red tape in the sector. The Sowetan newspaper of 13 March 2018 reported that about 40 doctors from the Democratic Republic of Congo, who passed their board examinations and got accreditation from the Health Professions Council of South Africa (HPCSA), were being rejected for internships at public hospitals (Sowetanlive, 2018). The doctors were forced to wash cars and work in salons or as security guards to make ends meet while waiting for their placements. Although the story can easily be misconstrued as another classic case of discrimination against foreign workers, South African medical students have also experienced challenges in securing paid internships. For example, in 2017 the National Health Care Professionals Association (NHCPA) had at least 80 unplaced doctors in its database (Pillay, 2017; Mahapo, 2018). This indicates two things i.e. (i) the Department of Health has budgetary constraints in meeting its constitutional mandate of availing enough paid internship posts, and (ii) the immigration policy seems oblivious to the said budgetary constraints as it continues to approve critical skills work visas for medical practitioners whom, although in genuine demand, cannot be regularized due to existential capacity constraints. The precarious situation of 105 foreign-trained medical doctors with work visas, but without internships in South Africa (Medical Brief, 2019), further exposed a clear discord between employment policy and migration policy.

Foreign academics, working in some South African institutions, succumb to brain waste as they are not only employed to tutor courses taught by people with lesser qualifications or experience, but they also get overlooked for promotions and are retained at the lowest ranks despite having published widely (Sehoole et al., 2019). However, the same study by Sehoole et al. about foreign academics glossed over how these academics retain some level of agency and still cope in the face of unfair conditions of participation, for example through their level of activism and their relationship with the South African labour unions. As one of us identified in a 2018 study with asylum seekers (Masuku, 2018), the strategies at the disposal of those facing skewed conditions of participation can vary, and may include bonding capital and other responses such as solidarism (Parkin, 1974). Mention in the study by Sehoole et al. (2019) of foreign academics' state of "powerlessness" and acute "vulnerability", nonetheless, suggests a poor rapport between the immigrant academics and relevant labour unions. This assumption is corroborated by Makonye's (2017) study of skilled immigrants in the education sector. He found that foreign teachers, who were mostly of Zimbabwean origin, "had no voice to raise complaints" even when made to work outside their job description. Skilled immigrants' subjugation to unequal conditions of participation also makes redundant the conventional concept of "collective bargaining" (through occupational unions), as South African citizens within the same occupation may not be subject to the same institutional biases.

A study of the University of Cape Town found that international academics tended to be promoted within a shorter period of time than the South African staff (Sadiq et al., 2018). Although, at face value, these findings seem to debunk Sehoole et al's (2019) study, further insight shows that such expedited career advancement is usually a result of foreign academics being appointed after having already advanced in their careers, whereas their local counterparts are appointed with lesser qualifications, in the interests of developing South African scholars. As such, international academics can more easily satisfy promotion criteria than South African academics. In its 2017 Draft Policy Framework for the Internationalization of Higher Education in South Africa (DHET, 2017), the Department of Higher Education and Training (DHET) calls for South African universities to establish global links and take advantage of the global labour market in recruiting scholars and scientists, but with a view to nurturing South Africa's own talent. A need exists for a balance between appointing the best possible people in academic positions, even if they are from outside South Africa, and meeting the need to develop and grow South African academic talent. This chapter underscores ways in which South African institutions may benefit from international talent. However, this is only theoretical, and is failing dismally in praxis as there is an existential failure by the South African government to find the balance between prioritizing its own citizens and the need to close the skills gap (Mhlanga et al, 2018).

Precarious careers and occupational closure

Zimbabwean engineers in South Africa are described in some of the literature on skilled immigrants in the country as being confronted with unsurmountable challenges in maintaining their professional status or getting work permits to practice their trade (Chikarara, 2019). By adopting Standing's (2011) notion of the precariat (defined as a class in the labour market that has minimal trust relationships with capital and the state), the precariousness of Zimbabwean engineers is conceptualized as partly stemming from a form of institutional closure, operationalized through the undervaluing of migrant engineers' academic qualifications by the Engineering Council of South Africa (ECSA). Chikarara's (2019) study also mentions a supposed reluctance by South African universities to acknowledge Zimbabwean qualifications as equal to South African ones, and claims that this adversely blocks the enrolment by Zimbabweans in postgraduate studies at South African universities. However, it is unclear whether this author considers the constitutionally mandated role of South African Qualifications Authority (SAQA) in not only the accreditation and evaluation of foreign qualifications, but also the registration of all professional designations for the purpose of the national qualifications' framework. A reduced agency for immigrant engineers stems not only from a precariousness of residence, labour and social protection, but also from their lack of social contract relationships and of associated labour securities provided to the proletariat as well as salariat. Most international immigrants, including skilled ones, and particularly foreign teachers (as Anganoo's 2014 study has shown), fall into this category as they encounter precarious careers and structural obstacles that inhibit their professional and career development.

Foreign truck drivers have also come under attack from the All-Truck Drivers Foundation (ATDF), an association of local truck drivers, whose members are demanding that South African trucking companies stop hiring foreign drivers. In a 2019 report, the Human Rights Watch (HRW) noted that "more than 200 people – mostly foreign truck drivers – have been killed in South Africa since March 2018". Foreign truck drivers have been subject to violence, including being shot at, stabbed and beaten, resulting in many of them losing their jobs despite having valid work permits. The attacks on foreign truck drivers exacerbates the shortage of skilled drivers in South Africa, and is another example of how a country can try to attract skilled labourers through a progressive immigration policy but still possess an employment sector that repels such immigration or integration. A domestic labour market that is in conflict with the progressiveness of the national immigration policy framework can thus subject the outsourced skilled labour to hostile conditions of participation. This can adversely affect their potential to make maximum use of their occupations, subsequently limiting the overall impact that skilled immigration will have on the receiving country's labour market. While the anti-immigration wave appears to be relatively more violent and perennial in South Africa than the rest of the world, labour market hostility towards foreigners, skilled or otherwise, is a growing phenomenon and can also be seen in the developed world. The growth of anti-immigration, nationalist and far-right political movements, such as Herman Mashaba's Action4SA, as well as viral social media campaigns under the banner #PutSouthAfricansFirst, are not exclusive to South Africa. In Germany, similar right-wing political formations include "Pegida" and the "Anti-Immigration Alternative" (Hatzigeorgiou & Lodefalk, 2017). Such extremist political formations have contributed to a new wave of employment related restrictions for immigrants across the global North.

The model of Waldinger et al. (1990) on immigrant entrepreneurship best explains the rate of entrepreneurialism amongst immigrants in South Africa. The country has attracted thousands of foreign entrepreneurs who set up their businesses in the country to take full advantage of its opportunities, resulting in the rise of immigrant entrepreneurship. Immigrant entrepreneurship, especially in the informal sector, has been the object of violent xenophobic attacks in the past. According to Bogoevska (2017), who investigated the experiences of immigrant entrepreneurs in Cape Town, foreign business owners face a number of challenges. These include barriers to entry in the market, violence, problems obtaining legal documentation, and lack of institutional support. Some of the businesspeople received business permits that they had to renew every three years. The fact that the renewal of the permit is not guaranteed adds uncertainty to the future of their businesses. Muchineripi et al. (2019) explored the experiences of foreign entrepreneurs in the Eastern Cape province of South Africa. Xenophobia, crime, hostile legislation, and lack of access to funding and local networks were some of the main challenges identified by immigrant entrepreneurs. The participants in the study said the cumbersome bureaucratic requirements involved in registering their businesses and opening a business bank account forced some of the immigrant entrepreneurs to operate illegally. Some immigrants resorted to getting into fake marriage arrangements with South Africans to get citizenship. Ngota et al. (2018) carried out a study about factors affecting the development and growth of African immigrant entrepreneurs and their enterprises in South Africa. These authors argued that Afrophobia amongst South Africans, which leads to jealousy over businesses owned by African immigrants, is a big obstacle. Lack of access to financial assistance, which is exacerbated by their lack of credit history and collateral security, saw many immigrant businesses suffer from shortage of capital. Moreover, language barriers also make doing business difficult for immigrant entrepreneurs, especially in terms of penetrating the market. In an extensive study of 120 African immigrant entrepreneurs in Cape Town, Katilanyi and Visser (2010) found that immigrants use their business acumen to create employment for South African citizens. However, despite some of them being successful, they often face the challenge of xenophobia.

Lack of secure residence

In 2013 the DHET reported the number of immigrant teachers on permanent employment as just 9%, meaning the rest were placeholders who could be removed once qualified citizens had been found. Zimbabwe's cultural and geographic proximity to South Africa explains why the majority of foreign teachers in the country are from Zimbabwe, but this proximity has not spared even the ethno-linguistic (Ndebele speaking) immigrants from skewed conditions of participation, common for most foreign workers (Siziba, 2013; Anganoo, 2014). As clear evidence of the limits to which assimilationist approaches can be used in 'exercising agency and negotiating exclusion' for skilled immigrants, some Zimbabwean Ndebele participants proficient in the South African IsiZulu (IsiNdebele and Isizulu are part of the dialects of the Nguni languages), were still encountering institutional and occupational closure (Makonye, 2017). Apart from being given short contracts of three to four months with the renewal of the contracts being always problematic (as they had to fight to get paid for their services), immigrant teachers were also offered low salaries as the school principals knew that they were desperate for income (Anganoo, 2014).

Lack of secure residence and tenure, and the associated disadvantages of contractual employment for skilled immigrants in South Africa, were also elaborated on in a study of Zimbabwean engineers working for the Gauteng provincial government on 5-year fixed term contracts (Chikarara, 2019). These skilled immigrants felt that the government was using them to train South African citizens who would take up their posts once their contracts expired (*ibid.*). Apart from a lack of job security, brain waste in the sector was a reality, with the South African Institute of Civil Engineering (SAICE) losing thousands of its members to emigration due to a lack of job security and exposure to international projects (IOL, 2019). Similarly, a lack of residence was identified as adversely impacting on the agency of foreign academics in South African universities. Some of the challenges these academics identified included getting work permits for their employment, as the Department of Home Affairs rejected their applications and demanded "additional" documents (Sehoole et al., 2019). In our earlier studies with forced immigrants in South Africa, we too observed how institutional biases can be effected through the demand of non-gazetted or "supplementary" documents by frontline bureaucrats (Masuku & Rama, 2020).

Partly as a consequence of the above, the Work Permit South Africa Critical Skills Survey conducted in 2018 showed that most companies in the country were finding it difficult to recruit individuals with requisite critical skills (see Figure 1). According to the survey, the most prominent cause for this was South Africa's inefficient visa regime, i.e., an existential disorganization and lack of coordination in the application and execution of the Immigration Act. This status quo has adversely contributed to the troubles facing skilled immigrants in South Africa, as mentioned in the above paragraph. South Africa's 124 embassies across the world are charged with receiving applications for various kinds of permits, including work and critical skills permits. However, Eisenberg (2019) queries why every embassy has got its own list of requirements, different from any of the other embassies. This leads to confusion and chaos, in a situation tantamount to South Africa having 125 immigration laws – one for each of the embassies and another for the Department of Home Affairs (*ibid.*). Requirements for specific visas are not the same in different embassies. For example, the embassy in France requires applicants for a critical skills visa to submit a contract of employment, yet this is not the case in embassies in the United Kingdom and Zimbabwe. This may be explained by the fact that only 30 of 124 embassies are run by the Home Affairs department, whereas others are under the control of the International Relations department, whose officials may have a poor grasp of the Immigration Act (Eisenberg, 2019). So decisions on visa applications are often affected by the arbitrary and subjective dispositions of the embassy officials. All this chaos becomes a stumbling block for ambitious policies, such as the earlier mentioned 2017 Draft Policy Framework for the Internationalization of Higher Education in South Africa, and for their drive to facilitate the flow of skilled migrant labour into the country.

Figure 1. Challenges in recruiting and solving the skills shortage in South Africa (Source: Work permit South Africa Critical Skills Survey 2018).

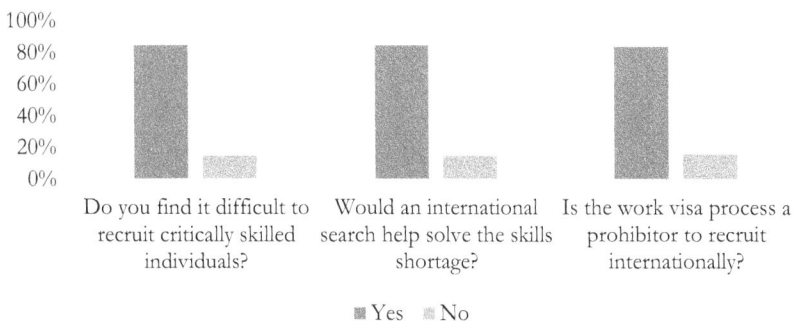

Conclusion

One of the legacies of the Apartheid regime in South Africa is a serious underinvestment in and underdevelopment of the skills of the majority black population. As democratic South Africa seeks to build a bigger and inclusive economy, its efforts in this regard are undermined by an acute shortage of skills. While on the policy side, inroads have been made to facilitate the entrance of skilled immigrants into the country, the impact of such immigration can only be maximized by formulating and promoting policies that ease immigrants' participation and contribution to the national economy. While this is true, in arguing for a less constricted focus on policy alone, this article has also shown that the agency of skilled immigrants and their ability to maximize their utility in the South African labour market is a variable contingent upon the many complex sociologies and historical politics dictating such participation.

While it is one thing to have an immigration system that makes it relatively possible for immigrants with desired skill cells to immigrate into the country, an increase in total factor productivity (through efficiency gains), can only be realized if the employment policy allows for such. In other words, an increased specialization of the labour force is only possible through a sound interaction between skilled immigrants and the host native-born working population (Waldinger et al., 1990). As highlighted in the article, several threats stand in the way of countries such as South Africa realising such gains, with the long-term effect being a normative underutilization of the skilled immigrant population. Some of these threats have been discussed in the article as including but not confined to the growing anti-immigration rhetoric within the public domain. Such predilections ultimately contribute to institutional/occupational forms of closure by negatively influencing the attitudes of employers, licensing boards and occupational associations in the country. The Migration Policy Institute's (2017) recommendations on maximizing efficiency gains from skilled immigration substantiate these findings and argue that employer biases and labour market tests (occupational licensing rules) are some of the factors impeding South Africa from realizing the full benefits of skilled immigration. Such bureaucratic red tapes (as well as the differential treatment of skilled immigrants in the labour market), not only hamper employment creation but also skills transmission. This, as has been argued throughout the article, has for the most part shaped the experiences of skilled immigrants in the country.

References

African Union. Agreement Establishing the African Continental Free Trade Area (2012. https://au.int/sites/default/files/treaties/36437-treaty-consolidated_text_on_cfta_-_en.pdf.

Anganoo, L.D. (2014). *Migrant teachers' experiences of teaching in primary schools in Johannesburg.* Doctoral thesis. University of KwaZulu Natal.

Bateman, C. (2012). Hope at last for foreign nurse recruitment?. *South African Medical Journal, 102*(9), 720–722.

Bezuidenhout, J. (2020). How the xenophobic network around #PutSouthAfricaFirst was born and then metastasised. https://www.dailymaverick.co.za/article/2020-08-18-ulerato_pillay-how-the-xenophobic-network-around-putsouthafricafirst-was-born-

and-then-metastasised/.

Bhorat, H., & Lundall, P. (2005). Employment, Wages and Skills Development: Firm-Specific Effects – Evidence from a Firm Survey in South Africa. *South African Journal of Economics*, *72*(5), 1023–1056. https://doi.org/10.1111/j.1813-6982.2004.tb00143.x

Bogoevska, A. (2017). Foreign Business Entrepreneurship in Cape Town: How To Start A Business - Stories of 6 Cape Town Based Immigrants. *Independent Study Project (ISP) Collection*. 2606. https://digitalcollections.sit.edu/isp_collection/2606

Chikarara, S. N. (2019). The Precariatization of Zimbabwean Engineers in South Africa. *Professions and Professionalism*, *9*(3), 1–15. https://doi.org/10.7577/pp.3303

Cleary, K, & Low, K. (2020). Maverick Citizen & Spotlight Exclusive: Leaked government strategy document shows billions needed to avert healthcare worker crisis. https://www.dailymaverick.co.za/article/2020-09-01-government-strategy-shows-billions-needed-to-avert-healthcare-worker-crisis/

Cohen, M., Naidoo, P., & Mbatha, A. (2020). Mboweni unveils the scale of shattered South African economy. https://www.biznews.com/budget/2020/06/24/mboweni-sa-economy.

Comins, L. (2020). Permit issues block bright foreign nursing graduate from attaining work. https://www.iol.co.za/mercury/news/permit-issues-block-bright-foreign-nursing-graduate-from-attaining-work-49007164

Daniels, R. (2007). Skills Shortages in South Africa: A Literature Review. https://papers.ssrn.com/sol3/papers.cfm?abstract_id=992111

Department of Home Affairs. (1997). Green paper on International Migration. http://www.dha.gov.za/index.php/notices/815-green-paper-on-international-migration.

Department of Home Affairs (2016). Green paper on the international migration. http://www.dha.gov.za/files/GreenPaper_on_InternationalMigration-%2022062016.pdf

Department of Home Affairs. (2017). White paper on international migration. http://www.dha.gov.za/files/dhawhitepaper.pdf.

DHET. (2013). Evaluation of Qualification Sets Submitted by Migrant Teachers in 2010, Report. Teaching Qualifications and Policy Directorate. (2013). https://www.dhet.gov.za/Commissions%20Reports/Annual%20Report%202012%20-%202013.pdf

DHET. (2014). List of occupations in high demand. https://www.dhet.gov.za/Gazette/List%20of%20occupations%20in%20high%20demand%202014%20.pdf.

DHET. (2017). Draft policy framework for the internationalisation of higher education. https://www.dhet.gov.za/Policy%20and%20Development%20Support/Draft%20Policy%20framework%20for%20the%20internalisation%20of%20Higher%20Education%20in%20Suth%20Africa.pdf

Eisenberg, G. (2019). Immigration Act upended by legal chaos. The Mail & Guardian https://mg.co.za/article/2019-05-31-00-immigration-act-upended-by-legal-chaos/

Facchini, G., & Mayda, A. M. (2012). Individual attitudes towards skilled migration: An empirical analysis across countries. *The World Economy*, *35*(2), 183–196.

George, A., Blaauw, D., Thompson, J., & Green-Thompson, L. (2019). Doctor retention and distribution in post-apartheid South Africa: tracking medical graduates (2007–2011) from one university. *Human Resources for Health*, *17*(1), 100.

Govender, P. (2020). Varsities condemn foreign quota call. https://www.timeslive.co.za/sunday-times/news/2019-09-15-varsities-condemn-foreign-quota-call/.

Handmaker, J., & Parsley, J. (2001). Migration, Refugees, and Racism in South Africa. *Refuge: Canada's Journal on Refugees*, *20*(1), 40–51. doi: 10.25071/1920-7336.21246

Hatzigeorgiou, A., & Lodefalk, M. (2017). *Anti-Migration as a Threat to Internationalization?* Ratio Working Paper 302. The Ratio Institute. https://ratio.se/app/uploads/2017/12/ah_mg_antimigration__threat_internationalization_302.pdf

Human Rights Watch. (2019). South Africa: Deadly Attacks on Foreign Truck Drivers. https://www.hrw.org/news/2019/08/26/south-africa-deadly-attacks-foreign-truck-drivers

Immigration Act 13 of 2002, South African Government. (2002). https://www.gov.za/documents/immigration-act.

IOL. (2019). Concern over engineers leaving SA to work abroad. https://www.iol.co.za/mercury/news/concern-over-engineers-leaving-sa-to-work-abroad-29052354

Katilanyi, V., & Visser, K. (2010). African Immigrants in South Africa: Job Takers or Job Creators? *South African Journal of Entrepreneurship and Management Studies*, *13*(4), 375–390.

Kleinsmidt, V., & Manicom, D. (2010). A policy analysis of the Refugee Act 130 of 1998. *Africa Insight*, *39*(4), 164–183.

Mahapo, Z. (2018). Foreign medics guard, wash cars. https://www.sowetanlive.co.za/good-life/health/2018-03-13-foreign-medics-guard-wash-cars/

Maisonnave, H., Decaluwe, B., & Chitiga, M. (2016). Does South African affirmative action policy reduce poverty? A CGE analysis. *Poverty and Public Policy*, *8*(3), 212–227.

Makonye, J. (2017). Migrant Teachers' Perceptions of the South African Mathematics Curriculum and Their Experiences in Teaching in the Host Country. *SAGE Open*, *7*(2), 1–9. doi: 10.1177/2158244017706713

Manpower Group. (2019). Closing the skills gap: What workers want. https://go.manpowergroup.com/hubfs/Talent%20Shortage%202019/2019_TSS_Infographic-South_Africa.pdf

Masuku, S. (2018). *The implementation of the refugee act 130 of 1998 in South Africa and the question of the social exclusion of forced migrants: a case study of DRC forced migrants in Pietermaritzburg.* Doctoral thesis. University of KwaZulu Natal.

Masuku, S., & Rama, S. (2020). Challenges to Refugees' Socioeconomic Inclusion: A Lens Through the Experiences of Congolese Refugees in South Africa. *The Oriental Anthropologist*, *20*(1), 82–96.

Mattes, R., Crush, J., & Richmond, W. (2000). The Brain Gain: Skilled Migrants and Immigration Policy in Post-Apartheid South Africa. SAMP Migration Policy Series 20. Waterloo, ON: Southern African Migration Programme.

Medical Brief. (2019). Foreign-trained SA doctors head to court over lack of internships. https://www.medicalbrief.co.za/archives/foreign-trained-sa-doctors-head-court-lack-internships/

Mhlanga, R., Gneiting, U., & Agarwal, N. (2018). Walking the Talk: Assessing companies' progress from SDG rhetoric to action. http://hdl.handle.net/10546/620550

Migration Policy Institute. (2017). Unlocking Skills: Successful Initiatives for Integrating Foreign-Trained Immigrant Professionals. https://www.migrationpolicy.org/research/unlocking-skills-successful-initiatives-integrating-foreign-trained-immigrant-professionals

Muchineripi, J. Chinyamurindi, W., & Chimucheka, T. (2019). A narrative analysis of barriers encountered by a sample of immigrant entrepreneurs in the Eastern Cape province of South Africa. *TD: The Journal for Transdisciplinary Research in Southern Africa*, *15*(1), 1–9.

National Development Plan 2030 (NDP): Our future – make it work. (2012). https://www.saferspaces.org.za/resources/entry/national-development-plan-2030-our-future-make-it-work#:~:text=The%20National%20Development%20Plan%20aims,leadership%20and%20partnerships%20throughout%20society.

National planning commission. (2021). Meeting the NDP's Labour Market Objectives: A Critical Review. https://www.nationalplanningcommission.org.za/assets/Documents/Meeting%20the%20NDP%E2%80%99s%20Labour%20Market%20Objectives_%20A%20Critical%20Review-%20February%202021.pdf.

Nattrass, N., & Seekings, J. (2019). *Inclusive Dualism: Labour-intensive development, decent work, and surplus labour in Southern Africa*. Oxford University Press.

Ndenze, B. (2020). *IFP seeking to regulate employment of foreign nationals*. https://ewn.co.za/2020/01/22/ifp-seeking-to-regulate-employment-of-foreign-nationals.

Nedlac. (2019). Annual Report. https://nedlac.org.za/wp-content/uploads/2020/12/FULL-NEDLAC-AR-201920.pdf

Ngota, B. L., Mang'unyi, E. E., & Rajkaran, S. (2018). Factors impeding African immigrant entrepreneurs' progression in selected small and medium enterprises: Evidence from a local municipality in South Africa. *South African Journal of Business Management*, *49*(1), 1–9.

Nyamnjoh, F. (2006). *Insiders and outsiders: citizenship and xenophobia in contemporary Southern Africa* (p. 34). London: Zed.

OECD/ILO. (2018). How Immigrants Contribute to South Africa's Economy. https://www.oecd.org/development/how-immigrants-contribute-to-south-africa-s-economy-9789264085398-en.htm.

Parkin, F. (1974). *Strategies of social closure in class formation. The social analysis of class structure* (pp. 1–18). Routledge.

Pillay, K. (2017). Scores of student doctors not placed on compulsory internship in SA. https://www.news24.com/witness/news/scores-of-student-doctors-not-placed-on-compulsory-internship-in-sa-20170704.

Rees, P. (2010). Senior South African politician wants Tendai Mtawarira to be deported. The Guardian. https://www.theguardian.com/sport/2010/jan/12/south-africa-tendai-mtawarira-deport.

Reitzes, M. & Crawhall, N. T. (1998). *Silenced by nation-building: African immigrants and language policy in the new South Africa*. Southern African Migration Project.

SADC. (2005). Protocol on Facilitation of Movement of Persons. https://www.sadc.int/documentspublications/show/800#:~:text=The%20SADC%20Protocol%20on%20Facilitation,people%20of%20the%20region%20generally.

Sadiq, H., Barnes, K. I., Price, M. Gumedze, F., & Morrell, R. G. (2018). Academic promotions at a South African university: Questions of bias, politics and transformation. *Higher Education*, *78*, 423–442.

Segatti, A., & Landau. L. B. (2011). The Role of Skilled Labour. In A. Segatti & L. B. Landau, (Eds), *Contemporary Migration to South Africa*. The International Bank for Reconstruction and Development: Washington DC.

Sehoole, C., Adeyemo, K. S., Ojo, E., & Phatlane, R. (2019). Academic mobility and the experiences of foreign staff at the South African higher education institutions. *South African Journal of Higher Education*, *33*(2), 212–229.

Sichone, O. (2008). Xenophobia and Xenophilia in South Africa: African Migrants in Cape Town. *Anthropology and the new cosmopolitanism: Rooted, feminist and vernacular perspectives*, *45*.

Siziba, G. (2013). *Language and the politics of identity in South Africa: The case of Zimbabwean (Shona and Ndebele speaking) migrants in Johannesburg*. Doctoral thesis. Stellenbosch: Stellenbosch University.

Sowetanlive. (2018). Foreign medics guard, wash cars. https://www.sowetanlive.co.za/good-life/health/2018-03-13-foreign-medics-guard-wash-cars/

Standing, G. (2011). Workfare and the precariat. *Soundings*, *47*(47), 35–43. doi: 10.3898/136266211795427549

Timeslive. (2019). Seven things we know about how NHI will work as revealed by health minister Zweli Mkhize. https://www.timeslive.co.za/news/south-africa/2019-07-12-7-things-we-know-about-how-nhi-will-work-as-revealed-by-health-minister-zweli-mkhize/

Van Rensburg, R. (2020). *The talent shortages in the South African labour market - talent shortage*. Solidariteit Wêreld. https://solidariteit.co.za/en/the-talent-shortages-in-the-south-african-labour-market/.

Waldinger, R., Aldrich, H., Ward, R., Ward, R. H., & Blaschke, J. (1990). *Ethnic entrepreneurs: Immigrant business in industrial societies*. SAGE Publications, Incorporated.

Work permit South Africa. (2018). Critical Skills Survey Results. https://www.workpermitsouthafrica.co.za/critical-skills-survey-results-2018/

IMMIGRANTS IN SKILLED OCCUPATIONS IN BRAZIL: ASSESSING THE FACTORS IMPACTING WAGES[1]

Renan Gadoni Canaan

Introduction

According to contemporary economic literature, the capacity of a given country to sustain steady economic growth over time is determined by its capacity to create and absorb new technologies. In turn, this capacity depends on the value of human capital (Romer, 1990; Barro & Lee, 2000). Technological innovation and absorption depend immensely on qualified workers in Science, Technology, Engineering, and Mathematics (STEM) fields, which are essential for the research, development, and innovation (R&D&I) activities that foster this technological development (Boyd & Tian, 2017). Economies heavily based on STEM professionals exhibit better economic outcomes, increased innovation, and higher levels of job creation (Rothwell, 2013). Therefore, scholars, leaders, and figures in both the private and public sectors mention increasing the STEM workforce as a top priority for economic development (Landivar, 2013).

There are two ways to increase STEM human capital in a country: high levels of investment in education, and immigrant attraction. As investment in education only yields results in the long term, the strategy for meeting short-term needs to increase human capital involves building a foreign workforce (OECD, 2015). Therefore, to design more attractive immigration policies and bring economic development to a given host country, it is essential to understand immigrants' decision-making process of location choice.

The gravity model of immigration, keeping with the social action theory, advocates that immigrants rationally weigh up the attractiveness of host countries to make their destination choice. On one hand, earnings levels play an important role in positively attracting skilled immigrants. On the other hand, wage gaps due to discrimination in host countries, particularly gender and ethnicity disadvantages, operate as negative incentives to move internationally.

The relative lack of human capital in Brazil is a major barrier to economic development (BNDES, 2018), and the attraction of STEM migrants could be a short-term and partial solution to this problem (Ruediger, 2015). Nonetheless, there are no studies that shed light on the landscape of STEM migrants' earnings in Brazil, particularly wage gaps due to minority discrimination. Consequently, there is no information on the positive and negative factors that impact the decision-making process of such migrants, hindering the elaboration of better immigration policies. Therefore, this chapter addresses the question: What are

---

[1] A short version of this chapter was presented and published in the proceedings of Tetovo Migration Conference 2020 under the title: "Skilled immigrants in Brazil: profile for Science, Technology, Engineering and Mathematics (STEM) occupations".

the factors impacting STEM immigrants' earnings in Brazil?

Our chapter contributes to the economic literature on immigration in various ways. For the first time, we describe the landscape of demographic, human capital, and occupational characteristics of STEM immigrants in Brazil using descriptive statistics. Moreover, we assess the key factors that determine earnings by immigrants in STEM occupations, disclosing intersectionalities that impact wages' discrimination. For this, we use ordinary least squares (OLS) multivariate regression and evidence comes from the Annual Social Information Report (RAIS).

The main findings point that, firstly, immigrants in STEM occupations in Brazil have higher average earnings compared to their Brazilian counterparts. However, their higher income is because a greater percentage of immigrants work in managerial occupations. However, when the occupational factor is controlled in the OLS analysis, differences in earnings are not significant. The conclusion is that there is no evidence of discrimination regarding earnings between foreigners and natives in STEM occupations in Brazil, which may be a positive aspect for the attraction and retention of migrant talents.

Secondly, we highlight the importance of demographic, human capital, and occupational factors in income earned by foreigners, concluding that immigrants, just like native-born Brazilians, face a historical system of discrimination based on racial and gender hierarchies in the workforce. This may impose motivational barriers to skilled female and black immigrants, and it is the case for policy implications to mitigate such discrepancies.

This chapter is structured as follows. Section two presents the theoretical framework of the decision-making process of destination choice by immigrants. This section also discusses how immigration could be a short-term solution to a lack of sufficient human capital in Brazil. Section three describes the primary data and presents the methodology used in assessing the composition of qualified immigrants as a group and analyzing the correlation between earnings and other key variables. Section four presents the landscape of immigrants and native-born skilled professionals in STEM occupations in Brazil. Moreover, this section discusses the lack of discrimination between immigrants and natives' wages. Section five debates the effect of demographic, occupational, and human capital characteristics on earnings and debates gender and race discrimination. Section six concludes the chapter.

Theoretical framework

Decision-making process of skilled migration

During their decision-making process to move internationally, skilled professionals compare several factors that might positively and negatively impact their location choice. They weigh up the attractiveness of destinations to choose a host country that maximises utility (Botezat & Ramos, 2020). This is the rationale for the canonical modern approach in the economic literature of migration studies, also known as the gravity model of immigration (Sjaastad,

1962). This model is in line with the social action theory, in which individuals are free to choose and evaluate the positive and negative consequences of their acts. As a result, they choose the most beneficial option in a given situation and make a rational choice (Christensen et al., 2017).

The factors affecting destination choice are related to two different components: earnings levels and taste for location (Ahlfeldt et al., 2015). Earnings in the host country are assumed to be the main positive incentive for skilled immigration choices (Ortega & Peri, 2013; Czaika, 2018). The state-of-art literature has demonstrated that skilled immigrants, willing to earn higher pays, choose high-income countries, being one of the main reasons for the vectorial migration flow from the Global South to North (Bailey & Mulder, 2017). The other component, taste for location, relates to the preference for host countries where immigrants may have equal opportunities relative to native-born professionals and other immigrants. Therefore, wage gaps due to discrimination may disincentive international mobility and play a role as a negative factor in the decision-making process (Le, 2020).

Regarding wage gaps, the extensive literature on migration studies of the Global North has demonstrated that, due to their foreign status, skilled migrants often face downward occupational mobility, and their posts are at lower pay levels compared to the native-born professionals (O'Dwyer & Colic-Peisker, 2016). Moreover, the same literature has already studied other factors that may positively affect earnings, such as the educational level (Silva et al., 2016, Picot & Hue, 2018), and work experience (Boyd & Tian, 2017). Also, demographic characteristics were assessed, such as country of origin (Picot & Hue, 2018). Particularly, two demographic factors are relevant to this work: gender and ethnicity.

At the beginning of migration studies in the 1960s and 1970s, the expression "migrants and their family members" meant "male migrants and their spouses and children". Immigrant women used to move internationally to join their husbands. Therefore, the model of male migrants as breadwinning and female immigrants as care providers for family persisted (Grubanov-Boskovic et al., 2020). However, over the last decades, the percentage of women immigrants is increasing significantly, and female professionals are increasingly moving independently seeking better jobs (Le Goff, 2016). Female immigrants are motivated by finding good job opportunities to bringing better economic outcomes for themselves and their families, and gender-equal pay levels may play an important role as a positive driver (Boucher, 2018).

Besides inherent difficulties faced by immigrants, female immigrants face additional difficulties upon immigrating for being women. The seminal paper on migration studies by Monica Boyd (1984) introduced the concept of double disadvantage, a combination of negative impacts of both gender and nationality status. This concept of double disadvantage has been widely implemented in migration studies (Ballarino & Panichella, 2018). Even if they are highly educated, female workers still suffer downgrading in their careers by employers in host countries (IOM, 2010), and discrimination by employers is part of the problem

(Cooke et al., 2013).

In regards to ethnicity, the race penalty in earnings has already been described extensively (Greenman & Xie, 2008) and immigrants' earnings vary by ethnicity (Villarreal & Tamborini, 2018). Wage gaps between white and non-white have been pointed by many authors. Boyd and Tien (2017) describe wage penalties in skilled black immigrants compared to their white counterparts in Canada. As well, Villarreal and Tamborini (2018) point that black immigrants do not catch up with white native-born Americans' earnings. These studies used quantitative methodologies that isolated the effects of group differences. Therefore, wage discrepancies are solely due to race discrimination. Wage gaps because of racial discriminatory barriers may impact the perception and taste for location of immigrants during the decision-making process for destination choice and work as a barrier to immigration.

Moreover, several intersection mechanisms affect the earnings of skilled migrants. The concept of intersectionality can be applied to migration studies since belonging to several minorities may lead to a situation of multiple disadvantages. Just as in the case of the double disadvantage of gender and migratory status, there is evidence that immigrants might be subject to double jeopardy situations concerning gender and race (Stypińska & Gordo, 2018). A combination of gender and race discrimination may also lead to lower pay levels, such as the case of Lebanese female skilled workers in France described by Al Ariss (2010). Also, Carangio et al. (2020) demonstrate that non-white female immigrants in Australia experienced additional forms of oppression compared to their white counterparts, indicating that employers frequently devalued and doubted their skills and work experience, reflecting on a wage penalty.

The shortage of STEM human capital in Brazil

In its 2018 report on Brazil's economic growth for 2018–2023, the National Bank for Economic and Social Development (BNDES) identified important barriers to progress, including infrastructure quality, commercial opening, the business environment, the tax structure, and human capital. The latter represents a major challenge for economic and social development, given the relatively low education level of the national workforce (BNDES, 2018). In line with this, Brazil has consistently placed among the top countries in an international talent shortage ranking (Manpowersgroup, 2015).

Although Brazil ranks higher when compared with other BRICS[2] countries in the Human Development Index, it comes last among this group for the availability of engineers and scientists (WEF, 2012). Moreover, the percentage of Brazilian graduates with STEM degrees (17%) is well below the average for developed countries (24%), and among all 46 OECD member and partner countries, Brazil only surpasses Argentina and Costa Rica on this measure (OECD, 2018). These numbers become even more relevant because only 15.3%

---

[2] BRICS is an acronym for the group of countries formed by Brazil, Russia, India, China and South Africa. These countries share two important characteristics: high economic growth since the year 2000 and implementation of public policies for developing their human capital (OECD, 2015).

of the population holds a high education degree (IBGE, 2015). Therefore, attracting foreign STEM professionals could be a solution that allows results in the short-run.

Brazil has an immigration policy that falls solely under federal jurisdiction, and a new law governing this field, approved in May 2017, considerably changed the framework for immigration management (Cavalcanti et al., 2018). Since the implementation of the new framework, there are two types of residence permits that cover work activities: (1) Previous Residence, for immigrants who are currently living outside Brazil; and (2) Residence Permits, for immigrants who already live in the country (BRAZIL, 2017). To obtain either of these work permits, applicants must have signed an employment contract covering a specific period of time. The General Immigration Council (CGI) assesses the employment contract as well as the compatibility between the skills of the applicant and those required for the job. Applicants must provide proof of their skills through official certificates and competencies, or official statements from organizations where they previously worked (CNIG, 2017).

As a job offer is an essential requirement for applying for a visa, Brazil's immigration process might be considered as a demand-oriented immigration policy, as defined by Czaika and Parsons (2017). Skilled immigrants meet the immediate needs of employers, without labour market reserve. This type of policy ensures that the migrant is incorporated to the labour market, without risk of being unemployed. However, contrary to a supply-oriented policy, i.e. score-based systems, this kind of migratory regulation is less efficient to attract skilled migrants (Czaika & Parsons, 2017). In line with this, foreigner represents only a very low portion of Brazil's workers, 0.3% (IBGE, 2010).

To increase skilled migration in Brazil, there must be a comprehension of motivational factors in the decision-making process of skilled migrants. Surprisingly, very few studies regarding skilled immigrants in Brazil exist, particularly those in STEM fields. Nothing is known about their wages or how subgroups affect earnings. As earnings levels and wage gaps are major drivers of the decision-making process of skilled immigrants, assessing the factors that impact earnings is a key aspect to disclosure incentives and barriers to immigration. This elucidation may shed light on the motivations of migrants in Brazil and provide information to design better policies to attract foreign STEM professionals.

Methodology

Primary data regarding the Brazilian labour market comes from the Annual Social Information Report (RAIS), which contains statistics derived from annual reports filed by all firms in Brazil to the Ministry of Labor and Social Security (MTE, 2017). The data covers all individuals employed at any time during the corresponding calendar year, including their demographic characteristics (such as age, gender, nationality, and color), education level, earnings, admission date, layoff date, and occupation. This study examines data spanning the period from

2010–2017 and is harmonized according to Furtado et al. (2018)[3].

Qualified Professionals and STEM occupations

Keeping with Simoes (2018), qualified professionals are defined as workers who hold at least a bachelor's degree. The term "education level" is comprised of the following subcategories: primary studies, secondary studies, incomplete high education degree, complete high education degree, M.Sc. degree, and Ph.D. degree.

Keeping with Picot and Hue (2018), the study population[4] contains individuals who were aged 25–54, which is the appropriate range for policy considerations concerning STEM immigrants (Schaafsma & Sweetman, 2001). In the earnings correlation analysis, the population included only those immigrants who had arrived prior to 2017, since new arrivals mid-year could not yet report a full annual income, they were omitted as their inclusion could bias the earnings correlation.

In line with other international studies, the classification of STEM occupations follows the methods used by the United States Census Bureau (Picot & Hue, 2018; Boyd & Tian, 2017; Landivar, 2013; Langdon et al., 2011; Lowell, 2010). In all these studies, each occupation has a corresponding Standard Occupation Classification (SOC) code, which can be matched and converted to the Brazilian Occupation Classification (CBO)[5] through a common code, the ISCO (International Standard Classification of Occupations). The final table with all CBO STEM codes can be found in Appendix A.

OLS Analysis for Key Factors in Earnings

Advanced quantitative methods, such as multivariate regression, have been used in canonical economic literature to compare group differences in earnings. Particularly, ordinary least squares (OLS) regression has been used as a common tool for earnings analysis (Malmberg, 2007). The main reason is that OLS regression can estimate the impact of factors, such as gender, home country, and minority status controlling for socio-demographic differences such as age and education (Picot & Hue, 2018). Therefore, the analyst may isolate the effect of each factor and assess its sole impact on earnings.

The dependent variable to be analysed in our regression model is the logarithm of earnings[6] per hour. The logarithm form is commonly used to adjust for skewness in the distribution of earnings (Boyd & Tian, 2017). Moreover, earnings were divided by the number of hours worked to adjust to differences in working hours. Because of the logarithm transformation, the analysis in this study is restricted to individuals who had positive earnings in 2017.

---

[3] Database available at: http://pdet.mte.gov.br
[4] Foreigners are individuals who do not hold Brazilian citizenship (born or naturalized).
[5] The CBO is the classification used in the RAIS survey for occupations.
[6] The 2017 RAIS collected information on individual annual earnings in the calendar year of 2017 directly from employers (Furtado et al., 2018).

In the economic literature, there are demographic variables that are often used as regressors for the logEarnings equation, namely gender, race, continent of origin and metropolitan region (Silva et al., 2016). Moreover, according to human capital theory (Becker, 1957), there are three key factors for productivity related to human capital: education level, work experience and experience at the current job. As work experience is not measured by most surveys (since it is difficult to know when the individual started to work), age is used as a proxy for this variable. All independent variables are summarized in Table 1.

Table 1. Demographic, Human Capital and occupational variables at the linear correlation model for immigrants' earnings in STEM occupations in 2017 in Brazil.

Characteristics	Variable	Type	Categories
Demographic	Gender	Dummy	Male, Female
	Race	Dummy	Indigenous, black, white, yellow, brown, others.
	Metropolitan Region	Dummy	Porto Alegre, Belo Horizonte, Rio de Janeiro, Sao Paulo, Brasilia, others.
	Origin Continent	Dummy	Africa, Asia, Europe, Latin America, Mercosur, North America, others.
	Years in Brazil	Continuous	
	Years in Brazil Squared	Continuous	
Human capital	Education Degree	Dummy	Bachelor, Master, Doctorate
	On-the-job time (months)	Continuous	
	On-the-job time squared	Continuous	
	Age	Continuous	
	Age Squared	Continuous	
Occupational	Occupation category	Dummy	Managerial, Technical

OLS analysis for discrepancies between earnings for foreigners and natives in STEM occupations

For the OLS analysis regarding discrepancies between immigrants and native-born Brazilians, the differences in earnings were assessed through the dummy variable "immigrant": (1) "Yes" for all foreigners, including naturalized Brazilians; and (2) "No" for Brazilian-born professionals (reference group).

We performed OLS analyses with four different models: Model 1 is unadjusted, showing only the relation between earnings and the variable "immigrant". Model 2 is adjusted for demographic characteristics. Model 3 is adjusted for demographic and human capital characteristics, and Model 4 for demographic, human capital and occupational characteristics.

All OLS analyses were tested for heteroscedasticity using the Breusch-Pagan test and corrected using robust standard errors. They were performed using R Studio, an open software for statistics.

The landscape of STEM immigrants in Brazil

Descriptive statistics

Skilled immigrants still represent only a small portion of those working in STEM occupations in Brazil, at 0.86% (3,924 overall). Males predominate in the workforce (82.6%), and this observation is in line with previous reports from the Ministry of Labour: one study of skilled immigrants in any formal job (not only in STEM fields) found that female workers comprised only 32.9% of this segment of the workforce (Simoes, 2018). Also, more than half of the STEM-occupied foreign workforce is employed either in the Sao Paulo or Rio de Janeiro metropolitan regions.

Europe and Latin America are the continents of origin for more than 60% of the foreign workforce in STEM jobs, a figure consistent with the study from the Ministry of Labour, which revealed that 74.3% of skilled immigrants came from those two continents (Simoes, 2018). Particularly, skilled immigrants in STEM occupations came from Argentina (12%), Portugal (10.2%), Peru (8.3%), France (7.5%), Colombia (7.4%), and China (6.9%). The majority of immigrants in STEM occupations in Brazil in 2017 are self-declared "white" (62.2%). In the same study from the Ministry of Labour, more than 72% fell under this category. Overall, the composition of the immigrant workforce in STEM fields does not differ much from the profile of skilled immigrants as a whole in Brazil.

The most common positions that STEM immigrants hold in Brazil are system development analyst, R&D manager, computer support analyst, civil engineer, IT project manager and production engineer. Moreover, managerial occupations represent more than 22% of all jobs occupied by foreigners in the STEM fields. As discussed by Ruediger (2015), one of the main drivers of skilled migration to Brazil is the transfer of supervisors and managers from firms in headquarter countries to new units in Brazil, what may explain the high number of skilled foreigners occupying such managerial jobs compared to skilled native-born professionals.

Finally, the average earnings of foreigners are 49.6% higher than those of their Brazilian counterparts (R$13,247.35 and R$8,852.80, respectively). The main characteristics of STEM-occupation immigrants are summarized in Table 2.

Table 2. Demographic, human capital and occupational characteristics for skilled immigrants and native-born Brazilians in STEM occupations in 2017.

	Immigrants	Natives
Total number	3,924	451,172
Average monthly earning	R$13,247.35	R$8,852.80
Sex	100.0%	100.0%
Male	82.3%	77.1%
Female	17.7%	22.9%
Average age	38.88	36.23
Metropolitan regions	100.0%	100.0%
Belo Horizonte	4.2%	5.6%
Porto Alegre	3.7%	3.1%
Rio de Janeiro	14.3%	9.7%
Sao Paulo	36.5%	30.7%
Brasilia	2.4%	3.7%
Others	39.0%	47.2%
Educational level	100.0%	100.0%
Bachelor's degree	89.6%	95.8%
Master's Degree	6.2%	3.2%
PhD degree	4.2%	1.0%
Origin continent	3,924	
Asia	559	
Europe	1,088	
Latin-America[7]	992	
Mercosur	470	
Africa	103	
North America	113	
Naturalized citizens of Brazil	230	
Others	369	
Race	100.0%	100.0%
Brown	14.1%	20.0%
White	62.2%	68.9%
Yellow	9.3%	1.8%
Black	2.4%	2.3%
Indigenous	0.8%	0.2%
non-declared	11.3%	6.9%
Occupation	100.0%	100.0%
technical	77.6%	91.4%
managerial	22.4%	8.6%

Elaborated by authors based on MTE (2017).

The lack of wage discrimination between immigrants and natives

To analyze the discrepancies in earnings between immigrants and native-born Brazilians in STEM occupations, OLS was performed[8]. Alike the descriptive statistics, OLS analysis also demonstrated that immigrants have higher average earnings compared to their Brazilian counterparts. According to the unadjusted

---

[7] Excluding Mercosur countries: Argentina, Uruguay and Paraguay.
[8] Regression coefficients are presented in Appendix B.

model (Model 1), immigrants earn 11.9% more than their native-born professionals (Table 3). Discrepancies can also be observed when demographic characteristics are controlled (Model 2) and human capital variables are controlled (Model 3): immigrants still earn more than their Brazilian counterparts (6.5% and 2.7%, respectively). However, when the variable for occupation is controlled, the results demonstrate no significant differences between the incomes of immigrants and native-born Brazilians in STEM occupations. This indicates that part of the discrepancy in earnings between immigrants and Brazilians may be explained by the fact that a greater proportion of immigrants occupy a managerial STEM job (22.4% against 8.6% for natives, Table 2), and that managerial jobs are top-status positions that command higher pay.

Table 3. Monthly earnings differentials, in percentage[9], between native-born Brazilians and immigrants (arrived 25 and older) in STEM occupations in Brazil in 2017.

	Immigrants	Natives
Model 1 (unadjusted)	+11.86	(rg)
Model 2	+6.47	(rg)
Model 3	+2.66	(rg)
Model 4	(ns)	(rg)

Elaborated by authors. Based on MTE (2017).

For implementing a demand-oriented immigration policy, Brazil has a lower potential to attract skilled migrants compared to supply-oriented migration policies, such as in Canada and Australia. To increase immigrants' participation in the Brazilian workforce and meet the need for a human capital increase in the short term, drivers of STEM immigration must be enhanced. Due to the fact of being a middle-income country that allows for lower pay levels compared to the Global North, STEM migrants are discouraged to settle in Brazil. This is perfectly illustrated by the fact that skilled immigrants represent only a small portion of STEM professionals in Brazil, as assessed by our study (0.86%).

However, skilled immigrants' destination choice is also immensely affected by his/her taste for the location, which is, in turn, impacted by the (lack of) wage discrimination. Skilled immigrants often face downgrading in their careers when moving internationally to the global North countries such as Canada, the US, and Australia and a wage gap due to migratory status has been extensively highlighted. Equal paying between foreigners and natives in Brazil diverges from such countries, and the fact that wage discrepancy is not demonstrated in the Brazilian context may be an important driver for skilled migration. Therefore, such a positive factor should be divulged and merchandised to counterbalance disadvantages in earnings levels.

---

[9] During ordinary least squares, the dummy effect on the dependent variable must be interpreted as in Halvorsen and Palmquist (1980), where the effect (%) is 100*[exp(d) − 1], where d is the linear regression coefficient for the dummy variable.

Human capital, occupational and demographic factors

OLS analysis[10] confirms a concave relationship (inverted "U" shape) between age and earnings. This pattern is well documented in the economic literature, since as age increases, so does the experience of the worker, thereby leading to higher productivity and earnings. But, at a certain point, incapacity due to age causes a decrease in productivity and, as a result, in earnings (Thornton et al., 1997). The analysis indicates a peak in earnings at the age of 57, after which point they decrease (Table 4). The same concave relationship can be observed with respect to time on the job. In their first years at work, employees integrate into their new jobs and activities, a process that increases worker's skills on the job and, as a result, his productivity. However, after a certain time on the same job, productivity decreases due to a lack of motivation to continue with the same activities in the same position, and there is a negative relation between time on the same job and ambition (Rhodes, 1983).

Furthermore, OLS analysis indicates a positive correlation between education variables and average earnings for STEM-occupied immigrants. This trend is in line with the economic literature both from Brazil and from other countries, which states that income increases in tandem with education level (Silva et al., 2016, Picot & Hue, 2018). Although foreign workers holding a master's degree do not earn more than those holding only a bachelor's degree, their counterparts that hold a doctorate earn 37.0% more (Table 4).

According to the 2010 Brazilian Occupation Classification, STEM jobs may be divided into two categories: (1) technical (professionals) and (2) managerial (directors and managers) (MTE, 2010). The activities of the first category require a Level-4 designation according to the ISCO-88 (International Standard Classification of Occupations), which denotes a high level of qualification. Those in the second category, although not receiving a specific level in the International Standard Classification of Occupations, can also be deemed highly qualified as a result of their elevated status and usually high earnings (MTE, 2010). OLS corroborates this observation, since immigrants that occupy a managerial position earn 44% more than other STEM immigrants. Thus, occupational role seems to be one of the most important factors defining income among immigrants in STEM occupations in Brazil.

Moreover, OLS analysis demonstrates that there are discrepancies in earnings related to the continent of origin of STEM-occupation immigrants. When compared to immigrants coming from Africa (reference group), North Americans, Asians and Europeans earn 93.9%, 81.9% and 55.7% more, respectively (Table 4). This might indicate discrimination on the basis of origin, but the discrepancy might also be related to where those immigrants were educated. Many studies relating income and origin indicate that the place where immigrants were educated – rather than nationality – is a key factor determining pay. In Canada, for example, when the "location of studies" variable is controlled, the evidence demonstrates that nationality has no effect on earnings (Picot &

---

[10] Regression coefficients for multivariate regression are presented at Appendix C.

Hue, 2018). The same might hold true in Brazil. This hypothesis cannot be tested because the RAIS database does not encompass data regarding "location of studies" and we may only conclude that origin affects earnings.

Table 4. Earnings differentials, in percentage, for immigrants in STEM occupations (arrived 25 and older in Brazil) by demographic, human capital and occupational characteristics in 2017.

Race	
Black	(rg[11])
Indigenous	(ns[12])
White	51.5
Yellow	60.0
Brown	46.1
Gender	
Male	(rg)
Female	-14.6
Continent of origin	
Africa	(rg)
Asia	81.9
Europe	55.7
Latin America	(ns)
Mercosur	37.9
Naturalized citizens of Brazil	(ns)
North America	93.9
Others	64.7
Metropolitan region	
Porto Alegre	(rg)
Belo Horizonte	(ns)
Brasilia	61.0
Rio de Janeiro	80.7
Sao Paulo	27.0
Other regions	(ns)
Age	11.4
Age squared	-0.1
Time on the job	6.6E-03
Time on the job squared	-1.1E-07
Education level	
Bachelor	(rg)
Master	(ns)
Doctorate	37.0
Occupation category	
Stem technical occupation	(rg)
Stem managerial occupation	60.9
Years in brazil	-2.9
Years in brazil squared	4.3E-02

[11] Reference group.
[12] Differences between the regression coefficients are not statistically different and deviations are not reported.

Gender and race discrimination

In Brazil, ethnoracial inequality studies rely on data provided by official agencies and surveys, such as the IBGE and RAIS which uses five different categories that form a skin color continuum: *branco* (white), *pardo* (brown), *preto* (black), *amarelo* (yellow), and *indigena* (indigenous) (Telles, 2009). Ethnoracial characteristics are important variables for earnings and the economic literature provides an extensive discussion about the influence of race on earnings in Brazil, and a consensus has emerged that racial discrimination affects earnings, even among professionals with the same education and demographic characteristics (Stamm & De Castro, 2017). In our study, OLS analysis shows a significant discrepancy in earnings among races, with self-declared "white" and "yellow" employees earning 51.5% and 60.0% more than the self-declared "black" reference group (Table 4). As discussed by Cavalcanti, Oliveira and Macedo (2018), immigrants are affected by this racial hierarchy as much as native-born Brazilians and are thus subjected to a historical system of discrimination in the workforce. The dummy variable for those self-declaring "indigenous" does not show any significance concerning the reference group. This might be due to the low number of self-declared "indigenous" employees, which may have impacted standard errors and – as a consequence – the p-value.

Gender inequality has also been a key factor influencing income in Brazil (Stamm & De Castro, 2017). Many studies point to gender discrimination as a major factor in the pay gap between men and women in the country (Barros & Mendonça, 1996; Bruschini & Lombardi, 2002; Stamm & De Castro, 2017). In the OLS analysis, gender assumes two values: 0 for men (reference group) and 1 for women. The results demonstrate that the regression coefficient for gender is significant, meaning that there is evidence of a discrepancy in earnings between male and female immigrants in STEM jobs (Table 4). Gender discrimination appears to be a key factor in determining income among these professionals, as women earn 14.6% less than men (Table 4). Therefore, just as native-born Brazilians, immigrants in STEM occupations appear to face the same discrimination based on gender. Such results keep with international immigration literature when stating that female skilled migrants encounter additional difficulties to immigrate, particularly wage gaps.

The gravity model of immigration asserts that, seeking for maximizing utility, skilled immigrants aim to move to host countries that might provide them with better conditions, such as the absence of wage discriminations. Because there is an observed earnings discrepancy due to gender discrimination such as the one assessed by our study, female skilled immigrants may be unwilling and unmotivated to move to Brazil. The same rationale may be applied to black immigrants and wage gaps due to ethnicity as exposed in the previous paragraph. Furthermore, intersectional groups, such as black female skilled migrants may face additional challenges when immigrating to Brazil that might be insurmountable. When adding up both negative effects due to racial and gender discrimination, black female STEM migrants earn 66.1% less than white male skilled immigrants. The concept of double disadvantage presented by Monica Boyd (1984) representing discrimination by origin and gender can be re-signified in Brazil. This concept is best applied to two distinct discriminations: gender and ethnicity.

Given that one of the main drivers for skilled immigrants' destination choice, i.e. taste for location, is impacted by wage discriminations, migration policies should not ignore such factors that might demotivate such groups from immigrating to Brazil. As an implication for immigration policies, there should be active regulations that incentive equal paying between male and female workers, and between different ethnicities as well. For example, since skilled immigrants are required to have a job offer to be given work visas in Brazil, a check by Brazilian authorities before authorizing work visas would be a tool to help to solve this issue.

Requiring a job offer only is not enough to ensure the incorporation of skilled immigrants into the Brazilian labour market. During the visa process, there should be mechanisms that ensure that there is no wage disparity regarding minority groups. This is particularly important because, according to Crenshaw (1991), the experience of being subject to multiple disadvantages simultaneously cannot be compared to any single-disadvantage experience.

Conclusions

This chapter demonstrated that skilled immigrants have higher average earnings compared to native-born Brazilians in STEM occupations. Part of the discrepancy in earnings may be explained by the fact that a greater proportion of immigrants occupy a managerial STEM job, which are top-status positions that command higher pay. However, no wage discrimination regarding migration status was observed. The lack of origin disadvantages may counterbalance the fact that Brazil is not a high-income country. Therefore, it is a positive factor for attracting and retaining more STEM talents to Brazil.

Moreover, this work highlighted that demographic, human capital and occupational characteristics are important factors defining income among immigrants in STEM occupations in Brazil. Immigrants, just like native-born Brazilians, face a historical system of discrimination based on gender and ethnoracial hierarchies in the workforce. As subjective preferences and tastes, including equal-paying, are the main positive drivers for skilled immigrants' choice, there should be public policies aiming at mitigating such discrepancies.

In line with the gravity model of immigration, within the scope of the social action theory, if Brazil is willing to increase its skilled foreign labour force in the short term and bring economic development to the country, it is suggested that public policies should target the positive incentives that drive skilled immigrants' choice of destination. Therefore, equal-paying between migrants and natives should be advertised. Moreover, active mechanisms that ensure no wage discrimination should be encouraged.

Acknowledgements

I express my acknowledgments to Associate Professor of Politics of Human Migration and Mobility at Carleton University, Dr. Martin Geiger, who supervised me during my research internship at the department of political science. I also would like to thank Mitacs Globalink that funded the project "Brazil and Canada in the Global Race for Talents".

References

Ahlfeldt, G. M., Redding, S. J., Sturm, D. M., & Wolf, N. (2015). The economics of density: Evidence from the Berlin Wall. *Econometrica*, *83*(6), 2127–2189.

Al Ariss, A. (2010). Models of engagement: migration, self-initiated expatriation, and career development. Career Development International, *15*(4), 338–358.

Ballarino, G., & Panichella, N. (2018). The Occupational Integration of Migrant Women in Western European Labour Markets. *Acta Sociologica, 61*(2), 126–142. https://doi.org/10.1177/0001699317723441.

Bailey, A., & Mulder, C. (2017). Highly skilled migration between the Global North and South: gender, life courses and institutions, *Journal of Ethnic and Migration Studies*, *43*(16), 2689–2703. doi: 10.1080/1369183X.2017.1314594

Barro, R., & Lee, J. (2000). International Data on Educational Attainment: Updates and Implications. *Oxford Economic Papers*, *53*(3), 541–563.

Becker, G. (1957). *Human capital*. New York: Columbia University Press.

BNDES. (2018). O crescimento da economia brasileira 2018-2023. Brasilia: BNDES. https://web.bndes.gov.br/bib/jspui/bitstream/1408/14760/1/Perspectivas%20201 8-2023_P.pdf.

Botezat, A., & Ramos, R. (2020). Physicians' brain drain - a gravity model of migration flows. *Global Health 16*(7). https://doi.org/10.1186/s12992-019-0536-0

Boucher, A. (2018). Female High-Skilled Migration: The Role of Policies. In M. Czaika (Ed.), *High-Skilled Migration, Drivers and Policies* (pp. 65–86). Oxford: Oxford University Press.

Boyd, M. (1984). At a Disadvantage: The Occupational Attainments of Foreign Born Women in Canada, *International Migration Review, 18*(4), 1091–1119. doi: 10.1177/019791838401800410.

Boyd, M., & Tian, S. (2017). STEM education and STEM work: Nativity inequalities in occupations and earnings. *International Migration*, *55*(1), 75–98.

BRAZIL. (2017). LEI N° 13.445. http://pesquisa.in.gov.br/imprensa/jsp/visualiza/index.jsp?jornal=1&pagina=1&data=25/05/2017.

Bruschini, C., & Lombardi, M. R. (2002). Instruídas e trabalhadeiras: Trabalho feminino no final do século XX. *Cadernos pagu*, (17), 157–196.

Carangio, V., Farquharson, K., Bertone, S., & Rajedran, D. (2021). Racism and White privilege: highly skilled immigrant women workers in Australia, *Ethnic and Racial Studies, 44*(1), 77–96. doi: 10.1080/01419870.2020.1722195

Cavalcanti, L., Oliveira, T., & Macedo, M. (2018). *Migrações e Mercado de Trabalho no Brasil. Relatório Anual 2018*. Observatório das Migrações Internacionais; Ministério do Trabalho/ Conselho Nacional de Imigração e Coordenação Geral de Imigração. Brasília, OBMigra.

Christensen, K., Hussein, S. & Ismail, M. (2017). Migrants' decision-process shaping work destination choice: the case of long-term care work in the United Kingdom and Norway. *European Journal of Ageing*, *14*, 219–232. https://doi.org/10.1007/s10433-016-0405-0

CNIG. (2017). Resolução normativa n° 02, de 01 de dezembro de 2017. https://portaldeimigracao.mj.gov.br/images/resolucoes_normativas/RN%2002%2

0-%202017.pdf>.

Cooke, F. L., Zhang, J. & Wang, J. (2013). Chinese professional immigrants in Australia: a gendered pattern in (re)building their careers, *The International Journal of Human Resource Management*, *24*(14), 2628–2645.

Crenshaw, K. (1991). Mapping the Margins: Intersectionality, Identity Politics, and Violence against Women of Color. *Stanford Law Review, 43*(6), 1241–1299. doi:10.2307/1229039.

Czaika, M. (2018). High-Skilled Migration: Introduction and Synopsis. In M. Czaika (Ed.), *High-Skilled Migration: Drivers and Policies* (pp. 1–19). Oxford: Oxford University Press

Czaika, M., & Parsons, C. (2017). The Gravity of High-Skilled Migration Policies. *Demography, 54*(2), 603–630. doi: 10.1007/s13524-017-0559-1

De Barros, R. P., & Mendonça, R. S. P. (1996). Diferenças entre discriminação racial e por gênero e o desenho de políticas anti-discriminatórias. *Revista Estudos Feministas, 4*(1), 183–193.

Furtado, A., Quintino, F., Dick, P., & Oliveira, A. (2018). Notas metodológicas. In: L. Cavalcanti, T. Oliveira, & M. Macedo (Eds.), *Migrações e Mercado de Trabalho no Brasil. Relatório Anual 2018* (pp. 8–18). Observatório das Migrações Internacionais, Ministério do Trabalho/ Conselho Nacional de Imigração e Coordenação Geral de Imigração. Brasília, OBMigra.

Greenman E, & Xie, Y. (2008). Double jeopardy? The interaction of gender and race on earnings in the United States. *Soc Forces, 86*(3), 1217–1244.

Grubanov-Boskovic, S., Tintori, G. & Biagi, F. (2020). Gaps in the EU Labour Market Participation Rates: an intersectional assessment of the role of gender and migrant status, Publications Office of the European Union, Luxembourg. doi:10.2760/045701.

Halvorsen, R., & Palmquist, R. (1980). The interpretation of dummy variables in semi-logarithmic equations. *The American Economic Review, 70*(3), 474–475.

IBGE (2010). Censo demográfico 2010. Características da população e dos domicílios: resultados do universo. Rio de Janeiro: IBGE, 2011.

IBGE (2015). Pesquisa Nacional por Amostra de Domicílios: síntese de indicadores 2014 / IBGE, Coordenação de Trabalho e Rendimento. Rio de Janeiro: IBGE, PNAD. https://biblioteca.ibge.gov.br/index.php/biblioteca-catalogo?view=detalhes&id=294935.

IOM. (2010). IOM gender and migration news: issue 34 April 2010, IOM, Geneva. https://publications.iom.int/books/iom-gender-and-migration-news-april-2010.

Landivar, L. C. (2013). *Disparities in STEM Employment by Sex, Race, and Hispanic Origin*. Report No. ACS-24. Suitland: US Bureau of the Census.

Langdon, D., Mckittrick, G., Beede, D., Khan, B., & Doms, M. (2011). *STEM*: Good Jobs Now and for the Future. ESA Issue Brief 03–11. Washington: Economics and Statistics Administration, US Department of Commerce.

Le, T. (2020). *Essays on economics of immigration*. PhD thesis. Chicago: The University of Chicago.

Le Goff, M. (2016). Feminization of migration and trends in remittances. *IZA World of Labor*. Iss. 220. Bonn: Institute for the Study of Labor (IZA). doi: 10.15185/izawol.220

Lowell, l. (2010). A Long View of America's Immigration Policy and the Supply of Foreign-Born STEM Workers in the United States. *American Behavioral Scientist, 3*(7), 1029–1044.

Malmberg, Å. (2007). *Evaluating the gender wage gap in Sweden*. Nationalekonomiska institutionen, Uppsala Universitet. http://www.diva-portal.org/smash/get/diva2:131299/FULLTEXT01.pdf.

Manpowersgroup. (2015). 2015 Talent Shortage Survey. https://www.manpowergroup.com.

MTE. (2010). Classificação Brasileira de Ocupações (CBO). http://www.ocupacoes.com. br/tabela-completa-da-cbo.

MTE. (2017). Relação Anual de Informações Sociais – RAIS. Brasília. http://pdet.mte.gov.br/.

O'Dwyer, M., & Colic-Peisker, V. (2016). Facilitating the professional transition of migrants in Australia: does gender matter? *The Australian journal of social issues*, *51*(1), 47–66. doi: 10.1002/j.1839-4655.2016.tb00364.

OECD (2015). *The Contribution of Labour Mobility to Economic Growth*. International Labour Organisation. 3rd meeting of G20 Employment Working Group, Cappadocia, 23–25 July 2015.

OECD (2018). *Education at a Glance 2018: OECD indicators*. Paris: OECD publishing. https://www.oecd-ilibrary.org/education/education-at-a-glance-2018_eag-2018-en

Ortega, F., & Peri, G. (2013). The effect of income and immigration policies on international migration, *Migration Studies*, *1*(1), 47–74. doi: 10.1093/migration/mns004.

Picot, G., & Hou, F. (2018). Immigrant STEM Workers in the Canadian Economy: Skill Utilization and Earnings. *Canadian Public Policy*, *44*(1), 113–124.

Rhodes, S. (1983). Age-related differences in work attitudes and behavior: A review and conceptual analysis. *Psychological Bulletin*, *93*, 328–367.

Romer, P. (1990). Endogenous Technological Change. *Journal of Political Economy*, *98*(5), 71–102.

Rothwell, J. (2013). *The Hidden STEM Economy*: The Surprising Diversity of Jobs Requiring Science, Technology, Engineering, and Math Knowledge. Washington: The Brookings Institution.

Ruediger, M. A. (2015). Análise e avaliação do desenvolvimento institucional da política de imigração no Brasil para o século XXI.: caderno de referência.

Schaafsma, J., & Sweetman, A. (2001). Immigrant Earnings: Age at Immigration Matters. *Canadian Journal of Economics*, *34*(4), 1066–1099.

Silva, V., França, J., & Neto, V. (2016). Capital humano e desigualdade salarial no Brasil: uma análise de decomposição para o período 1995–2014. *Estudos Econômicos*, *46*(3), 579–608.

Simoes, A. (2018). A Inserção dos Migrantes Qualificados no Mercado de Trabalho Formal Brasileiro: Características e Tendências. In L. Cavalcanti, T Oliveira, & M. Macedo (Eds.), *Migrações e Mercado de Trabalho no Brasil. Relatório Anual 2018* (pp. 128–147). Observatório das Migrações Internacionais, Ministério do Trabalho/Conselho Nacional de Imigração e Coordenação Geral de Imigração. Brasília, OBMigra.

Sjaastad, L. A. (1962). The Costs and Returns of Human Migration, *Journal of Political Economy, 70*(5), 80–93.

Stamm, C., & De Castro, B. N. (2017). Diferenças salariais de gênero e raça no mercado de trabalho brasileiro uma análise estatística e econométrica. *Anais*, 1–20.

Sturman, M. (2003). Searching for the Inverted U-Shaped Relationship Between Time and Performance: Meta-Analyses of the Experience/Performance, Tenure/Performance, and Age/Performance Relationships. *Journal of Management*, *29*(5), 609–640.

Stypińska, J., & Gordo, L. R. (2018). Gender, age and migration: an intersectional approach to inequalities in the labour market. *European Journal of Ageing, 15*, 23–33. doi: 10.1007/s10433-017-0419-2.

Telles, E. E. (2009). The Social Consequences of Skin Color in Brazil. In E. N. Glenn (Ed.), *Shades of difference: why skin color matters* (pp. 9–24). Stanford, Calif.: Stanford University Press.

Thornton, R., Rodgers, J., & Brookshire, M. (1997). On the interpretation of age-earnings profiles. *Journal of Labor Research*, *18*(2), 351–365.

Villarreal, A., & Tamborini, C. R. (2018). Immigrants' Economic Assimilation: Evidence from Longitudinal Earnings Records. *American Sociological Review, 83*(4), 686–715.

doi:10.1177/0003122418780366

Walsh, J. (2015). The impact of foreign-born scientists and engineers on American nanoscience research. *Science and Public Policy*, *45*(1), 107–120.

WEF. (2017). The Global Competitiveness Report 2017–2018. Geneva: World Economic Forum. http://www3.weforum.org/docs/GCR2017-2018/05FullReport/TheGlobal CompetitivenessReport2017%E2%80%932018.pdf.

Winters, J. (2014). STEM graduates, human capital externalities, and wages in the U.S. *Regional Science and Urban Economics, 48*, 190–198.

Appendix A

CBO codes corresponding to STEM occupations. Based on MTE (2010).

142005	202120	211110	213125	213425	214280	214435	214805
142510	203005	211115	213130	213430	214305	214505	214810
142515	203010	211120	213135	213435	214310	214510	214905
142520	203015	211205	213140	213440	214315	214515	214910
142525	203025	211210	213145	214005	214320	214520	214915
142530	203105	211215	213150	214010	214325	214525	214920
142535	203110	212205	213155	214205	214330	214530	214925
142605	203115	212215	213160	214210	214335	214535	214930
142610	203120	212305	213165	214215	214340	214605	214935
201105	203125	212310	213170	214220	214345	214610	214940
201110	203205	212315	213205	214225	214350	214615	221105
201115	203210	212320	213210	214230	214355	214705	221205
201205	203215	212405	213215	214235	214360	214710	222105
201210	203220	212410	213305	214245	214365	214715	222110
201215	203225	212415	213310	214250	214370	214720	222115
201220	203230	212420	213315	214255	214405	214725	222120
201225	203405	213105	213405	214260	214415	214730	222205
202105	203410	213110	213410	214265	214420	214735	222215
202110	203415	213115	213415	214270	214425	214740	
202115	203420	213120	213420	214275	214430	214750	

Appendix B

Coefficients[13] for OLS model concerning monthly earnings differentials between native-born Brazilians and immigrants (arrived 25 and older) in STEM occupations in Brazil in 2017.

Variables	Unadjusted		Model 2		Model 3		Model 4	
	coefficient	S.E.	coeffi cient	S.E.	coefficie nt	S.E.	coefficient	S.E.
IMMIGRANT								
no	(rg)		(rg)		(rg)		(rg)	
yes	1.12E-01	1.19E-02 ** *	6.27 E-02	1.15 E-02 ***	2.62 E-02	1.02 E-02 **	-1.02 E-02	1.02E-02 (ns)
RACE								
Black	(rg)		(rg)		(rg)		(rg)	
indigenous			2.01 E-01	2.66 E-02 ***	1.51 E-01	2.36 E-02 ***	1.39 E-01	2.34E-02 ***
white			2.51 E-01	7.14 E-03 ***	1.96 E-01	6.32 E-03 ***	1.84 E-01	6.27E-03 ***
yellow			4.60 E-01	1.05 E-02 ***	3.26 E-01	9.31 E-03 ***	3.19 E-01	9.23E-03 ***
brown			3.53 E-02	7.42 E-03 ***	6.19 E-02	6.57 E-03 ***	5.66 E-02	6.52E-03 ***
others			3.70 E-02	8.11 E-03 ***	8.73 E-02	7.18 E-03 ***	7.72 E-02	7.12E-03 ***
GENDER								
Male			(rg)		(rg)		(rg)	
Female			- 1.78 E-01	2.54 E-03 ***	-1.60 E-01	2.25 E-03 ***	-1.64 E-01	2.23E-03 ***
METROP. AREA								
Porto Alegre								
Others			- 9.39 E-02	6.24 E-03 ***	-7.92 E-02	5.52 E-03 ***	-7.59E-02	5.48E-03 ***
Belo Horizonte			- 1.53 E-02	7.57 E-03 *	1.45 E-03	6.70 E-03	4.40 E-03	6.64E-03
Brasilia			1.52 E-01	8.27 E-03 ***	1.46 E-01	7.32 E-03 ***	1.53 E-01	7.25E-03 ***
Rio de Janeiro			2.93 E-01	6.94 E-03 ***	2.37 E-01	6.14 E-03 ***	2.42 E-01	6.09E-03 ***
Sao Paulo			4.05 E-02	6.34 E-03 ***	8.78 E-02	5.61 E-03 ***	7.69 E-02	5.56E-03 ***
EDUCATIONAL LEVEL								
Bachelor					(rg)		(rg)	
Master					3.80 E-01	5.38 E-03 ***	3.70 E-01	5.33E-03 ***
Doctorate					6.09 E-01	9.53 E-03 ***	6.17 E-01	9.45E-03 ***
TIME ON THE JOB					4.13 E-03	3.52 E-05 ***	4.13 E-03	3.49E-05 ***
TIME ON THE JOB SQUARED					-6.66 E-06	1.20 E-07 ***	-6.59 E-06	1.19E-07 ***
AGE					1.22 E-01	1.21 E-03 ***	1.15 E-01	1.21E-03 ***
AGE SQUARED					-1.24 E-03	1.57 E-05 ***	-1.18 E-03	1.56E-05 ***
OCCUPATION CATEGORY								
Technical occupation							(rg)	
Managerial occupation							2.96 E-01	3.36E-03 ***

[13] Significance levels: *** p <0.001, ** p < 0.01, * p < 0.05, . p<0.1.

Appendix C

Coefficients for OLS model regarding earnings differentials for immigrants in STEM occupations (arrived 25 and older, in Brazil) by demographic, human capital and occupational characteristics in 2017.

Variables	Coefficient	S.E.	Significance
(INTERCEPT)	6.007E+00	5.18E-01	***
YEARS IN BRAZIL	-2.908E-02	5.93E-03	***
YEARS IN BRAZIL SQUARED	4.275E-04	1.29E-04	***
TIME ON THE JOB	6.629E-05	7.82E-06	***
TIME ON THE JOB SQUARED	-1.131E-09	2.87E-10	***
ETHNORACIAL CATEGORY			
"Black"	(rg)		
Indigenous	1.417E-01	2.29E-01	
"White"	4.155E-01	1.33E-01	**
"Yellow"	4.698E-01	1.58E-01	**
"Brown"	3.793E-01	1.39E-01	**
EDUCATION LEVEL			
Masters' degree	4.236E-02	7.85E-02	
Doctorate degree	3.151E-01	9.37E-02	***
GENDER			
Male	(rg)		
Female	-1.584E-01	5.08E-02	**
CONTINENT OF ORIGIN			
Africa	(rg)		
Asia	5.983E-01	1.54E-01	***
Europe	4.425E-01	1.37E-01	**
Latin America	2.635E-01	1.36E-01	.
Mercosur	3.214E-01	1.42E-01	*
Naturalized citizens of Brazil	2.826E-01	1.50E-01	.
North America	6.624E-01	1.75E-01	***
Others	4.991E-01	1.42E-01	***
METROPOLITAN REGION			
Porto Alegre	(rg)		
Belo Horizonte	4.737E-02	1.35E-01	
Brasilia	4.760E-01	1.50E-01	**
Rio de Janeiro	5.915E-01	1.08E-01	***
Sao Paulo	2.393E-01	1.01E-01	*
Other regions	1.354E-01	1.01E-01	
AGE	1.138E-01	2.57E-02	***
AGE SQUARED	-1.105E-03	3.19E-04	***
OCCUPATIONAL CATEGORY			
Technical	(rg)		
Managerial	4.756E-01	4.86E-02	***

CONTRACTUAL OBLIGATION, INDIVIDUAL AUTONOMY, AND SANCTION IN TARGETING BENEFITS FOR THIRD-COUNTRY NATIONALS' WORK PROMOTION IN AUSTRIA, FINLAND, AND CZECH REPUBLIC

Eddy Bruno Esien

Introduction

Over the past century, budget deficit, fiscal constraints, and demographic necessities that confront the industrialized society have forced policy makers under intense pressure to structure welfare provision for unemployed people around targeting benefits. Several studies have revealed that targeting benefits emphasize public resources are distributed on a measure of financial need instead of universal transfers to the entire population, but the governance faces challenges in terms of equity and efficiency as the programs may not reach all intended beneficiaries (Neil, 2004; Devereux & Sebates-Wheeler, 2004; Devandas 2017; Andries, 1996; Bitran & Munoz 2000; Jill, 2001; Peck, 2003). Until now, little importance has been given to the studies in Central Eastern European (CEE), Western European, and Nordic countries explaining eligibility criteria in public assistance programs. Studies of contractual obligation, individual autonomy, and sanction-induced behavioural criteria under targeting benefits and its implication to young third-country nationals' (TCNs) heterogeneous subgroups' transition from welfare to work are rare and require clarification.

This study will deserve a careful analysis of targeting benefits' eligibility models to understand the implication of behavioural criteria for work promotion. The study analyses contractual obligation, individual autonomy, and sanction-induced behavioural criteria in public assistance programs under targeting benefits to understand young third-country immigrants' (TCIs) transition from welfare to work in Austria, Finland, and Czech Republic. Unemployed young TCIs in this study are non-EU nationals who voluntarily and legally move to one of the EU member's states with visa and residence permits (European Union, 2008). The main research question of this study is: How do contractual obligation, individual autonomy, and sanction-induced behavioural criteria in the realm of public assistance programs under targeting benefits enable young third-country immigrants' transition from welfare to work? The sub questions are: How do the criteria contrast and (b) what is the implication for immigrants?

Based on a qualitative cross-country case-oriented research approach with fewer country comparisons, documents, reports, published and unpublished scholarly texts are collected to shed light on this seemingly complex phenomenon. The research data analysis methods include the technique of document and content analysis. This article begins with next section discussing the targeting benefits eligibility in legal behavioural governance to promote work.

After that, the author of this article presents the methods of the study. Next section presents the findings in the selected entities. Finally, the article ends with a conclusion and recommendations.

Targeting benefits eligibility in legal behavioural governance

Research in targeting benefits represents one of the oldest modes of interventions in advanced democracies (Spicker, 2005). It revolves around the drift towards means-tested benefits (Neil, 2004). Otto von Bismark (German Chancellor 1862–1890) in 1884 first denounces targeting benefits more than 100 years ago to the initial design of old-age pension (Social Security, 2021; Clotet, 2020). Targeting benefits governance emphasizes public resources, which are distributed on a measure of financial need instead of universal transfers to the entire population (Neil, 2004). Nevertheless, the governance is imperative to challenges in terms of equity and efficiency that infringe social solidarity and reinforce a divisive society (Neil, 2004; Devereux & Sebates-Wheeler, 2004; Devandas, 2017). The governments manage these uncertainties through regulatory pre-specify behavioural requirements that recipients must satisfy to remain eligible (Mead, 2011). Hence, a targeting benefits regulative model is relevant for this study to capture the three following interrelated dimensions – contractual obligations, individual responsibilities, and sanction – and thus offers an empirical lens to understand young TCIs transition from welfare to work.

Contractual obligation dimension

Contractual obligations refer to a quid-pro-quo approach to welfare relief through effectively attitudinal features and moral agreement (Mead, 1997) that requires claimants to give up "something" in return for the benefits received (Paz-Fuchs, 2008; Neil, 2004). Attitudinal features refer to target pre-specify reproductive behaviour to remain eligibility for public and social welfare benefits. Activation contracts, for instance, conditioned (immigrants) beneficiaries to perform work requirements and remain eligible for public/social assistance benefits (Act Governing the Employment of Foreign Nationals (AUSlBG), 2017; Act on the Promotion of Immigrant Integration (1386/2010), 2010; 435/2004 Col. Act of 13 May 2004 on Employment, 2004). In contrast, moral agreement encompasses claimants' behaviour with an inherent ethical value and utilizes various mechanisms of social control. However, governments face challenges to balance rights over responsibilities on the obligation in disfavour of poor people (Neil 2004; Esien 2019a; Esien, 2020a). This contravenes the broad philosophical and ethical principle functional gains from conditional benefits (Standing, 2008). In Maynard's (1997) and Mead's (1997) opinions, this endorses more "austere" and "paternalistic" roles in redistributive policymaking and activation governance that constrains and takes away benefits from the poor. In short, contractual obligation reproduces moralise attitude that governs claimant's behaviour to remain eligible. Despite pre-specify obligations, there are other legal behavioural criteria to shrink the people eligible for benefits.

In the next subsections, I discuss individual autonomy and then sanction-based regulatory instruments.

120

Individual autonomy dimension

Individual autonomy refers to the individual's capacity for self-directed, independent action (Mead, 1986; Anderson, 2003) and reciprocity bond (Bothfeld, 2008). Self-directed action serves as a prerequisite to the capacity of independence choice to act and control over one's own rights in decision making (Bothfeld, 2008). In Ulrich's (2004) and Bothfeld's (2008) opinions, it is a self-reflection from external constraints or choice for autonomous actions. Activation programs, for instance, sought to place (immigrant) claimants in public works with the requirements either to accept any offer of employment or to seek work "actively" or "genuinely" on their own (435/2004 Coll., Act of 13 May 2004 on Employment; Act on the Promotion of Immigrant Integration (1386/2010), 2010). However, people are not free from the influence of the effect of social and institutionally transmitted norms and values that influence their environment and the development of their own personal option (Bothfeld, 2008). In contrast, reciprocity established a bond between the individual and the community (Bothfeld, 2008) over the realisation of individual's needs (Forst, 1996). Labour Office activation plan (435/2004 Coll., ACT of 13 May on Employment), for instance, enforce collective principles, norms, or benefits with socially approved behaviour and (immigrants) claimants' rights over the realisation of individual needs to remain eligible (Act on the Promotion of Immigrant Integration (1386/2010), 2010; Neil, 2004; Forst, 1996). However, to maintain the bond to the community during social change is challenging (Bothfeld, 2008). Thus, in respect to social differences, individuals (internalised) moral demands can form dilemmas of quite different intensity between their needs and social expectation place on them (ibid). To repeat, individual autonomy is part of regulative reforms to reproduce socially approved behaviour, activate benefit systems, and administer eligibility governance. Despite personal autonomy conditionality, the governments still face challenges to administer job seekers performance that further target claimant's behaviour to access benefits based on sanction regulative tool.

In the next subsection, I discuss sanction-based conditionality in targeting beneficiaries' behaviours.

Sanction-based conditions dimension

Sanctions-based conditions refer to a regulative and restrictive tool institutionalized under the Employment Act. Regulative tools convey a distinct meaning of rules to limit beneficiary's choice and actions (Zinyama, 2014). There are, for example, coding guidelines, process definition or control rules to guide welfare claimants in activation programs. In contrast, restrictive tools represent penalties that place "good work" habits and individual responsibilities at the centre of social citizenship relation (Mead, 1986; Esien, 2019b, Esien, 2020b; Clasen & Clegg, 2007). Active Labour Market Policy programs, for instance, penalized (immigrant) beneficiaries' "immoral" (Mead, 1986) or "anti-social behaviour" with financial penalties or withdrawal of benefits (Clasen and Clegg, 2007) when violating legislative behavioural conditionality (Act on public employment and business service, 2012; 435/2004 Coll. ACT of 13 May 2004 on

Employment, 2004). However, sanction bears transaction and high administrative cost to monitoring compliance activities. Moreover, benefits sanctions may cause "bubble effects", intensify poverty, and lower the likelihood of sustainable employment and income over time (Neil, 2004; Classen & Clegg, 2007). Briefly, sanction disciplines beneficiaries' action and punishes registered unemployed claimants conduct for violating legislative behavioural conditionality. Despite the regulatory mechanism, the government cannot sustain costs and fully control claimant's behaviour that results to consequences and causes of targeting benefits. In the next paragraphs, I will discuss the consequences, followed by the causes of targeting benefits in legal behavioural criteria governance for work protection.

A considerable amount of literature has been published on the consequences of regulatory reductive governance of targeting benefits. In Garcia-Jaramillo and Miranti (2015), Desai (2017), Slater and Farrington (2009), Devereux, (2016), Devereux et al., (2015), and Kidd and Althias (2019) views, there are following consequences: (a) targeted program is imperative to inaccuracy because the information needed to identify the poor is often imprecise to resolve this issue; (b) targeted programs' design is sometimes too complex and uncoordinated; (c) targeting benefits play burdens on state administrators which may not be cost-effective and efficient. The programs are usually designed for short term perspective to reduce current poverty and inequalities, but may fail to focus on the subsequent efforts to ensure the long term alleviation of poverty; (d) targeting benefits involve the tendency of politicians to abuse these programs by converting them into instruments of patronage; and (e) targeting benefits generate ethical reasons as it can lead to social divisiveness and perceptions that excluding others from benefits are socially unjust. That means, it can potentially increase social tension and exacerbate social division and inequalities by including specific groups and leaving out others. Despite such consequences, there are different causes behind targeting benefits that play a crucial role in shrinking the categories of people eligible for public and social benefits.

Data from several studies have identified the causes of targeting benefits in the policy studying process. In Garcia-Jaramillo and Miranti (2004), Slater and Farington (2009), Neil (2004), Fellowes and Gretchen (2004), and Tweedie (1994) opinions, the following causes are behind the design of proliferative policies to targeting benefit in redistributive policy decisions: (a) targeting benefits focus on the group who are most in need or to give the poor a higher amount of transfers, but income raise the threshold of eligibility; (b) targeting benefits are influenced by constituency pressure through public liberalism with an increase on government spending to welfare dependent families and children when citizens' opinion towards welfare becomes more liberal, less racist, or less bias, but reduces when state becomes diverse because of racial/ethnic diversity and class differences to pass welfare programs that are less generous; (c) targeting benefits are influenced through the paternalistic role of the government to actively endorse more austere and a moral agenda of reproductive citizen's behaviour that may influence policymakers decision about redistribution policies, but they may act to make welfare increasingly less attractive when "immoral" behaviours grow, since welfare may be seen as a viable source of funds for "immoral" behaviour; (d) targeting benefits are influenced through welfare dependency to decrease welfare generosity. As the proportion of the population receiving assistance increases, policymakers may act to make welfare less generous to discourage further enrolment; and (e) targeting is influenced through state financial resources pressure on welfare budgets. State with more resources provides more generous benefits than a less wealthy state since wealthier states may have more slake resources to afford more generous welfare expenditure than less wealthy states. In addition, state competition over resources also influences targeting benefits because when neighbouring states reduce benefits, a state will reduce their own benefits as to avoid becoming a "welfare magnet" for enterprising welfare clients that influence the pattern of targeting benefits programs.

Overall, targeting benefits model shows the reductive approach of behavioural requirement to shrink the categories of people eligible for social and/or public assistance benefits in employment-related policy process (see Figure 1). This regulatory tool serves as a policymakers' compass to uphold eligibility threshold in public assistance system, target labour market performance and individual responsibility. Although most researchers in the field agree that targeting benefits pattern of the policy process faces challenges in terms of equity and efficiency (Spicker, 2005; Devereux, 2016). There is still little investigation in Central Eastern European (CEE) countries and other European countries explaining behavioural criteria in the public and/or social assistance employment-related program under targeting benefits to interpret young third-country immigrants' transition from welfare to all types of work in Austria, Finland, and Czech Republic. Thus, targeting benefits in reductive governance is imperative to analyse the implication of contractual obligation, individual autonomy, and sanction-induced behavioural requirements to understand young third-country immigrant transition from welfare to all types of work.

Figure 1. Targeting benefits conceptual framework with the three interrelated behavioural requirement dimensions (Source: Author).

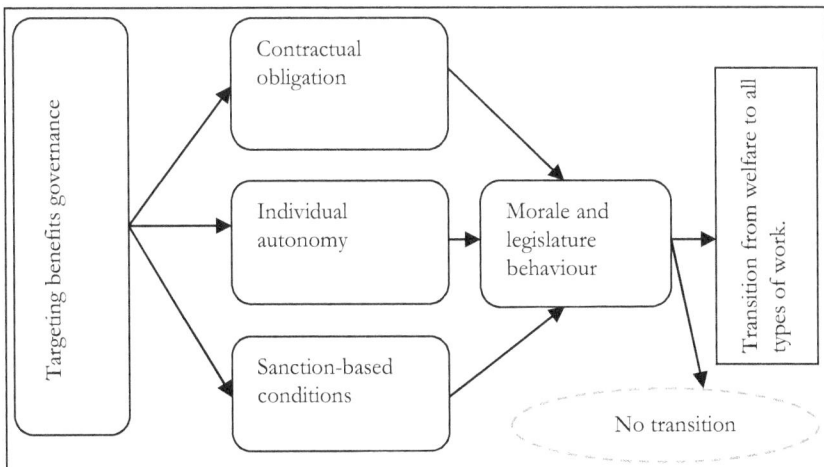

In the next section, I discuss the methodology and materials part to investigating the phenomenon and derived findings to answer the research questions.

Methodology and methods

The design of this study is based on a comparative cross-national case-oriented research approach with a fewer-country comparison (Lor, 2011). The methodology has several advantages, such as the notion that it relies on a constructivist philosophical position about how the complexities of a socio-cultural world are experienced, interpreted, and understood in a context (Atteslander, 1971). Limitation of the study includes the notion that fewer countries may have different data sets for the same category (Hantrais, 2009). In addition, the study is limited to Austria, Finland and Czech Republic that indicate selectivity, universalism, and mixed targeting benefits approaches accordingly. Moreover, a suitable and exact countries' choice is critical (Lor, 2011) with low external validity making the generalization of the phenomenon difficult to countries not included in the study (Ragin, 1987). However, the findings may generalize a theory in the way social scientists' theory-generate findings from one case study to the other (Yin, 2003).

Data were gathered from a triangulation of Employment Acts on the promotion of immigrant integration, authorized official immigrant employment reports and an overview of existing scholastic literature to offer corroboration and/or supportive evidence (Mayring, 2002) from Austria, Finland, and Czech Republic. The use of multiple-purpose sample (Yin, 2003) is applied to select the documents that have a long history and physical evidence to explain human behaviour on the promotion of third-country nationals' employment-related integration. The documents are investigated during the author's time in Prague, Tampere, and Linz between 2018–2020. The documents were in German, English, Finnish, and Czech. The researcher asked colleagues to translate and use on-line official English versions in databases such as OECD, ILO, European Union, and selected country's websites. For the on-line search and choice, the researcher inserted, for instance, "Targeting benefits and eligibility criteria", "Social Assistance Act", "Employment Act", "Third-country Nationals", "Ethnic Minorities" in the search machine rubric. This generated a diversity of documents and materials that mark a major advantage of this research plan with a source that is less subject to error (Mayring, 2002).

Furthermore, the passages are extracted with themes derived from targeting benefits conceptual-led deductive categories (Mayring, 2002) for young third-country nationals work promotion. In the initial round of the coding process, the author reviewed phrases, sentences, and paragraph segments from the documents and other sources to code the data. In the first round of the coding process, the researcher developed the following suitable categories to enable the analysis: (I) contractual obligation – This code represents targeting that links eligibility for social welfare benefits to contractual obligations. How are the contractual obligations of beneficiaries regulated? (II) Individual autonomy – How are the individual responsibilities of claimants conditioned? How is behaviour managed? How is the behavioural responsibility of beneficiaries' families and household condition in social welfare eligibility governance? and (III) Sanctions - How are the behaviour regulated for "immoral" behaviours? And the fines, for instance, that punish claimants' misconducts?

After several rounds of code deduction and all the evidence from the documents, reports, and scholarly text creating a big picture of the way in which the implication of behavioural criteria in targeting public and/or social benefits developed, interrelated, and implicated young-third country immigrant transition from welfare to work, the processes of data collection and analysis were completed and arrived saturation to answers the research question.

In the next chapter, the findings are presented to understand the phenomenon and answer the research question.

The implication of behavioural criteria in targeting benefits to enable young TCIs transition from welfare to all types of work.

The previous section examined the document and content analysis process. This section will look at the findings. It consists of three themes that emerged in the previous data analysis section, namely (I) contractual obligations, (II) individual autonomy, and (III) sanction-based behavioural conditionality to shrink eligibility in targeting benefits governance and answers the research question(s).

Contractual agreement for participation in programs

In the study, firstly, it may be useful to consider the notion of how contractual obligation evolves redistributive politics decision-making in the social protection system to investigate and analyses the notion of targeting benefits by behavioural criteria in public and/or social benefits programs for work. This section looks at the issue, discuss the findings surrounding behavioural criteria under targeting benefits to shrink the category of people eligible for public and/or social assistance[1] benefits and its implications with a conclusive remark.

For each of the comparative entities (Austria, Finland, and Czech Republic), there is a centralized targeting governance framework that arranges contractual agreement for third-country national's activation programs service delivery. In Austria, the central direction and local/regional Labour Offices are the administrative level responsible for contractual agreement (European Commission, 2012; Esien 2019a). The Labour Office contract out activation programs for young third-country nationals work promotion such as counselling and/or career guidance service delivery to external entities- private companies, third-sector organizations, and mixed consortium (European Commission, 2012). Procurement of service delivery takes place through a public call for tender, direct bargain, and other forms. Contractual agreement implementation

---

[1] Social assistance is a benefit in cash or in-kind, financed by the state (national or local) and usually provided based on a means or income test (Howel, 2001).

is through fix prices and/or cost-reimbursement[2]. Services are for the benefit of all jobseekers rather than a particular group but in favour of other hard to place groups and employers (ibid.).

In Finland, the local/regional Labour Offices are the administrative level responsible for contractual agreement (European Commission, 2012). The Labour Offices contract out service delivery for young third-country nationals work's promotion to private companies, third-sector organization, and other public agencies (European Commission, 2012). Procurement contract methods are often through public tender and direct bargain. Contractual arrangement implementation is through cost reimbursement and fixed price. Services are targeted to all jobseekers instead of a particular group but in favour of long-term unemployed, youth, older, disabled, immigrants/ethnic minorities, other hard to place groups, redundant workers and not employers (ibid.).

In Czech Republic, the central direction and local/regional Labour Offices are the administrative level responsible for contractual agreement (European Commission, 2012). The Labour Offices do not work directly with the third sector but signed contracts with mixed consortia that may include third-sector organizations to deliver activation programs (European Commission 2012; Act No. 137 of 14 March 2006 on Public Contracts §10). Procurement contract methods are often through a "public call for tender" (Act No. 137 of 14 March 2006 on Public Contracts § 17). Contractual arrangement implementation is through fixed price[3] and/or outcome or performance[4]-based contracts. Services are for the benefit of all jobseekers instead of groups but in favour of employers (European Commission, 2012).

The governments of this study comparative entities, for instance, in 2018 spent in direct job creation so that needy families that include young third-country immigrants participate in any of the intended benefit activation programs. In Austria, the public expenditure for a direct job account to 205,496 million euro on 8,678 participants to gain working habits for work. In Finland, public spending on direct job-creation account to 457,139 million euro on 33,725 participants. Meanwhile, Czech government spent 75,01 million euro for direct job creation with 10,594 participants in the programs (Eurostat, 2020) to enable unemployed registered job seekers to improve their human capital. However, other studies found deficiencies in contractual agreement design with decreasing proportion of funds going to the short-lived relief character of programs, which

---

[2] In cost-reimbursement contracts, providers receive payment for the expenses they incur. Generally, costs must fall within a budget approved during the procurement process. Some cost-reimbursement contracts specify performance standards, but payment is not dependent on meeting them (European Commission, 2012).

[3] Fixed-price contracts arrangements establish a set fee for subcontractors, regardless of performance or the actual cost of providing services. As with cost-reimbursement contracts, the contracts may include performance measures, but a contractor's performance does not directly affect payments (European Commission, 2012).

[4] Under outcome or performance-based contracts, providers are paid some or all the payments based on achieved job placement results. Performance contracts specify a wide range of measures which may include job outcomes, but also other factors, such as assessments made, action plans agreed, and so on (European Commission, 2012)

does not enable access to any permanent source of income (Muqtada, 1989; Dejardin, 1996). Moreover, there is a consensus that the social and labour offices face administrative capacity with limited staff and time capacities to consider individual cases in line with the behavioural requirements (Večerník, 2004; 2005). Another study found irregularities in the procurement environment with large-scale shortcomings of contracting out agreement cases (European Commission, 2016)

In short, the comparative entity's contractual agreement governance relies on Labour Offices as enables than providers in service delivery (Esien, 2019a; Esien, 2020a). Unlike in Finland, where the units of responsible administrative level in contracting agreement are local/regional, they are similar in Austria and Czech Republic (central direction and local/regional). The comparative country's contractual arrangements are fixed prices, but also cost-reimbursement (Austria and Finland) and outcome/performance (Czech Republic) to identify the mutual tasks between the two parties and determine the values of the contracted-out agreement for third-country immigrants employment-related activation measures delivery (European Commission, 2012). Moreover, the comparative entity's authorities use public call for tender. In addition, Austria and Finland also use direct bargain. Interestingly, Austria, also employ "other" form of contractual arrangement. However, there are large-scale irregularities with shortcomings in the contractual agreement for employment-related measure's environment. These findings suggest that management increase flexibility and performance to improve quality service in public sector`s performance (Räutä, 2014); but face inadequate administrative capacity in the effective management of contractual agreement to target (Hood, 1991) registered unemployed immigrant public and/or social beneficiaries needs that may mislead, disguise, or confuse participants in contracting out service delivery (Barney & Ouchi, 1986; Eisenhardt, 1985). This indicates the tendency to target self-decision making with lack of transparency, efficiency, and solidarity may infringe public accountability and beneficiary's eligibility to access public and/or social assistance benefits when looking at issues such as transition from welfare to work of young third-country immigrants and disadvantage group of people in behavioural requirements of targeting benefits setting.

This subsection has argued that targeting through contractual obligatory regulatory categorical devices has several implications that may heavily affect the safety nets of minority groups' jobseekers and incur a bubble effect. The next subsections will look at individual autonomy and responsibility management.

Individual autonomy for personal moral commitment

Reforms of public and/or social assistance programs for each of these countries embody the extensive use of regulatory instruments to couple benefits with socially approved moral commitment (Neil, 2004). In Austria, registered unemployed third-country immigrant beneficiaries must fulfil work requirements – job search, apply for job vacancies and accept suitable jobs, etc. (Hofer & Helmut, 2003; Act Governing the Employment of Foreign Nationals). Labour Office does not require other conditions for beneficiaries that include conditional cash transfers (CCTs). Targeting behaviour is based on the unit of individual claimants (Regional Hunger and Vulnerable Program – RHVP, n.d.; Federal Ministry of Labour, Social Affairs, Health and Consumer Protection – BMAGSK, 2018; Federal Ministry of Social Affairs, Health, Long-term care, and Consumer Protection – BMSGPK, 2020; Law Gazette, LGBl. No. 41/2008). There is no legal behavioural requirement for other members of the household (Federal Ministry of Labour, Social Affairs, Health and Consumer Protection (BMAGSK), 2018; Regional Hunger and Vulnerable Program – RHVP, n.d.).

In Finland, registered unemployed young third-country immigrant social assistance claimants are responsible to fulfil work requirement conditions in activation programs (Act on the Promotion of Immigrant Integration (1386/2010); Act on public employment and business service). There are no other conditions for registered unemployed social assistance beneficiaries in public assistance programs that include CCTs. (RHVP, n.d.). Targeting on social assistance beneficiaries is based on the unit of households (RHVP, n.d.). There may be a legal behavioural requirement applied also to other adults living in the same household as the social assistance claimants (Act on public employment and business service).

In Czechia, young third-country immigrant claimant's behaviour is constrained with work requirement conditions (Act No 435/2004 Coll., of 13 May 2004 on Employment). Targeting is based on the unit of household to remain eligible for benefits (RHVP, n.d.). Legal behavioural requirements for work availability and job search requirements apply to all members of the claimant household (Act No 435/2004 Coll., of 13 May 2004 on Employment, 2004). Beneficiaries in activation programs are jointly assessed with their families and people living in the same household (Kalužná, 2008). The Labour Office may also request long-term job seeker's claimants to participate in targeted Public Employment Service (PES) programs (No. 435/2004 Coll., ACT of 13 May 2004 on Employment, 2004; Kalužná, 2008).

For registered unemployed young third-country immigrants to partake in any of the intended benefits activation programs, for instance, the government spends on needy families. In 2018, the overall government expenditure on social protection in % of GDP for family and children in these countries accounted for 2.1 % (Austria), 3.0 % (Finland), and 1,7 % (Czech Republic). The government expenditure assists disadvantaged families in need with programs temporarily that include activation measures to encourage young third-country immigrants to engage in more active traditional social behaviours with individual responsibility and enter work. Other studies and reports confirmed that Finland and Czech Republic also initiated behavioural requirements that impose parental responsibility to ensure that they also search jobs and receive the standardized immunizations (Kalužná, 2008; Kotýnková, 2007; Sirovátka & Kulhavý, 2008).

In short, reforms in the comparative entities approved socially legal morale requirements. Unlike Finland and Czechia, Austria's registered unemployed young third-country immigrant public and/or social assistance claimants' commitment in activation programs is based on the individual. Whereas in

Finland and Czech Republic it is based on the unit of the household where there may be a legal behavioural criterion imposed on other adults living in the same household as claimants. These findings suggest that in general the government spent for people in need, but the policy design and administration are based on asymmetric power, pressure, punishing the poor, and moralise punitive measures (Schram, 2010; Wacquant, 2009; Serano-Pascual, 2013; Serano-Pascual 2007; Salais et al, 1986; Topalov 1994; Foucault, 1975). These procedures and policy process deemphasized rights to universal allocation of income and emphasizes on selective targeting compulsory individual responsibilities (Bauman, 2001; Franssen, 2003; Mead, 1986; Holden, 2003; Neil, 2004) as the treatment of poverty in terms of managing behaviour based on moral issue, reciprocity norm and the creation of standardized individual (Schram, 2000, Serano-Pascual, 2013; Serano-Pascual, 2007; Večerník, 2004). One possible reason could be the emphasis on recipients to behave like responsible citizens might be the result of a shift in the nature of the problem being tackled where rather than being a fight against poverty, it is, now above all a fight against (welfare) dependency. This policy outcome may impair young third-country national and socio-economically ethnic minority groups' eligible for social benefits in targeting benefit setting for work promotion.

The next subsection looks at behavioural requirement in targeting benefits eligibility based on sanction with punishments.

Sanction-induced condition for performance monitoring

The previous subsection emphasizes parental responsibility in individual autonomy as the basis of people eligible for public and/or social assistance benefits. This subsection looks at another aspect of sanction-induced regulatory reform in behavioural conditionality.

In Austria, the government agrees with young third-country immigrant claimants in Integration Action Plan. The plan includes actions across all policy areas that are crucial for integration to support labour market participation. The agreement "represents a clearly defined task" and "timetable" for both the case worker and the job seeker. Labour Office defines the "terms" and "conditions" that regulates the "rights and obligations" at a more general level (Federal Ministry of Labour, Social Affairs, Health and Consumer Protection – BMAGSK, 2018). These guidelines regulate job seekers' behaviour to fulfil institutionalised tasks. However, this approach stimulates workers to reduce their search (that is lock-in effect) instead of increasing it (that is skill-enhancement effect). Moreover, if an unemployed young third-country immigrant "does not take over a job" or a "place on a course" that has been offered, they "lose their entitlement to assistance for the duration of their refusal" (Federal Ministry of Labour, Social Affairs, Health and Consumer Protection – BMAGSK, 2018; Federal Ministry of Social Affairs, Health, Long-term care, and Consumer Protection – BMSGPK, 2020).

In Finland, registered unemployed public and/or social assistance third-country immigrant claimants shall "adhere to the activation plan and regularly attend a Finnish or Swedish course" and participate in other measures (Act on the Promotion of Immigrant Integration (1386/2010); Act on public employment and business service, issued in Helsinki 28 December 2012). However, failure to participate and for refusal of job, suffer severe benefits sanctions (Immervoll & Knotz, 2018). In addition, part of the integration plan emphasizes that if third-country national's job seekers have no valid reasons for his or her refusal of job referral, "his or her right to the benefits paid as integration assistance may be restricted" (Act on public employment and business service, issued in Helsinki 28 December 2012, chapter 4, Section 4 (1); Employment Contracts Act (55/2001, amendments up to 204/2017 included).

In Czech Republic, the registered unemployed third-country national's public and/or social assistance beneficiaries job seeker is "obliged to cooperate" with the Regional Branch of the Labour Office in "preparing," "updating" and "evaluating" the individual action plan (Act No 435/2004 Coll., of 13 May 2004 on Employment). In doing so, job seekers shall "comply with the deadlines" specified by the Regional Branch of the Labour Office and "meet the conditions laid down therein" (Act No 435/2004 Coll., of 13 May 2004 on Employment). Furthermore, registered unemployed public and/or social assistance jobseekers in the Czech Republic require to participate in retraining or job-creation programs if it is essential for their futures (Ministry of Labour and Social Affairs (MoLSA), 2019). Noncompliance implies exclusion from the register when there is no serious reason to refuse job referral (Act No 435/2004 Coll., of 13 May 2004 on Employment, Section 30 (2)).

Briefly, sanction regulatory tool discipline and restrict unemployed third-country immigrant's public and/or social assistance claimants under specific legislatures with sanction and punishment. These findings suggest that the Labour Office exercise compliance rules generally (Rehfuss, 1993) with sanction and fines to limit registered unemployed young third-country immigrant public and/or social assistance claimant's choice (Zinyama, 2014; Fama, 1980), but face challenges to discipline beneficiaries fully (Heilemann & Lukits, 2017; William, 1985). One possible reason for these administrative challenges could be a loss of proper control on registered unemployed public and/or social assistance claimants' action. This makes compliance governance imperative to uncertainties and difficulties to administer that may impair beneficiaries' access to benefits when looking at issues such as transition to work of young third-country immigrants and socio-economically disadvantaged groups of people in behavioural criteria for targeting benefits setting.

To sum up, the governments sign work contracting agreements to create job opportunities for registered unemployed young third-country immigrant's public and/or social assistance beneficiaries with regulations. The reforms embody an extensive use of a condition with rights and obligation attached to sanction and punished beneficiaries in case of noncompliance. The tendency to punish registered unemployed young third-country immigrant's public and/or social assistance beneficiaries jobseekers' behaviour might suggest raising threshold of eligibility and targeting benefits to those most in need that may stigmatize and impair beneficiaries' development when looking at issues such as employment-related transitions of third-county immigrants and disadvantaged young people in targeting behavioural requirement's setting.

Despite similarity in convergence towards selective targeting based on the means-tested need and sanctions, the comparative cases are diverse in their behavioural requirement's institutional context (see Table 1) to administer young third-country immigrant's transition from welfare to all types of work. In Austria, behavioural criteria in targeting benefits are based on the individual basis. There is no legal behavioural requirement for other members of the households. In Finland, targeting is based on the unit of households. There may be a legal behavioural requirement applied also to other adults' obligations and commitments living in the same household as the claimants. In Czech Republic, targeting is based on the unit of household. Beneficiary's personal behaviours in activation programs are jointly assessed with their families and people living in the same household (Kaluzna, 2008). Noncompliance implies denial or limited benefits for parents and children who are already in welfare. These procedures and policy process deemphasized rights to universal allocation of income and emphasizes on compulsory individual responsibilities (Bauman, 2001). One possible reason could be the emphasis on recipients to behave like responsible citizens might be the result of a shift in the nature of the problem being tackled where rather than being a fight against poverty, it is, now above all a fight against (welfare) dependency. This policy outcome may jeopardize young TCNs employment-related transition.

Table 1. Legal behavioural requirements in targeting public and/or social assistance benefits governance to administer unemployed registered young third-country immigrant's transition from welfare to all types of work in Austria, Finland, and Czech Republic.

	Legal behavioural requirements institutional settings		
	Individual Basis	Units of Household (HH)	Noncompliance Sanction
A	Yes		Yes
FI		Yes, but may applied to other adults' obligations and commitments living in the same HH as claimants.	Yes
CZ		Yes, but beneficiary's personal behaviours in activation programs are jointly assessed with their families and people living in the same household	yes

A (Austria), FI (Finland), and CZ (Czech Republic)

Conclusion and recommendations

This study investigated contractual obligation, individual autonomy, and sanction-induced behavioural requirements under targeting benefits to enable young TCIs' transition from welfare to all types of work in Austria, Finland, and Czech Republic. The research design consisted of a qualitative cross-national case-oriented research approach with a fewer-country comparison between Austria, Finland, and Czech Republic.

The study has shown that contractual agreement for participation in programs, individual autonomy, and sanction-induced condition for performance monitoring regulatory tools, is a major perceived influence in targeting benefits governance. An important finding to emerge in this study is the bureaucrats' morale agenda (Fellowes & Gretchen, 2004) that has encouraged social tension and divisiveness (Neil, 2004). These uncertainties are challenges to officials' capacity to manage beneficiaries' behaviours. Despite similarities in the conditional redistributive policy process, the institutional framework in Austria is dissimilar to those of Finland and Czech Republic, because it is based on the individual basis. Meanwhile, Finland and Czech Republic focus on the units of households. This research confirms previous findings and contributes to our understanding that targeting benefits generate ethical issues, create inequalities and/or stigma, and divisiveness in the regulatory redistributive governance. This suggests deemphasized rights to universal allocation of income as social rights and emphasizes on compulsory, moralistic, and individualized punitive model (Wacquant, 2009; Jill, 2001; Fellowes & Gretchen, 2004; Neil, 2004; Kidd & Althias, 2019; Kidd, 2017, 2018; Serano-Pascual, 2007; Serano-Pascual, 2013; Peck, 2003), which may impair recipients of welfare, disabilities, and public assistance access to benefits, when looking at issues such as employment-related transition of young third-country immigrants and socio-economically disadvantaged groups in targeting behavioural criteria settings.

However, several limitations need to be considered. The study indicates a "whole-nation bias" (Lijphart, 1975) and cannot be generalized to explain other countries leading to low external validity. Nevertheless, it may be generalized into a theory in the way scholar's theory-generate findings from one case study to the other (Yin, 2003). The study appears to support the argument for a marginal adjustment and improvement on the design, governance, and implementation of the public assistant benefits eligibility policy process, especially to regulate third-country nationals and/or vulnerable people's transition to all types of paid work. Further research should concentrate on young TCIs' personal experience in the realm of targeting public assistance benefits eligibility for employment-related integration policy process and implementation.

In short, the governance of targeting benefits indicates a sign of neo-liberal realpolitik (Peck, 2003) and a new paternalistic policy mode with an administrative cost containment and regulatory tools that targets individual responsibilities and labour market performance in times of austerity policy approach to allocate scarce resources and steers young TCIs' transition from welfare to all types of work. If lack of transparency, ethical standards, and solidarity in the design of eligibility criteria and the effective functioning of targeting eligibility regimes persist, problem of public accountability, power asymmetry, stigmatization, democratic deficits, and political inequalities may prevail not only to impair minority group's belongings but jeopardize social cohesion, economic prosperity, sustainable public finance, and participatory democracy.

Acknowledgement

The work on this article has been supported by the Charles University Specific Academic Research Projects Competition (project No. 260462).

References

Anderson, P. S. (2003). Autonomy, Vulnerability and Gender. *Feminist Theory*, 4(2), 149–164.

Andries, M. (1996). The Politics of Targeting: The Belgian Case. *Journal of European Social Policy*, 6(3), 209–223.

Areily, D. (2008). *Predictability Irrational: The Hidden Forces that Shape Our Decision*. New York: Harper Collins.

Atteslander, P. (1971). *Methoden der empirischen Sozialforschung*. Berlin: deGruyter.

Barney, J. B., & Ouch, W. G. (1986). *Organisational economics: Toward a new paradigm for understanding and studying organisations*. San Francisco: Jossey-Bass.

Bauman, Z. (2001). *In Search of Politics*. Cambridge: Polity Press.

Bitran, R., & Munoz, C. (2000). *Targeting Methodologies: Conceptual Approach and Analysis of Experiences*. PHR and USAID. http://www.paho.org/hq/documents/targeting methodologiesconceptualapproachandanalysisofexperiences-EN.pdf

BMAGSK. (2018). *Basic Information Report: Labour Market Policy- Institutions, Legal Framework and Procedures, Measures- Reporting Year 2016/2017*. Vienna: Federal Ministry of Labour, Social Affairs, Health and Consumer Protection. https://broschuerenservice.sozial ministerium.at/Home/Download?publicationId=237

BMSGPK. (2020). *Overview of the horizontal issue of disability in Austria*. Vienna: Federal Ministry of Labour, Social Affairs, Health and Consumer Protection. https://broschuerenservice.sozialministerium.at/Home/Download?publicationId=4 41

Bothfeld , S. (2008). *Individual autonomy: A normative and analytical core of democratic welfare statehood*. The Annual Conference of the RC/19/ISA "The Future of Social Citizenship: Politics, Institutions and Outcomes", 4–6 Sept 2008 in Stockholm. Stockholm: ISA Conference.

Clasen, J., & Clegg, D. (2007). Levels and Levers of Conditionality: Measuring Change within Welfare States. In J. Clasen , & N. A. Siegel (Eds), *Investigating Welfare State Change: The "Dependent Variable Problem" in Comparative Analysis*. (pp. 166–197). Cheltenham: Edward Elgar Publishing.

Clotet, M. (2020). *How an Industrial German Elite Could Have Shaped the Modern World in the late 19th Century*. https://mclotet200.medium.com/how-an-industrial-german-elite-could-have-shaped-the-modern-world-in-the-late-19th-century-f904f09d167e

Dejardin , A. K. (1996). *Public Works Programmes, a Strategy for Poverty Alleviation: The Gender Dimension, Issues in Development*. Discussion Paper 10. Geneva: ILO. https://www.ilo.org/wcmsp5/groups/public/---ed_emp/documents/publication/ wcms_123436.pdf

Desai, R. M. (2017). *Rethinking the universalism versus targeting debate*. https://www.brookings. edu/blog/future-development/2017/05/31/rethinking-the-universalism-versus-targeting-debate/

Devandas, C. A. (2017). Social protection and persons with disabilities. *International Social Security Review*, 70(4), 45–65. doi:https://doi.org/10.1111/issr.12152

Devereux, S. (2016). Is targeting ethical? *Global Social Policy*, 16(2), 166–181. doi:https://doi.org/10.1177/1468018116643849

Devereux, S., & Sabates-Wheeler, R. (2004). *Transformative social protection. IDS Working Paper 232*. Brighton, UK: Insititure for Development Studies. https://www.unicef. org/socialpolicy/files/Transformative_Social_Protection.pdf

Devereux, S., Edoardo , M., Rachel , S.-W., Michael, S., Althea-Maria, R., & Dolf, T. L. (2015). *Evaluating targeting effectiveness of social transfers: A literature review.* IDS Working Paper 460 and CSP Working Paper 12. Brighton: IDS. https://opendocs.ids.ac.uk/opendocs/bitstream/handle/20.500.12413/6606/Wp460.pdf;jsessionid=6ECACA41E454080994C05E6DBBBC30CE?sequence=1

Eisenhardt, K. M. (1985). Control: Organizational and Economic Approaches. *Management Science, 31*(2), 123–248. doi:https://doi.org/10.1287/mnsc.31.2.134

Esien, E. B. (2019a). Activation and Unemployed Third-country Nationals: The Implication of Work-related Incentives to Promote Work in Austria, Finland, and Czech Republic. *Proceedings of the International Scientific Conference ECONOMIC AND SOCIAL POLICY. Economic and Social Challenges for European Economy* (pp. 167–180). Opava: Vysoka Skola PRIGO. https://www.narodacek.cz/wp-content/uploads/2019/12/Proceedings-of-the-International-Scientific- Conference_2019-179-192.pdf

Esien, E. B. (2019b). Principal-Agent Relation and Contracting-out for Employment Case Management to Enable Third-country Nationals' Transition to Work. *Journal of Public Administration and Policy, 12*(2), 9–28. doi: https://doi.org/10.2478/nispa-2019-0012

Esien, E. B. (2020a). Enabling State and Third-country Nationals: In Local Government and Private Agencies Contracting for Counselling. *Karierove poradebstvo v teorii a praxi,* 21–43. https://www.euroguidance.sk/document/casopis/17/03_kpj_1-2020_17_esien_en.pdf

Esien , E. B. (2020b). Enabling State and Unemployed Third-country Nationals: Direct Measures, Psychological Plane, and Supportive Service for Work Protection. *Social Transformations in Contemporary Society, 8*(1), 88–99. http://stics.mruni.eu/wp-content/uploads/2020/06/STICS_2020_8_88-99.pdf

European Commission. (2012). *Forms of contracting arrangements between employment services. Small Scale Study* . Brussels: European Commission.

European Commission. (2016). *Public Procurement- a study on administrative capacity in the EU: Czech Republic Profile.* Luxembourg: European Commission. https://ec.europa.eu/regional_policy/sources/policy/how/improving-investment/public-procurement/study/country_profile/cz.pdf

European Union. (2008). *Employment in Europe: The Labour Market situation and impact of recent thrid-country migrants.* Brussel: European Union.

Eurostat. (2020). *Social protection statistic – Social Benefits, Data from November 2019.* Eurostat.

Fama, E. F. (1980). Agency Problems and the Theory of the Firm. *Journal of Political Economy, 88*(2), 288–307. http://www.jstor.org/stable/1837292

Fellowes, M. C., & Gretchen, R. (2004). Politics and New American Welfare States. *American Journal of Political Science, 48*(2), 362–373. doi:https://doi.org/10.2307/1519888

Forst, R. (1996). "Politische Freiheit". *Deutsche Zeitschrift für Philosophie, 44*, 211–227.

Foucault, M. (1975). *Surveiller et punir.* Paris: Editions Gallimard.

Franssen, A. (2003). "Le sujet au Coeur de la nouvelle question sociale". *La revue nouvelle, 17*(12), 10–50.

Garcia-Jaramillo, S., & Miranti, R. (2015). *Effectiveness of targeting in social protection programs aimed to children: Lessons for a post-2015 agenda.* UNESCO. http://unesdoc.unesco.org/images/0023/002324/232421e.pdf

Hantrais, L. (2009). *International comparative research: theory, methos and practice.* Basinstoke, England: Palgrave Macmillan.

Heilemann, S., & Lukits, R. (2017). *The Effectiveness of Return in Austria: Challenges And Good Practices Linked to EU Rules And Standards.* Vienna: EMN Austria and IOM Austria. https://ec.europa.eu/homeaffairs/sites/homeaffairs/files/01a_austria_return_study_2017_final_en.pdf

Hofer, A., & Helmut, W. (2003). *Active Job-search Promising Tool. A Macroeconometric Evaluation for Austria.* Vienna, Austria: IRIHS. https://irihs.ihs.ac.at/id/

eprint/1490/1/es-131.pdf

Holden, C. (2003). Decommodification and the Welfare State. *Political Studies Review, 1*(3), 303–316. doi:https://doi.org/10.1111/1478-9299.t01-2-00001

Hood, C. (1991). A Public Management for All Seasons? *Public Administration, 69*(1), 3–19. doi:https://doi.org/10.1111/j.1467-9299.1991.tb00779.x

Howel, F. (2001). *Social Assistance - Theoretical Background.* https://gsdrc.org/document-library/social-assistance-theoretical-background/

Immervoll , H., & Knotz, C. (2018). *How Demanding Are Activation Requirements for Jobseekers?* Bonn (Germany): Institute of Labor Economics (IZA). http://ftp.iza.org/dp11704.pdf

Jill, D. B. (2001). Targeting Social Welfare in the United State: Personal Responsibility, Private Behaviour, and Public Benefits. In G. Neil (Ed.), *Targeting Social Benefits: International Perspectives and Trends* (pp. 135–143). New Brunswickm N.J.: Transaction Publisher .

Kalužná, D. (2008). *"Main Features of the Public Employment Service in the Czech Republic".* Paris: OECD Publishing Paris. doi:https://doi.org/10.1787/230150403603

Kidd, S. (2017). Social exclusion and access to social protection. *Journal of Development Effectiveness, 9*(2), 212–244. doi:https://doi.org/10.1080/19439342.2017.1305982

Kidd, S. (2019, September 19). *Who really benefits from poverty-targeting in social protection: the poor or the rich?* http://www.developmentpathways.co.uk/blog/who-really-benefits-from-poverty-targeting-in-social-protection-the-poor-or-the-rich/

Kidd, S., & Athias, D. (2019). *Hit and miss: An assessment of targeting effectiveness in social protection.* Orphington (Sweden) and Nairobi (Kenya): Development Pathways. https://www.developmentpathways.co.uk/wp-content/uploads/2019/03/Hit-and-Miss-March13.pdf

Kotýnková, M. (2007). *The Social Assistance System in the Czech Republic: How to Find a Balance between Protecting People from Poverty and Motivating Them to Work.* Geneva: International Social Security Association. https://ww1.issa.int/html/pdf/warsaw07/2kotynkova.pdf

Lijphart, A. (1975). The comparable-case strategy in comparative research. *Comparative political studies, 8*(2), 158–177. doi:https://doi.org/10.1177/001041407500800203

Lor, P. (2011). *International and Comparative Librarianship.*

Maynard, R. A. (1997). Paternalism, Teenager Pregnancy Prevention, and Teenage Parent Service. In L. Mead (ed.), *The New Paternalism: Supervisory Approaches to Poverty* (pp. 89–129). Washington: Brookings Institution Press.

Mayring, P. (2002). *Einführung in die Qualitative Sozialforschung.* Weiheim and Basel: Belz Verlag.

Mead , L. (1986). *Beyond Entitlement: The Social Obligations of Citizenship.* New York: Free Press.

Mead, L. (1997). *The New Paternalism: Supervisory Approaches to Poverty.* Washington: Brookings Institution Press.

Mead, L. (2011). Reply to Ruth Patrick, the wrong prescription: Disabled people and welfare conditionality. *Policy and Politics, 39*(2), 281–282. doi:https://doi.org/10.1332/147084411X574572

MoLSA. (2019, August 6). *Employment.* https://www.mpsv.cz/web/en/employment

Muqtada, M. (1989). *The Elusive Target: An Evaluation of Target-Group Approaches to Employment Creation in Rural Asia.* Geneva: ILO.

Neil, G. (2004). *Transformation of the Welfare State: The Silent Surrender of Public Responsibility.* New York: Oxford University Press.

Paz-Fuchs, A. (2008). *Welfare to Work: Conditional Rights in Social Policy.* Oxford: Oxford University Press. doi:10.1093/acprof:oso/9780199237418.003.0001

Peck, J. (2003). The rise of the workfare state. *Kurswechsel: Zeitschrift für gesellschafts-, wirtschafts- und unweltpolitische Alternativen, 3*, 75–87.

Ragin, C. C. (1987). *The comparative method: Moviong beyond qualitative strategies.* Berkeley (CA): University of California Press.

Räutä, E. (2014). A Decision-making Model for Public Management: The Existence of a Policy Framework for Performance in Romania. *International Review of Social Research (IRSR), 4*(1), 57–74. doi: 10.1515/irsr-2014-0005

Rehfuss, J. (1993). *Contracting out water and sanitation services. Case studies and analysis of service and management contracts in developing countries.* Lough Borough University.

RHVP. (n.d.). *Targeting Social Transfer.* Social Transfer.

Salais , R., Bavarez, N., & Reynaud, B. (1986). L'invention du chomage: histoire et transformation d'une categorie en France des annees 1890 aux annees 1980, 1986 (Coll, Economie en Liberte). *Droit et Societe, 4.* https://www.persee.fr/doc/dreso_0769-3362_1986_num_4_1_1529_t1_0473_0000_3

Schram , S. (2000). In the Clinic: The medicalization of welfare. *Social Text, 18*(1), 81-107. https://muse.jhu.edu/article/31865

Schram, S. F. (2010). Review of Punishing the Poor: The Neoliberal Government of Social Insecurity, by Loic Wacquant. *Social Service Review, 84*(1), 685–689. https://repository.brynmawr.edu/cgi/viewcontent.cgi?article=1014&context=gsswsr_pubs

Serrano-Pascual , A. (2007). Activation Regimes in Europe: A Clustering Exercise. In M. Lars , & Amparo Serrano-Pascual (Eds.), *Reshaping Welfare States: Activation Regimes in Europe* (pp. 275–316). Brussel: P.I.E.- Peter Lang S.A. Editions Scientifiques Internatuonales.

Serrano-Pascual , A. (2007). *Reshaping Welfare States: Activation Regimes in Europe.* Brussel: P.I.E. Peter Lang S.A.

Serrano-Pascual, A. (2013). The European strategy for youth employment: a discursive analysis. In B. A. Lopez , W. McNeish, & A. Walther (Eds.), *Young People and Contradictions of Inclusion: Towards Integrated Transtition Policies in Europe* (pp. 85–105). Bristol: University of Bristol Press.

Sirovátka, T., & Kulhavy, V. (2008). *Implementation of the New Policies of Activation and their Effects for Labour Market Inclusion of the Vulnerable Groups in the Czech Republic.* IAB/DGS Conference.

Slater , R., & Farrington, J. (2009). *Targeting of Social Transfer; A review for DFID, Final Report.* London: Oversee Development Institute (ODI). https://www.odi.org/sites/odi.org.uk/files/odi-assets/publications-opinion-files/5494.pdf

Social Security. (2021). *Social Security History.* https://www.ssa.gov/history/ottob.html

Spicker, P. (2005). Taregting, risidual welfare and related concepts: modes of operation in public policy. *Public Administration, 82*(2), 345–365. doi:https://doi.org/10.1111/j.0033-3298.2005.00453.x

Standing , G. (2008). How cash transfers promote the case for basic income. *Basic Income Studies, 3*(1), 1–30. doi:https://doi.org/10.2202/1932-0183.1106

Standing, G. (2011). Behavioural Conditionality: Why the nudges must be stopped- an opinion piece. *Journal of Poverty and Social Justice, 19*(1), 27–38. doi:http://dx.doi.org/10.1332/ 175982711X559136.

Topalov, C. (1994). *La naissance du chomeur 1880–1910.* Paris: Albin Michel .

Tweedie, J. (1994). Resources Rather Than Needs: A State-centred Model of Welfare Policymaking. *American Journal of Political Science, 38*(3), 651–672. doi:https://doi.org/10.2307/2111601

Ullrich , C. G. (2004). Aktivierende Sozialpolitik und individuelle Autonomie. *Soziale Welt, 55*(2), 145-158. https://www.nomos-elibrary.de/10.5771/0038-6073-2004-2-145.pdf?download_full_pdf=1

Večerník, J. (2004). *Structural Tensions in the Interface Between the Labour Market and Social Policy in the Czech Republic.* Prague.

Večerník, J. (2005). *Process of Social Inclusion in the Czech Republic- Third report.* Prague: Group of non-governmental experts in the fight against poverty and social exclusion.

http://ec.europa.eu/employment_social/social_inclusion/docs/3cz_en.pdf

Wacquant, L. (2009). *Punishing the Poor: The Neoliberal Government of Social Insecurity* . Durham: DUKE University Press.

William , O. (1985). *The economic institutions of capitalism* . New York: Free Press.

Yin, R. K. (2003). *Case study research: Design and Methods*. Thousand Oak, CA: SAGE.

Zinyama, T. (2014). Contracting out: What Works, What doesn't and Why? *International Journal of Public Policy and Administration Research, 1*(2), 64–79. http://www.conscientiabeam.com/pdf-files/eco/74/ijppar-2014-1(2)-64-79rev.pdf

Legal documents

Austria

Act Governing the Employment of Foreign Nationals (AuslBG). https://www.migration. gv.at/fileadmin/downloads/gesetzestexte/AuslBG_englisch_1_10_2017.pdf (last accessed 15.08.2020)

Federal Ministry of Labour, Social Affairs and Consumer Protection (2020) Law Gazette, LGBl.No.41/2008.https://www.sozialministerium.at/cms/site/attachments/5/2/8 /CH3434/CMS1450780318640/un_disability_rights_convention_first_report_austri a.pdf (last accessed 14.07.2020).

Finland

Act on the Promotion of Immigrant Integration (1386/2010). https://www.finlex.fi/ fi/laki/kaannokset/2010/en20101386.pdf (last accessed 17.05.2020)

Act on public employment and business service (Issued in Helsinki 28 December 2012). NB: Unofficial translation, legally binding only in Finnish and Swedish Ministry of Employment and the Economy. https://www.finlex.fi/fi/laki/kaannokset/2012/en 20120916.pdf (last accessed 14.07.2020).

Employment Contracts Act (55/2001, amendments up to 204/2017 included). https://www.expat-finland.com/pdf/employment_contracts_act.pdf (last accessed 15.12.2020).

Czech Republic

Act on Employment, 435/2004 Coll. Dated 13th May 2004. https://portal.mpsv.cz /sz/obecne/prav_predpisy/akt_zneni/act_no._435_2004_coll._1.1.2018.pdf (last accessed 14. 07. 2020).

Act No 137 of 14 March 2006 on Public Contracts. 134/2006 Coll., ACT of 19 April 2016 on Public Procurement. https://sovz.cz/wp-content/uploads/2017/08/act-no.- 134_2016-coll.-on-public-procurement.pdf (last accessed 15.12.2020).

CONTRIBUTORS TO THE IMPROVEMENT OF EMPLOYER-EMPLOYEE RELATIONSHIPS: THE CASE OF THAI MIGRANTS IN ISRAEL

Parkpoom Kuanvinit

Introduction

Thai unskilled workers started finding employment in Israel in the late 1980s after the First Intifada or Palestinian uprising in 1987, which caused severe labor shortages in Israel (Kaminer, 2019). Due to the growing number of Thai workers in Israel, both Thai and Israeli governments decided to implement a bilateral agreement to provide Thai agricultural migrant workers in Israel with a fair and transparent recruitment system and labor rights protection mechanisms (Huguet & Chamratrithirong, 2011).

Whereas numerous impoverished Thai workers regard employment in the agricultural sector of Israel as a prosperous opportunity to escape poverty in Thailand, some international organizations and media criticized the efficiency of the right protection mechanisms provided through the bilateral agreement. Human Right Watch (HRW) (2013) reflected the problems of underpayment, poor living and working conditions, and other labor rights violations from their interviews with 173 Thai workers in various agricultural settlements in Israel. Likewise, British Broadcasting Corporation (BBC) (2018) voiced concern over unsafe working practices, unsanitary accommodations, and many unexplained deaths experienced by Thai workers in Israel. Also, psychosocial distress was another problem that Thai workers were vulnerable to, as Griffin and Soskolene (2003) pointed out. Kashti (2018) from Haaretz also expressed worries over an alarming rate of suicidal attempts and mental health issues among Thai workers in Israel. The rights abuse and mental health issues that Thai workers experienced are presumed to be interrelated.

Thai workers are not the only group of migrants experiencing hardship in Israel because an amount of literature discussed the poor interpersonal relationship between Israelis and non-Israelis as a fundamental cause of diverse direct and structural violence such as sexual exploitation, social exclusion, and other forms of discriminations (e.g., Seltenreich, 2004; Rajiman, 2011; Shauer & Kaminer, 2014). The associations between the qualities of relationship and the degrees of right abuse as well as psychological distress among migrant workers are one of the foci in this study.

This research also explores factors influencing relationships' qualities by applying the positive social contact and cooperative conflict management approaches that were championed by Rajiman (2011) and Yi-Feng and Tjosvold (2007) in the situation of Thai workers in Israel. These approaches could aid in assessing the potential contributors to the improvement of relationships between the two groups.

The purposes of this research are mainly classified into two aspects. On the one hand, it explores the association of relationship between Israeli employers and Thai workers toward the vulnerability of rights abuse and psychological distress among Thai workers. On the other, it studies the roles of social contacts, as well as conflict management approaches applied among Israeli employers and Thai workers toward the qualities of relationships between two groups.

The study was conducted under four main research questions; (I) How are qualities of employer-employee relationships related to the possibility that Thai workers suffer rights abuse ?; (II) How are qualities of employer-employee relationships related to the vulnerability to psychological distress experienced by Thai workers?; (III) How do social contacts play roles in relationships between Israeli employers and Thai workers?; and (IV) How do conflict management approaches play roles in relationships between Israeli employers and Thai workers?

Literature review and theoretical framework

As pointed out by much literature, Israeli people can easily generate discriminatory attitudes toward foreigners, which leads to grievances and miseries among non-Israelis (e.g. Seltenreich, 2004; Griffin & Soskolne, 2003; Ash-Kurlander, 2014). To illustrate, female Eritrean asylum seekers were vulnerable to sexual exploitation and objectification in Israel (Gebreyesus et al., 2018). Furthermore, Ethiopian migrants were prone to living difficulties due to political, social, and economic exclusions (Ringel et al., 2016).

Thai workers also suffered various forms of hardship in Israel. HRW (2013) found that a considerable number of Thai workers encountered labor rights abuse such as underpayment, poor housing conditions, and excessive working hours. BBC (2018) also reported unsafe working practices, unsanitary accommodations, and many unexplained deaths experienced by Thai workers in Israel. The situations reflected the inefficiency of the right protection mechanism provided by the state-to-state memorandum. Kaminer (2019) interestingly argued that Israeli employers intentionally paid migrant workers the lower wage to oppress and marginalize them as an inferior class in the society.

The psychological distress among Thai workers in Israel was also discussed in a quantitative study conducted by Griffin and Soskolne (2003). In numerous studies, psychological distress is defined as a vulnerable emotional state indicated by visible signs of depression and anxiety (e.g. Drapeau et al., 2012; Daly et al., 2011; Ridner, 2004). Psychological distress typically stems from a particular stressor which means that an individual can recover from psychological distress if the stressor is addressed and eliminated or if an individual can adapt to the stressor (Arvidsdotter et al., 2015). Migrant workers can be prone to psychological distress due to separation from home and pressure from adaptation to new cultures and environments during transnational movement. For this reason, psychological distress experienced by migrant workers has been primarily discussed in many studies. Mucci et al. (2019) cited socio-environmental factors (separation from home, discrimination, and lack of social status) as the main instigators of psychological distress among migrants. Other studies (Lee et al., 2012; Lurie, 2009; Zhong et al., 2013; Holumyong et al., 2018; Bhugra, 2004) conceptualized acculturative stress (difficulty in cultural adaptation, social exclusion, and discrimination) and healthy migrant effect (varying immunity to migration stressor based on pre-existing migration experiences) as the predominating causes.

The means to improve intergroup relationship has provoked interest in many studies. The qualities and frequencies of social interaction and how the conflicting parties manage the conflicts are some of the proposed factors contributing to the improvement of interpersonal relationships. Cook (1984) argued that the interpersonal relationship positively changed due in part to the frequent social interactions. Rajiman (2011) extended these findings by positing positive social contact as a contributor to a lower degree of prejudice between Israelis and non-Jewish people.

Conflict management approaches can also influence the qualities of a relationship. The term "conflict" in this study reflects the situations when employers and employees have contrasting needs and goals. For example, an Israeli employer may expect higher work capacity from a worker to achieve his or her business goals. In contrast, the worker might concern about his or her work safety and health condition. That is why they would feel reluctant to enhance their capacity to meet the employer's need. While traditional views assumed the uncompromising nature of conflicts, many scholars have postulated that conflict management, rather than the conflict itself, navigates the consequences (Edmondson et al., 2001; Lovelace et al., 2001). According to several cross-national studies (Yi-Feng & Tjosvold, 2007; Graham et al., 1988; Triandis et al., 1990; Tse et al., 1994), conflict management can be classified into three approaches, namely cooperative, competitive, and avoidance. Yi-Feng and Tjosvold (2007) argued that the cooperative one is the most effective relationship improvement approach, referring to their studies into the intergroup relationship between foreign employers and Chinese employees. The cultural context of the present research and the study conducted by Yi-Feng and Tjosvold bears resemblance because both studies look into the intergroup relationship between Asian and non-Asian culture. Moreover, both studies address the employer-employee relationship.

While much literature shed light on the factors stimulating the exclusionary attitude of Israeli people, very few literature (Griffin & Soskolne, 2003; Ringel et al., 2016) have been conducted to convey the perspectives of the migrants. Thus, the present research was conducted to fill in the gaps and complement previous studies by emphasizing the Thai migrants' perspectives. Moreover, many scholars studied the causes of rights abuse of migrants in Israel through the top-down perspective. Still, the relationship between employers and employees through the narratives of the workers, which is considered a bottom-up approach, is lacking.

Moreover, this study also extends the knowledge of previous studies by investigating the associations of migration stressors and psychological distress using both quantitative and qualitative methodology. Despite the empirical findings from prior quantitative studies, without narratives from the migrants and employer-employee relationship as one of the variables toward migration stressors, the quantitative studies were inadequate to explore the complex reality.

The study not only explores how qualities of relationships are associated with right abuse and psychological distress but also the factors contributing to the improvement of relationships using the theories regarding the influence of social contacts and conflict management approaches toward the qualities of interpersonal relationships. Below theoretical framework posits positive social contact and cooperative conflict management approach as contributors to the high-quality relationship. With a positive relationship, the degrees of right abuse and psychological distress are likely to be lower (see Figure 1).

Figure 1. Developed theoretical framework.

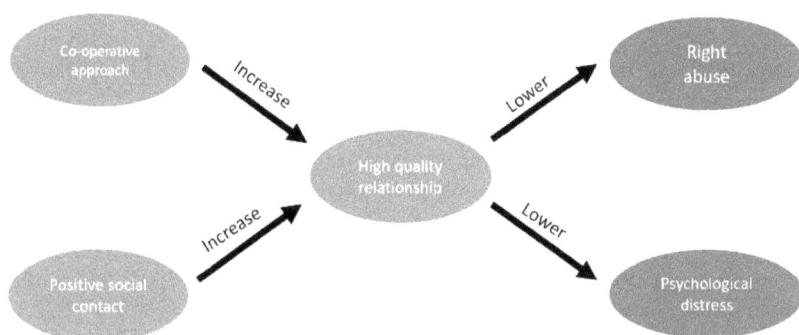

Research methods and results

Participants

The present study applied in-depth interview, semi-structured interview, and survey to investigate the associations that employer-employee relationship have toward right abuse, psychological distress, social contacts, and conflict management approaches. The data collection and analysis were carried out mostly in a qualitative manner. The psychological distress was the only aspect analyzed both qualitatively and quantitively for triangulation.

Nineteen Thai agricultural workers in Israel volunteered to give interviews. All participants were members of a Facebook page called "Rang Ngan Thai Pai Tai Krong Karn Kwam Ruam Mue Thai-Israel" (http://www.facebook.com/groups/142545962580579. After receiving permission from the page administrator, the Facebook page was used as a channel to get in touch with the interview participants. Most importantly, the readers were well-informed that 1) the interview would be implemented only after the researcher receives informed consent from the participants, 2) their personal information would be strictly kept confidential, and 3) they would have the right to skip any questions which they did not feel comfortable to answer as well as to withdraw from the interview at any time. The demographic attributes required in this study include gender (male and female), ages (21–30 and 31–40), region (central, north, and south), types of farms (Kibbutz and Moshav[1]) and type of work (cultivation and animal breeders).

The nineteen participants consisted of fourteen male and five female workers. Seven of them were aged between 21–30 years old, while the other twelve between 31–40 years old. Interestingly, one worker worked at three different places and acquired working experiences in three different regions, types of farms, and types of works. Therefore, there were nineteen Thai workers with twenty-one experiences participating in this study. The total number of respondents is summarized in Table 1.

Table 1. Numbers of respondents.

Gender		Types of farm	
Male	14	Kibbutz	7
Female	5	Moshav	14
	19		**21**
Age		**Types of work**	
21-30	7	Plants	16
31-40	12	Animals	5
	19		**21**
Region			
Central	10		
North	7		
South	4		
	21		

Data gathering

Five sets of questionnaires and one set of the survey were created for each respondent to share their experience regarding right abuse, psychological distress, social contacts, conflict management approaches, and relationship with their employers. The interviews took approximately 10–45 minutes and were tape-recorded with the interviewees' informed consents.

---

[1] Kibbutz refers to agricultural settlement operated cooperatively and with vital standardization, while Moshav farm owners are relatively independent, resulting in varying financial status (Israel Ministry of Foreign Affairs, n.d.).

Data analysis

Relationship analysis

The qualities of relationships between nineteen Thai workers and their Israeli employers in this study somewhat vary. In contrast to previous studies, half of the respondents appreciated their relationships with their employers. Some answered without hesitation that they trusted and loved their employers as if they were families. However, despite a small number, a few workers experienced poor treatment and aggressive behaviors from their employers, resulting in feelings of hostility and resentment between employers and employees.

The excerpts from some narratives below reflect two different extremes in the degrees of interpersonal relationship. The first one illustrates the level of positive relationship at the personal level characterized by a relatively low social hierarchy perception between employers and employees. In contrast, the following narrative expresses the negative relationship defined by the employer's discriminatory attitude.

My employer is very nice. He always ensures all the workers that he will try his best to protect our rights and he never fails to keep his words... He's so funny and approachable. He treats me like a friend, not an employee. (Mr. Sombat)

The employer never sees Thai workers as humans; He never cares about our safety or conditions, ... He always describes Thai people as typically lazy, cowardly, and have poor English skills... (Mr. Prayoon)

Among all workers who defined their relationship with their employers as positive, there are two distinct cases of workers who regarded their employers as friends and families, while others as respectable supervisors. The terms "Positive (personal)" and "Positive (professional)" are used to describe the former and latter relationships. Other respondents describe their relationships with employers as neutral and negative. The numbers of all respondents are summarized in Table 2.

Table 2. Numbers of Thai workers with different relationship qualities with Israeli employers.

Qualities of relationship	Number of respondents
Positive (personal)	2
Positive (professional)	8
Neutral	8
Negative	3
Total	21

Right abuse analysis

This study emphasizes four labor rights, including wage, working hours, accommodations, and work safety referring to the employment contract and other legal documents (CIMI et al., 2018). The varying degrees of right abuse are acknowledged when Israeli employers violate one or more of these rights. Clear examples of the right abuse include underpayment, excessive working hours, lack of sanitary and ventilation in the accommodation, and shortage of protective gear in the hazardous work environment. Among four rights, the wage is prioritized over others for two main reasons. Both Human Right Watch (2013) and BBC (2018) agreed in their criticisms that the workers expressed the most concern regarding the wage issue. Their arguments are in line with the interviews with all nineteen workers, which indicate that the wage is the most significant right and the principal motive for them to secure employment in Israel. The level of rights abuse is moderate for the participants who experienced violations of wages but not others. It is classified as high in case other rights were also abused on top of the wages. If other rights apart from the wages were abused, the level is identified as low.

The right abuse is not a prominent phenomenon in this research because more than half of respondents experienced right abuse at a low level. Some experiences regarding rights violation mostly are relevant to underpayment issues, substandard accommodations, and lack of safety kits and instructions for chemicals-related work.

It is worth noting that the degrees of right abuse are measured by comparing the workers' actual conditions and the legal documents, not their feelings. A lot of workers whose rights were violated did not recognize the abuse either because they were not fully aware of their rights or they were happy with their current conditions compared to pre-migration precarity. To clarify, many workers did not take the underpayment as a right violation as long as it was higher than their income in Thailand. The numbers of all rights abuse levels are summarized in Table 3.

Table 3. Numbers of Thai workers with different levels of rights abuse.

Level of rights abuse	Number of respondents
Low	11
Moderate	5
High	5
Total	21

Psychological distress analysis

The Kessler Psychological Distress Scale (K10) survey was preliminarily applied to detect the sign of psychological disorders quantified into different levels. The respondents also gave in-depth interviews for further narrative analysis. Based on both methods' results, there was only one case of psychological distress at a high level. However, the workers whose scores from the survey indicate a healthy mental state reflected varying degrees of distress and emotional states through their narratives. With the in-depth analysis of the narratives, four workers were identified with a moderate level of psychological distress. The level of psychological distress of the other sixteen respondents was classified as low (see Table 4).

Table 4. Levels of PD from in-depth interviews.

Levels of PD from in-depth interview	No. of cases
Low	16
Moderate	4
High	1
Total	21

The results from both the survey and in-depth interview are following each other. Those whose score from the survey indicate vulnerability to psychological distress mentioned negative aspects from living in Israel which had negative effects on their daily lives – *"I thought coming to Israel is a wrong decision, and I cannot go back until I save enough money (Mr. Pichet)"* while those likely to be mentally well according to the survey mostly shared positive things and hardly shared the negative ones in their narratives

– *"Israel gave me a new better life… I should have come a long time ago (Mr.Anurak)"*.

Social contact analysis

Social contacts in this study are conceptualized through the qualities and frequencies of social interactions between Israeli employers and Thai workers. Influenced by Rajiman's (2011) theory, social contacts in this research are classified into positive, negative, and no.

The social contacts of thirteen respondents are defined as positive. The social activities reflect friendly and intimate interactions such as hanging out after work, having dinner together, and talking about personal issues. Seven workers shared that they hardly or never interacted with their employers. The social contacts in this scenario are defined as no. One worker experienced frequent aggressive confrontation and dispute with his employer, signifying negative social contact (see Table 5).

Table 5. Number of Thai workers with different levels of rights abuse.

Social contacts	Number of respondents
Positive	13
No	7
Negative	1
Total	21

Conflict management approaches analysis

The workers were asked about how they approached the employers when conflicts arose and how the employers reacted. Seven workers in this study applied a cooperative approach to settle the conflict. Eleven and two opted for avoidance and competitive, respectively (see Table 6).

To clarify, the cooperative approach reflects the situation when the conflicting parties tried to reach mutual goals that satisfy both parties. Avoidance refers to every case when the negotiation or confrontation never took place. The conflict approach was applied by employers and workers who aimed only at fulfilling their needs without concerns for the other party.

Table 6. Number of Thai workers with different conflict management approaches.

Conflict management approach	Number of respondents
Cooperative	7
Avoidance	11
Competitive	2
Total	**20**[2]

Findings and discussion

Association between right abuse and qualities of relationship

The results from the interviews depicted varying degrees of right abuse as well as levels of relationship. To answer the first research question, "How are qualities of relationships related to the possibility that Thai workers suffer right abuse?", the levels of right abuse and qualities of relationship are compared to each other to analyze their associations through the respondents' narratives.

Two workers who defined their relationship with their employers as negative echoed some associations between the relationship quality and right abuse in his narratives. When they heard the question, "Does the employers protect your rights as agreed in the employment contract?", both had a very similar reaction. In contrast, for the workers who had a high level of right abuse and neutral relationships, the two aspects arose in parallel without transparent interconnection.

After hearing the question, Mr. Prayoon tilted his head to the other side with a weak chortle as if he was listening to a stupid question. He then shared his experiences about the rights violation and poor treatment from his employer and believed most Thai workers suffered rights abuse to some extent and that Israeli employers have no interest in protecting the rights of the migrants. The rights abuse clearly exacerbated the interpersonal relationship between him and his employer.

Nothing is as agreed according to the contract. The employer never cares about our living conditions and safety. He does not see us as humans and always forces us to work too excessively. I couldn't stand reacting impolitely when he treated us very rudely and without respect. He never cared about us. Why do we need to care about him... (Mr. Prayoon)

Most of the respondents in this study who had a low level of right abuse enjoyed a positive relationship with their employers. They shared similar responses about appreciations toward their employers' willingness to protect

---

[2] One worker did not apply any CMA because the employer and worker have never had conflict against each other.

their rights which resulted in their feelings of loyalty, respect, and high commitment to work. The development of a friendly and proximate relationship was, as a result, visible.

Mr. Isaret was one of the workers who repeated several times with cheerful smiles during the interview how much he felt thankful for his employer's kindness. He firmly believes that the more he shows honesty and loyalty to his employer, the better his right is protected.

> ….I try to show that I'm a dedicated worker. When we can make them believe that we love and are loyal to them, they will give love and respect back to us. I think the employer tries his best to protect my right because he recognizes me as one of his family and wants me to have a better life… (Mr. Pichet)

Regarding the moderate level of right abuse, it is worth considering the pre-arrival experiences and precarity of the workers because all five respondents shared that their income and living conditions in Israel were better off than those of their prior migration experience. Therefore, they still appreciated the employment in Israel and did not feel offended. Besides, since the underpayment issue was relatively common in Israel, they perceived it as an acceptable norm. For these reasons, the association between a moderate level of right abuse and the employer-employee relationship is not salient. However, while they seemed satisfied with the current conditions, the workers believe that a positive employer-employee relationship can potentially minimize the degree of right abuse.

To answer the research question, the employer-employee relationship and level of right abuse have a reciprocal correlation to each other. The negative relationship has a connection with the high level of right abuse, while the positive relationship is interconnected with the low level of rights abuse.

Association between psychological distress and qualities of relationship

The second research question addresses the correlation between relationship qualities and degrees of psychological distress. The comparison between relationship qualities and psychological distress level and the respondents' narratives from the in-depth interview was applied for the association analysis.

Only one worker in this study exhibited a high level of psychological distress. Both groups of workers with moderate and low levels similarly shared the gratitude toward relatively high earnings in Israel, which was regarded as a life encouragement. Their negative attitudes toward living in Israel in some respects can gradually decrease, while their savings were getting higher. All the workers also pointed out the development of self-esteem and confidence due to higher income. Most workers entered Israel with the hope to financially support their families in Thailand. Thus, the goal achievement generated a sense of pride and appreciation toward living in Israel. A few workers even perceived their significant roles not only at the household but national level. They realized that the remittance transferred to Thailand could benefit the economy at the macro level. Moreover, the agricultural techniques and knowledge in Israel can also be applied to develop the agricultural industry in Thailand in the future.

Strong attachment and a sense of belonging in the Thai workers' community were stressed as other factors contributing to a positive mental state. None of the workers mentioned any conflicts or social problems among Thai workers. Instead, community members with the same linguistic, identical, and cultural backgrounds helped them continue their everyday lives smoothly. The strong ties in the community also played a critical role in relieving stress and loneliness due to separation from home. Two respondents mentioned the socialization and positive relationship at the personal level with Israeli employers as a major factor preventing them from psychological distress. Interestingly, both workers seemed to have an exceptionally low level of psychological distress because they did not mention anything negative about living in Israel.

Other factors vary from one person to another. This is also arguably due to the prior migration experiences and predicaments in Thailand. Many workers in the study compared Israel's living conditions to their precarious lives in Thailand or worse miseries when they had migrated to other countries. The prior lives experienced also helped the workers develop problem-solving skills, communication skills, stress management, and patience, which also play a part in strengthening their psychological health. The degrees of these survival skills can differ from person-to-person, reflecting varying levels of immunities against psychological distress.

Even though most workers in this study did not experience severe psychological disorders themselves, they are aware that a large number of Thai workers in Israel suffered and are vulnerable to mental disorders so much that it could lead to miserable phenomena such as drug abuse, self-harm, or suicidal attempts. They also shared similar thoughts about the stressors from living in Israel.

While financial stability contributes to a healthy mental condition, financial problems can be a leading instigator of stress. More than half of the workers were certain that individuals could suffer high stress if they fail to reach their financial goals. Stress from financial distress can potentially be associated with harmful behaviors like gambling and drug use. It will become a vicious cycle because gambling and drugs exacerbate the individuals' financial status. The result is worsened psychological distress.

Respondents cited excessive use of work-related chemicals and pesticides as the other instigator of psychological distress. The substance in the chemicals is not only physically but also mentally harmful. The insufficient provision of protective gear and instruction of use can affect their mental health. This is in line with a study conducted by Beard et al. (2014), which indicated that the consecutive use of chemicals tends to affect the nervous system and instigate the vulnerability to depressions. Rusiecki et al. (2016) conducted a comparative study between two groups of farmers who were not and highly exposed to the use of pesticides. Their finding depicted that the latter has been diagnosed with intense symptoms of depression and likely to generate suicidal thoughts.

Even though the interview participants did not exhibit severe signs of psychological distress, they were likely to experience some negative emotional states like stress, anxiety, loneliness, and occasional regret over the decision to come to Israel at a level that did not disturb their daily lives. The feelings stem from varying causes such as diverse and harsh weather, physically demanding work, lack of rest, lack of privacy, and rights abuse. Female workers mainly express concerns about insecurity and discomfort because the female workers' population is significantly small compared to males.

In summary, the factors, which can potentially instigate and prevent psychological distress shared by all nineteen workers are shown in Table 9.

Table 9. Factors preventing and instigating psychological distress (PD).

Factors preventing PD	Mentioned by	Factors instigating PD	Mentioned by
High income	13 workers	Lack of self-control	10 workers
Goal orientation	9 workers	Gambling, and drug abuse	9 workers
Socialization with coworkers	8 workers	Overuse of chemicals	6 workers
Sense of pride	6 workers	Gender balance in the workplace	4 (female) workers
Prior life experience	2 workers	Physically demanding work	4 workers
Encouragement from family	2 workers	Pressure from family	3 workers
A positive relationship with employers	2 workers	Rights abuse	3 workers
		Separation from home	3 workers
		Harsh diverse weather	2 workers

Among varying factors affecting psychological distress, the interviews with nineteen Thai workers depicted no clear and direct association with the interpersonal relationship with Israeli employers. However, it is worth considering that two workers who mentioned the interconnection between the positive relationship with their employers and the exceptionally low level of psychological distress developed the positive relationship at the personal level. They also expressed high gratitude toward living in Israel through the statements such as *"Israel gave me a new better life"*, *"I and my family have never been happier (Mr. Pichet),"* and *"I should have come to Israel a long time ago (Mr. Anurak)."* Their narratives reflected the close association of the two extremes (exceptionally low level of PD and positive relationship at the personal level). Also, as right abuse can be regarded as one of the instigators of psychological distress, this study suggested that psychological distress has an indirect association with the relationship considering the association between degrees of right abuse and qualities of relationship discussed in the previous section.

Association between social contacts and qualities of relationship

The third research question is "How do social contacts play roles in the relationships between Israeli employers and Thai workers?". In line with the theories proposed by Rajiman (2011) and Brewer (1999), positive social contact is associated with the relationship. However, Mr. Suradet defined his relationship with his employer as negative but social contact as positive. The negative relationship is characterized by a low level of trust as well as frequent arguments. Despite his profoundly hostile attitude toward his employer, he maintained positive social contact, such as friendly and casual conversations with his employer.

I don't feel uncomfortable talking to him. We talk a lot even about personal matters, but deeply I don't trust him and never perceive him as a friend... As I still need this job, I think it's a better idea to interact with him positively no matter how I actually feel (Mr. Suradet).

It was obvious for the workers who hardly or never interact with their employers to have impassive feelings about their employers. Furthermore, the negative social contact like verbal abuse, disputes, and threatening behaviors ignited the hostile attitudes between the workers and employers in this study.

To answer the research question, positive social contact is mostly but not necessarily always associated with a positive relationship. The absence of social contact is also likely to result in a neutral relationship, while the negative social contact and a negative relationship are interrelated.

Association between conflict management approaches and qualities of relationship

The last research question, "How do different types of conflict management approaches have impacts on the relationship between Israeli employers and Thai workers?", was formulated to study the role of the conflict management approach toward the employer-employee relationship.

A negative relationship explains the application of competitive conflict management approaches found in two cases. Both respondents shared that it was unlikely for them to settle the conflicts with employers in a cooperative because of the mutual discriminatory attitudes between conflicting parties. The approach even worsened the relationship, which illustrated the bidirectional association between the competitive approach and the negative relationship.

When the relationship is positive, characterized by mutual empathy and deep concern for each other, it was common, according to five respondents, for conflicting parties to compromise and reach the mutual goals that satisfy both parties. This points out the association between positive relationships and the cooperative approach.

Whereas many respondents with a neutral relationship applied the avoidance approach, the correlation between the two elements is not clear. According to the narratives of all eight participants, they all agreed that the relationship played no significant role in the selection of approach. They avoided a confrontation when the conflict arose either because they did not see the conflict as a big problem and preferred not to approach the employers for safety reasons. Also, they prioritized employment opportunities in Israel over their well-being. In this sense, the cultural background and concern for employment security explain the reason for selecting the avoidance approach, not the employer-employee relationship quality.

To summarize, negative relationships and competitive conflict management approaches are closely interrelated to each other. Likewise, the positive relationship and cooperative conflict management approaches are also associated. Even though most workers and employers who applied the avoidance conflict management approach have a neutral relationship with each other, the association between a neutral relationship and the avoidance conflict management approach is not salient.

The interviews with nineteen Thai agricultural migrant workers in Israel depicted positive associations between cooperative conflict management approach and positive social contact and high-quality relationship, which was following the developed theoretical framework (Rajiman, 2011; Yi-Fen & Tjosvold, 2007). Furthermore, the findings complemented previous studies by providing detailed information about the selection of conflict management approaches and social contacts. With the pre-existing optimistic attitudes of both employers and employees, they potentially opt for a cooperative approach and develop positive social contact. Such an attitude can also influence the employer-employee's positive relationship at the personal level. As opposed to the discriminatory attitude from Israeli employers against foreigners as an instigator of poor-quality relationships (Rajiman, 2013), the pre-existing optimistic attitude can be considered a factor contributing to the high-quality ones.

The theories proposed by Rajiman (2011) and Yi-Fen and Tjosvold (2007) perceived unidirectional association from social contact, along with conflict management approach, toward the relationship qualities. However, this research suggests that the qualities of the relationship also influence the application of conflict management approaches and social contacts. Thus, the association is somewhat reciprocal.

Another significant finding of this research is that relationship quality and right abuse level are associated. The improvement of the relationship is likely to contribute to a low degree of right abuse. While the connection between relationship qualities and levels of psychological distress is not salient, the indirect association is presumed, thanks to the interconnection between levels of psychological distress and right abuse. The associations between the five elements were illustrated in a new theoretical framework (see Figure 2).

Figure 2. Theoretical framework (2) based on this research's findings.

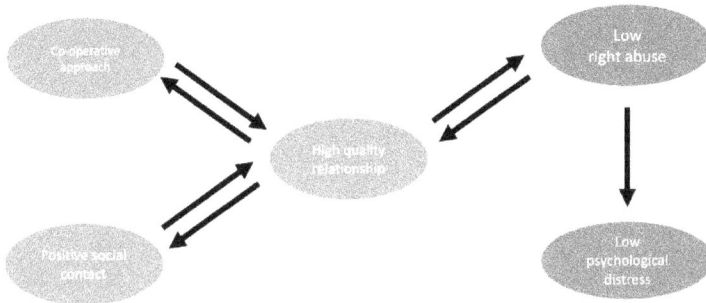

Conclusion and implications

In agreement with previous studies (Rajiman, 2011; Yi-Feng & Tjosvold, 2007), this research suggests that positive social contact and cooperative conflict management approach can be considered potential tools for the improvement of the relationship between Israeli employers and Thai workers. With the positive interpersonal relationship between Israeli employers and Thai workers, the degree of right abuse is likely to be diminished. Despite insufficient evidence supporting the association between levels of psychological distress and relationship qualities, the indirect association was assumed because right abuse is one of the main instigators of psychological distress.

Based on these findings, the research makes recommendations to government authorities and practitioners involved in the deployment and right protection of Thai workers in Israel. Related bodies are recommended to consider the improvement of the interpersonal relationships between Israeli employers and Thai workers as another way to facilitate right protection on top of the enactment of legal instruments. Consideration into social contacts and conflict management approaches can be one of the concrete solutions for the improvement of the relationship. The psychological distress issue is also expected to be relieved through the assured right protection. As the departing Thai workers must attend pre-departure orientation provided by the Thai government, it can be within their capacity to include the subjects on positive social contact and cooperative conflict management approach. The workers should be educated to resolve conflict collaboratively and improve relationships with their employers through positive social contact. Israeli government authorities, NGOs, and other counterparts also work very closely with both Israeli employers and Thai agricultural workers in Israel. With the fruitful insights and understandings about Israeli and Thai people, they are recommended to initiate events and recreational activities to provide space for employers and employees to interact more with each other and strengthen their mutual understanding.

This research encountered some challenges and limitations. First, it was conducted into the group of Thai workers only using 15- to 45-minute semi-structured interviews. The voices of Israeli employers about how they socially interact and solve the conflicts with Thai workers are lacking. Regarding the research method, interpersonal relationships can take time and rely on social and cultural factors. Thus, the ethnographic study suits the study method because the nature of on-site learning and observation can provide insightful details of changes in the relationship between two groups. Future research may further investigate the issue by applying ethnographic observation methodology and collecting data from the employer's side.

Acknowledgments

The author would offer special thanks to Professor Katayanagi Mari, Professor Kawano Noriyuki and Associate Professor Tomotsugu Shinsuke from Hiroshima University, as well as nineteen Thai workers who volunteered to be the interview participants in this study.

References

Arlozorov, M. (2018). Netanyahu's adviser: foreign workers will receive less than the minimum wage. *The Marker*, April 10, 2018.

Arvidsdotter, T., Marklund, B., Kylén, S., Taft, C., & Ekman, I. (2015). Understanding persons with psychological distress in primary health care. *Scandinavian Journal of Caring Sciences*, *30*(4), 687–694. doi:10.1111/scs.12289

Ash-Kurlander, Y. (2014). Immigration for agricultural labor in Israel in the shadow of the bilateral agreement between Israel and Thailand. *Emek Hefer*: Ruppin Academic Center [Hebrew].

BBC. (2018). *Thai labourers in Israel tell of harrowing conditions*. BBC News. https://www.bbc.com/news/av/world-middle-east-46311922.

Beard, J. D., Umbach, D. M., Hoppin, J. A., Richards, M., Alavanja, M. C., Blair, A., Sandler, D. P., & Kamel, F. (2014). Pesticide exposure and depression among male private pesticide applicators in the agricultural health study. *Environmental health perspectives*, *122*(9), 984–991. https://doi.org/10.1289/ehp.1307450

Bhugra, D. (2004). Migration and mental health. *Acta Psychiatr Scand 109*(4), 243–258 Combating Discrimination against Migrants. (n.d.). https://www.ohchr.org/EN/AboutUs/Pages/DiscriminationAgainstMigrants.aspx

Brewer, M. B. (1999). Intergroup Discrimination: Ingroup Love or Outgroup Hate? *The Cambridge Handbook of the Psychology of Prejudice*, 90–110. https://doi.org/10.1017/9781316161579.005

Center for International Migration and Integration (CIMI), the Department of Policy Planning at the Population and Immigration Authority (PIBA) and Hercowitz-Amir, A. (2018). Labor Migration to Israel. Tel Aviv, Israel. Cook, S. (1984). Cooperative interaction in multiethnic context. In N. Miller & M. Brewer (Eds.), *Group in contact: The psychology of desegregation* (pp. 156–86). New York: Academic Press.

Daly, M., Delaney, L., Doran, P. P., & MacLachlan, M. (2011). The role of awakening cortisol and psychological distress in diurnal variations in affect: *A day reconstruction study*. *Emotion*, *11*(3), 524–532. doi:10.1037/a0022590

Drapeau, A., Marchand, A., & Beaulieu-Prevost, D. (2012). Epidemiology of psychological distress. *Mental Illnesses – Understanding, Prediction and Control*. doi:10.5772/30872

Edmondson, A. C., Roberto, M. & Watkins, M. (2001). Negotiating asymmetry: A model of top management team effectiveness. *Paper presented at Academy of Management Meetings*, August, in Washington, DC.

Gebreyesus, T., Sultan, Z., Ghebrezghiabher, H. M., Tol, W. A., Winch, P. J., Davidovitch, N., & Surkan, P. J. (2018). Life on the margins: The experiences of sexual violence and exploitation among Eritrean asylum-seeking women in Israel. *BMC Women's Health*, *18*(1). doi:10.1186/s12905-018-0624-y

Graham, J. L., Kim, D. K., Lin, C., & Robinson, M. (1988). Buyer–seller negotiations around the pacific rim: Differences in fundamental exchange processes. *Journal of Consumer Research, 15*, 48–54.

Griffin, J., & Soskolne, V. (2003). Psychological distress among Thai migrant workers in Israel. *Social Science & Medicine*, 57, 769–774.

Holumyong, C., Ford, K., Sajjanand, S., & Chamratrithirong, A. (2018). The Access to Antenatal and Postpartum Care Services of Migrant Workers in the Greater Mekong Subregion: The Role of Acculturative Stress and Social Support. *Journal of Pregnancy*, 2018..

Huguet, J. W., & Chamratrithirong, A. (2011). *Thailand Migration Report: Migration for development in Thailand: Overview and tools for policymakers.* Bangkok, Thailand: International Organization for Migration, Thailand Office Organization for Migration, Thailand Office.

Human Rights Watch. (2013). *A Raw Deal: Abuses of Thai Workers in Israel's Agricultural Sector* (Rep.). United States of America: Human Rights Watch.

Israel Ministry of Foreign Affairs (n.d.). Kibbutz and Moshav. https://mfa.gov.il/MFA/AboutIsrael/Maps/Pages/Kibbutz-and-Moshav.aspx

Kaminer, M. (2019). At the zero degree/Below the minimum: Wage as sign in Israel's split labor market. *Dialectical Anthropology*, *43*(3), 317–332.

Kashti, O. (2018). Sudden adult death syndrome takes toll on Thai workers in Israel. https://www.haaretz.com/israel-news/.premium-sudden-adult-death-syndrome-hits-thai-workers-in-israel-1.5453502

Lee, H., Ahn, H., Miller, A., Park, C. G., & Kim, S. J. (2012). Acculturative Stress, Work-related Psychosocial Factors and Depression in Korean-Chinese Migrant Workers in Korea. *Occup. Health* 2012, 54, 206–214.

Lovelace, K., Shapiro, D., & Weingart, L. R. (2001). Maximizing cross-functional new product team's innovativeness and constraint adherence: A conflict communications perspective. Academy of Management Journal, *44*, 779–793.

Lurie, I. (2009). Psychiatric care in restricted conditions for work migrants, refugees and asylum seekers: experience of the open clinic for work migrants and refugees, Israel 2006. *Israel Journal of Psychiatry and Related Sciences, 46*(3), 172–181.

Mucci, N., Traversini, V., Giorgi, G., Tommasi, E., Sio, S. D., & Arcangeli, G. (2019). *Migrant Workers and Psychological Health: A Systematic Review. Sustainability*, *12*(1), 120.

Rajiman, R. (2011). Foreigners and Outsiders: Exclusionist attitudes towards labour migrants in Israel. *International Migration, 51*(1), 136–151. doi:10.1111/j.1468-2435.2011.00719.x

Ridner, S. H. (2004). Psychological distress: Concept analysis. *Journal of Advanced Nursing*, *45*(5), 536–545. doi:10.1046/j.1365-2648.2003.02938.x

Ringel, S., Ronell, N., & Getahune, S. (2005). Factors in the integration process of adolescent immigrants. *International Social Work*, *48*(1), 63–76. doi:10.1177/0020872805048709

Rusiecki, J. A., Beane Freeman, L. E., Bonner, M. R., Alexander, M., Chen, L., Andreotti, G., Kamel, F., & Baccarelli, A. (2016). High pesticide exposure events and DNA methylation among pesticide applicators in the agricultural health study. *Environmental and Molecular Mutagenesis*, *58*(1), 19–29. https://doi.org/10.1002/em.22067

Seltenreich, Y. (2004). Jewish or Arab Hired Workers? Inner Tensions in a Jewish Settlement in Pre-state Israel. *International Review of Social History*, *49*(2), 225–247.

doi:10.1017/s0020859004001506

Shauer, N., & Matan, K. (2014). Below the minimum – violation of wage laws in the employment of migrant farmworkers. Tel Aviv: Kav LaOved tinyurl.com/below-min-heb.

Thai labourers in Israel tell of harrowing conditions. (2018). https://www.bbc.com/news/av/world-middle-east-46311922/thai-labourers-in-israel-tell-of-harrowing-conditions

Triandis, H. C., McCusker, C., & Hui, C. H. (1990). Multimethod probes of individualism and collectivism. *Journal of Personality and Social Psychology, 59*, 1006–1020.

Tse, D. K., Francis, J., & Walls, J. (1994). Cultural differences in conducting intra- and intercultural negotiations: A Sino Canadian comparison. *Journal of International Business Studies, 24*, 537–555.

Yi-Feng, C., & Tjosvold, D. (2007). Cooperative conflict management: An approach to strengthen relationships between foreign managers and Chinese employees. *Asia Pacific Journal of Human Resources, 45*(3), 271–294. doi: 10.1177/1038411107082274.

Zhong, B. L., Liu, T. B., Chiu, H. F., Chan, S. S., Hu, C. Y., Hu, X. F., Xiang, Y. T., & Caine, E. D. (2013). Prevalence of psychological symptoms in contemporary Chinese rural-to-urban migrant workers: an exploratory meta-analysis of observational studies using the SCL-90-R. *Social psychiatry and psychiatric epidemiology, 48*(10), 1569–1581. https://doi.org/10.1007/s00127-013-0672-4

THE "UNSEEN" IN MIGRATION AND REMITTANCES: THE CASE OF SOUTH ASIAN MIGRANT WORKERS IN CAMERON HIGHLANDS, MALAYSIA[1]

Prakash Arunasalam and Thirunaukarasu Subramaniam

Introduction

In migration research involving migrant workers, the often "seen" aspect is the determinants of migration, migration processes and patterns, income earned and the remittances made. However, there is another dimension of migration and remittances that often receive less or no attention which is the "unseen" aspect. The "unseen" aspect is related more to the sacrifices made by migrant workers which underlies the determinants of migration, migration processes and pattern, income earned and remittances made. The sacrifices made by the migrant workers often receive less attention in previous studies despite the sacrifices made by them are instrumental to the social and economic well-being of the migrant workers and their families. They are willing to make various sacrifices because their goal is to maximize the remittances made to their home countries. The income earned by migrant workers has two main uses namely for expenditure and savings purposes. The savings made while working abroad are the money which is sent by South Asian migrant workers to their home countries as remittances. This implies that the more the sacrifices are made, the higher will be the amount saved, therefore the higher will be the remittances.

This study as such attempts to identify those dimensions of sacrifices made by the migrant workers using an in-depth face-to-face interviews as the main method of data collection. This study intends to uncover and refine those sacrifices made by migrant workers in a more detailed and systematic manner by looking at various dimensions of sacrifices which was captured loosely in previous studies (see Tonder & Soontiens, 2014; Schwenken & Eberhardt, 2008; Garabiles et al., 2017; Appleyard, 2001 among others). The second section of this article will focus on literature review, the third section covers the conceptual framework used in this study, the fourth section discusses the research methodology employed, the fifth section focuses on research findings and discussion while the final section concludes.

This study focuses on migrant workers from South Asia who are employed in the agriculture and plantation sectors in Cameron Highlands, Malaysia which is known for its agrotourism. South Asian migrant workers in this study hail from two South Asian countries namely Bangladesh and India. Ravenstein's (1885) Laws of Migration proposed that economic factors are the main cause of migration. Undoubtedly, economic factors remain as the main cause that motivated migration, however the underlying aspect of the economic motivation

---

[1] This paper was presented in The Migration Conference 2020 held as Online Conference at Tetovo, North Macedonia from 8-11 September 2020 (Session 10A: Remittances and Development).

would be the sacrifices made by the migrant workers working abroad.

Literature review

Sacrifices made by migrant workers are less emphasized in previous studies, except for the study done by Subramaniam, et al. (2011). The authors focused on two dimensions of sacrifice namely "sacrifice of life comfort" and "sacrifice of being separated from the loved ones". The migrants workers are willing to make those sacrifices as they are more concerned in ensuring that remittances are made on a regular basis. Also, the sacrifices made implies that the greater the sacrifice, the higher is the amount of remittances sent to their home countries and this in turn enables the family members left behind to have better access to health care, education and improved standard of living.

Tonder and Soontiens (2014) in their research highlighted that migrant worker have to sacrifice a lot of the things that they were used to do and simultaneously take on different roles and different activities. In another study, Schwenken and Eberhardt (2008) distinguished women worker going abroad to send remittances to her family is regarded as a good mother who cares for her children by sacrificing herself or she may even consider herself as a "better mother" than those who stay and do not support towards their children education and health care through remittances. Philam Life BalikBayani Program (n.d) highlighted that Filipinos working overseas are normally away from their families for years before returning home and they miss out on a lot of important family moments and this is regarded as a huge sacrifice, which they are willing to do because they want to provide a good life for their families. Likewise, Garabiles et al., (2017) view migration of Overseas Foreign Workers (OFWs) in the Philippines as a sacrifice that women make to serve their families and migration as impermanent and the sacrifice of being separate is transient and finite.

Appleyard (2001) contended that while labour migration gave access to earnings and empowerment in economic, social and family contexts, the gains too often came with a cost in the form of sacrificed family life, women mistreated through physical or verbal abuses, restricted in their freedom of movement or in contacts with family, and not paid agreed salaries. The decision to migrate may emanate from an autonomous decision to sacrifice short-term individual wellbeing (e.g. being separated from your loved ones; the alienating experiences of living in a strange society) from the (instrumental) wish to improve the long-term wellbeing of the family (after return or family reunion) (see de Haas, 2014).

Hall et al. (2019) succinctly mentioned that remittances sent home are the embodiment of sacrifice by migrant workers. Even though they pointed out that appreciation comes from the family members, the author observed that being separate from one's family as a form of sacrifice. Xiao (2014) likewise seems to agree that money that was earned from the migration embodied a parents' hardship and sacrifice. Loganathan et al. (2019) mentioned that migrant worker's tendency to prioritise remittance of income over all else, including healthcare and food and the salary is not touched because they want to send the money back for their children's education. ILO (2004; 2010) highlighted that many migrate, often knowing it will involve great personal sacrifice, working in difficult conditions, and tend to spend very little of their earnings so that they can send most of their savings home to their families.

On the other hand, sacrifice made by children of migrant workers were highlighted by Xiao (2014) and the children acknowledge the significance of their parents' migration as well as learn to appreciate the sacrifices they were making to provide for them. Even though the author stressed that parents' money making as sacrifice and love, the missing dimension in parent-child relations emerges including parents' better care, stricter supervision and education. Another dimension remains untouched is when migrants sacrifice themselves in occupations for which they are over-qualified for example, a large number of skilled women migrant workers enter domestic work (see ILO, 2010).

Conceptual framework

An investigation of the conceptual framework employed in previous studies found that most previous studies only emphasized on push and pull factors, migration processes as well as the effects of migration (see Nurhazani & Nur Syafiqah, 2011; Bodvarsson & Van den Berg, 2013; Timmerman, Heyse & Van Mol, 2010; Nijkamp & Voskuilen, 1996). The conceptual framework developed in this study includes the drivers and the motivations that encourage economic migrants from South Asia to work in the agriculture and the plantation sector in Malaysia. The underlying motivation of this article is to probe the "unseen" aspect of migration and remittances. Maximization of the "unseen" sacrifices leads to maximum remittances. Every single remittances made by the migrant workers hide a story of sacrifice underneath it. Those sacrifices will be traced from various dimensions as depicted in Figure 1.

Figure 1. Conceptual framework – the "unseen".

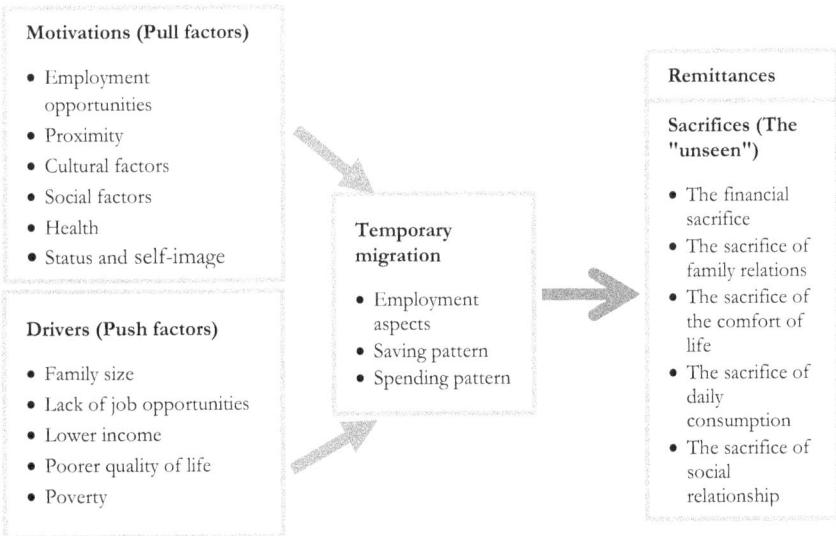

Research methodology

(a) Data collection

This study uses in-depth face-to-face interview method to collect qualitative data in order to uncover the "unseen" aspect in migration and remittances. The in-depth face-to-face interviews used in this study provide us with valuable information regarding the sacrifices made which could be difficult to be obtained through quantitative processes. For that purpose, 11 informants comprising migrant workers that came from Bangladesh (five) and India (six) were taken as informants. Previous studies generally do not emphasize on the sacrifices made by migrant workers working in the host countries. The questions posed to the selected informants are based on five aspects of sacrifices namely (a) aspects related to financial sacrifice; (b) aspects related to family relations sacrifice; (c) aspects related to sacrificing the comfort of life; (d) aspects related to daily use sacrifice; and (e) aspects related to social relations sacrifice.

To fullfill the consent and ethical approval requirement, verbal informed consent was obtained from all the participants included in the study. All procedures performed in studies involving human participants were in accordance with the ethical standards of the 1964 Helsinki Declaration and its later amendments or comparable ethical standards.

(b) Data analysis

Data obtained through qualitative methods were analyzed using a thematic analysis approach. Braun and Clarke (2006) and Braun et al. (2019) have used thematic analysis approach and this approach is suitable for qualitative data not only in the field of psychology but also beyond the field of psychology. The questions posed to the selected informants are questions that focus on the five aspects of sacrifices mentioned above.

Research findings and discussion

(a) Sociodemographic characteristics of migrants and general working conditions

The first part of this section uncovers the socio-demographic characteristics of migrant workers employed in the agricultural and plantation sector in Cameron Highlands, Malaysia (see Table 1). It is obvious that Indian migrant workers are mainly in their prime working age. Most of the informants (seven out of 11) were unemployed and the main reason to migrate is due to poverty (ten out of 11). Several aspects characterizes the working conditions of migrant workers in Cameron Highlands namely long working hours, lower wage and absence of health benefits as the employment in agriculture and plantation sector in Malaysia is often labelled as 3D sector (dirty, dangerous and difficult).

Table 1. Socio-demographic characteristics of South Asian migrants.

Informant	Age	Country of origin	Nearest city	Marital status	Number of children	Number of dependents (including wife, children, parents and others)	Last employment in the country of origin	Main reason to migrate
I1	46	Bangladesh	Dhaka	Married	2	3	Unemployed	Poverty
I2	32	India	Kanpur, Uttar Pradesh	Married	6	7	Unemployed	Poverty
I3	30	India	Madurai, Tamilnadu	Single	-	4	Unemployed	Poverty
I4	25	India	Chennai, Tamilnadu	Single	-	7	Driver. Also worked in Dubai.	Unsatisfactory work condition in Dubai.
I5	26	India	Uttar Pradesh	Single	-	2	Unemployed	Poverty
I6	30	India	Thanjayur, Tamilnadu	Married	2	5	Temporary employment	Poverty
I7	48	Bangladesh	Dhaka	Married	NA	NA	Unemployed	Poverty
I8	46	Bangladesh	Sylhet	Married	1	30	Rice Farmer	Poverty
I9	52	Bangladesh	Natore	Single	-	2	Unemployed	Poverty
I10	59	Bangladesh	Dhaka	Married	2	4	Unemployed	Poverty
I11	28	India	Kanpur, Uttar Pradesh	Single	-	5	Furniture Company	Poverty

Note: NA – Not available.

(b) Sacrifices

The second part of this section discusses various aspects of the sacrifices made by South Asian migrant workers who are working in the agriculture and plantation sectors in Cameron Highlands. Five main aspects of sacrifices that are considered in this study are: (i) financial sacrifice; (ii) family relations sacrifice; (iii) sacrifice of the comfort of life; (iv) daily use sacrifice; and (v) social relationship sacrifice.

(i) The financial sacrifice – debt and remittances

The first aspect of sacrifice focused in this study is the financial sacrifice made by the South Asian migrant workers who are working in the agriculture and plantation sectors in Cameron Highlands. The financial sacrifices had to be made as they had to tighten their belts while living in Malaysia as they need to ensure that the debt incurred to enable them to come and work in Malaysia is settled promptly. The following verbatim reveals the extent of the debt burden faced by South Asian migrant workers.

I7 who hails from Bangladesh said;

"The amount of money I send to Bangladesh is Taka 4000.00 every month. The amount borrowed was Taka 80,000.00 and I only brought Taka 2000.00. Taka 2000.00 which I brought was sufficient as I came with a "Calling Visa". I am not scared because my boss is here. He paid for everything." (I7, 48 years old, Bangladesh)

I6 from India said;

"The amount of money that I send to India each month is between MYR700–MYR900. Before coming to Cameron Highlands, I borrowed from friends, relatives and money lenders a total sum of Rps60,000.00. I had to borrow money because there are no savings. My income here is not enough for food and to send money to my home country." (I6, 30 years old, India)

I4 said;

"I borrowed Rps50,000.00. A total of Rps45,000.00 for agent fees and Rps5000.00 for my friend. I came here with Rps2000.00 because I was called by my present employer. Every month I will send Rps4,500.00 to my family through Western Union. My income is not enough. I used to work in Dubai, and my paycheck was great. I had to go back to India and come to Malaysia because I do not like Dubai. There are no friends and I disliked it." (I4, 25 years old, India)

Another informant, I5 who is also from India related how he has to sacrifice to increase his remittances as follows;

"The amount to be sent to my home country is MYR1000.00 a month. I borrowed Rps120,000.00. A total of Rps60,000.00 was payment for agent fees and the remainder was for visa fees and plane tickets. I have to cut down my expenses to increase my savings and remittances." (I5, 26 years old, India)

From the verbatim, it is evident that remittances need to be made on a regular basis as it enables those left in the home country to settle the debt taken to cover the cost of migration. In terms of remittances, the following verbatim reveals the amount remitted on a regular basis either monthly or quarterly. According to I4 from India;

"The amount of money I sent to India is not the same every month, sometimes more and sometimes less than MYR1000.00. This is because I would borrow money from my employer for any event or celebration in my home country. I just borrowed MYR4000.00 from my employer in April because my sister was getting married. After that, my employer will deduct from my salary." (I4, 25 years old, India)

I4 contended further by saying;

"The quality of life here and in my home country is almost the same. In my home country, I didn't have enough money. My life is rather difficult here because I have to cut down my expenses to settle the debt. The drop in the exchange rate makes the situation even worse and makes me feel the same." (I4, 25 years old, India)

The financial sacrifices made by the migrant workers interviewed in this study who are working in Cameron Highlands, Malaysia, have one aim that is to send as much money as possible to their home countries. Firstly, they want to ensure that the debt taken to come to Malaysia is settled the soonest. Secondly, their desire is to save as much money as possible to ensure that their family members will enjoy a better standard of living in their home countries. As such, this requires a financial sacrifice to be made by those migrant workers as they have to cut down on all the unnecessary expenses (as mentioned by I4 and I5) and even many life pleasures such as going for movie or even going for tours.

(ii) The sacrifice of family relations – separation with the beloved

The sacrifice of family relationship is the greatest sacrifice made by the migrants for the purpose of earning a living. For married informants, they have to sacrifice family relations as they have to leave their wives and their children. For unmarried informants, they have to sacrifice family relations by leaving their parents or close relatives and friends behind. The following verbatim reveals this aspect of sacrifice.

Several informants expressed their sadness over separation with the loved ones as follow:

"I have a wife, two children, a mother, and a father. I feel sad because I'm separated from my family. I'll call them every day. The only occasion I was unable to attend, was my father's retirement ceremony and prayer for a new house." (I6, 30 years old, India)

"I have a wife and a child. When I came to Malaysia, my wife was pregnant. I haven't had the chance to see my son's face. I feel sad and want to see the face of my son." (I8, 46 years old, Bangladesh)

"I have a wife, a son, a daughter and a mother. My father had passed away. After getting the news of my father's death, I tried to return to Bangladesh, but I had no money. My heart is sad." (I10, 59 years old, Bangladesh)

I9 and I4 shared how they were not able to participate in important family functions such as marriage in the following verbatims;

"My mother and sister always call me. My sister is getting married, I could not attend the ceremony. I do not have money to go back." (I9, 52 years old, Bangladesh)

"My family members are my mother, father, and sister. I miss them because I haven't seen them for years. I always call them, at least once a day. I am very sad as I was not able to attend the wedding of my sister. I was only able to send MYR4000.00." (I4, 25 years old, India)

According to I3,

"I have a mother, a younger brother, and a younger sister. I love them and I miss them." (I3, 30 years old, India)

The sacrifice of family relations is the biggest sacrifice made by migrant workers as they made the decision to work in Malaysia. Married informants left their wives and children in their home countries. This is an enormous sacrifice made by the migrant workers from South Asia. For the unmarried ones, they sacrifice family relations too because they have to leave their mothers, fathers or siblings in their home countries. Some of the informants have never returned home while working abroad. Even more emotionally moving is when they are unable to attend important ceremonies such as wedding functions of their siblings or the death of their parents or close family members, relatives or friends. Their sacrifices are so significant that most of these ceremonies such as weddings are held using the money earned and remitted by these migrant workers, yet they are unable to attend those ceremonies especially wedding events of their close family members which are suppose to be a joyous occasion of gathering.

(iii) The sacrifice of the comfort of life

The third aspect of sacrifice that is examined in this study will divulge the sacrifices related to the comfort of life. Normally, when one leaves the home country, they will be willing to let go various comforts of life they had earlier. This aspect of sacrifice will probe whether the presence of facilities in the host country is better than that of the country of origin. Informant I11 who compared the comfort of accommodation in Cameron Highlands with that of his home country in Bangladesh said;

"Living in my home country is more comfortable and organized. Here the room which I live in is very narrow and small. Nonetheless, the room, the toilet and showers is in good condition." (I11, 28 years old, Bangladesh)

I2 who hails from India, agreed with the opinion of I11 and stated that;

"The quality of life is better in India. Living in Malaysia is just okay."

(I2, 32 years old , India)

According to another informant, I3, who also came from India:

"Living in my home country is very comfortable and good. Here, the room in which I live is very narrow and small. This small space has to be shared with many people." (I3, 30 years old, India)

Generally the informants agree that lives in their home countries is better and they would potentially have made more sacrifices of comfort of life in the host country. Often a small room is shared by many in order to minimise the cost of rental in the event that the employer fails to provide accomodation. This causes them to live in cramped spaces (see Wahab, 2020), thus sacrificing their comfort of life.

(iv) The sacrifice of daily consumption – clothing and food

The sacrifice of daily consumption include various purchases that have to be sacrificed such as purchasing clothes, food, cigarettes and other needs and wants to tighten their belts in order to ensure that more money saved by South Asian migrant workers who are working in Cameron Highlands. The main daily consumption involves purchase of clothing and food intake. The following verbatim reveals various narrative related to this aspect of sacrifice.

"I buy things like clothes only when I desperately need it. At first, I just wanted to stifle the desire to buy clothes because I need to send money to my family. But since I was in need of clothes, I had to buy it." (I10, 59 years old, Bangladesh)

"In my opinion, I have to sacrifice everyday items such as clothes. In my country, I often buy clothes because they are cheap. It is expensive here. I am only able to buy at the bundle store." (I3, 30 years old, India)

There are also informants who highlighted how they missed the food cooked by their family members in the country of origin. I6 who hails from India said;

"I really missed the food my family cooks, because I cook nonchalantly. I cook only to fill my stomach. In India, spices are grounded but here everything is sold in packages. Taste is different. In my home country, my mother and my wife would be cooking. I cook on my own here because the food sold in restaurant is expensive and I need to save money." (I6, 30 years old, India)

According to another informant, I4 who is also from India;

"I miss my favorite food which is my mother's cuisine cooked with love. My mother would grind chillies until smooth for fish and chicken curry. She would choose the right chillies and serve me with love. Unlike in the shop downstairs (the restaurant next to the workplace) sells mainly Indonesian cuisine such as soup. The chicken curry is runny. It doesn't taste like curry. Our own cooking taste somewhat like those sold at the restaurant. I have eaten food prepared by my mother for more than 20 years which has made me dislike other dishes."

He added further by saying;

"Sometimes the income I received is insufficient to buy the things I want, just enough to buy the things I need. As such I need to cut my expenses."

(I4, 25 years old, India)

I1 too felt the same as I6 and I4. He said;

"I cook myself. It is not delicious. I miss my family's cooking. I do not sacrifice everyday stuff because I brought what I need. If I run out of things, I will buy it here. Everything is the same. I will buy if I need it this month, and the following month, I will send more money."

(I4, 46 years old, Bangladesh)

Although sacrifices of daily consumption are made by South Asian migrant workers, their sacrifices are more focused on the use of clothes and food. Most of them will only buy items such as clothing when it is absolutely necessary. As

India and Bangladesh are the leading countries for textile exports, the price of clothes is much lower compared to the price in Malaysia and as such this may hinder them from buying clothes unless they are badly in need. Sacrifice in terms of food consumption is more focused towards cutting expenses on food purchase at restaurants which is less appealing compared to the food consumed in their home countries. Often food bought from restaurant is found to be less tasty by these migrant workers and they tend to cook for themselves. The sacrifice of daily consumption either in food concsumption or purchase of clothing ensures that the maximum amount of money is remitted to their home countries.

(v) The sacrifice of social relations

The final aspect of sacrifice investigated in this study is the sacrifice of social relations. The sacrifice of social relations occurs when an individual moves from one place to another, which causes social relations especially with friends in their home countries to become increasingly distanced. The South Asian migrant workers often reminisced their relationship with friends in their home country as can be seen from the following verbatim. I9, I4 and I8 recalled their social relations in the country of origin as follow;

"I used to play football with my friends in my village."

(I9, 52 years old, Bangladesh)

"I have an Indian friend from the same village who lived here for 3 years. He returned in 2015. I was very sad. Normally, during my free time in India, I bathed in the river and caught fish." (I4, 25 years old, India)

"I missed my friends in my hometown. We would play whatever we want because we do not have any other work to do." (I8, 46 years old, Bangladesh(

It is interesting to note how I6 relayed his opinion on the sacrifice of social relations made by saying that the separation is meant to be temporary.

"I normally play football with my friends when I was in India. At present, I am separated from my friends in India and this separation is only temporary as I have to work abroad." (I6, 30 years old, India)

Generally, several informants interviewed in this study felt that they have sacrificed social relations with friends in their home countries. In Malaysia, social activities such as playing football or other games have become very limited as they have to devote more time to work. Any opportunities that they have are used wisely to generate as much income as possible as this is the main motive for them to come to Malaysia. In addition, the debt taken serves as an incentive for them to sacrifice their social activities in order to ensure that more income generated and more money remitted.

(c) Policy implications

As policy implication, some recommendations can be offered. First, this study has highlighted various aspects of sacrifices made by migrant workers from South Asia as the migration undertaken involves high costs. High migration costs incurred due to the presence of various elements of fraud and agent monopolies. Hence, the need to maximize returns from migration arises because the sacrifices made by migrant workers are overwhelming. The need to reduce migration costs has been widely publicized, including in the UN Secretary General's Eight-Point Agenda, presented at the UN General Assembly High Level Dialogue on Migration and Development (see United Nations, 2013). In the past, the G-to-G (government-to-government) mechanism implemented by Bangladesh with the Malaysian government through a Memorandum of Understanding (MOU) between the two countries for the recruitment of Bangladeshi workers signed on 26 November 2012 establishing a recruitment system the state-managed recruitment system successfully reduced the migration cost. The G-to-G mechanism as such need to be revived. According to Piyasiri (2016),

"...roughly (it is) estimate(d) that the cost of migration has been reduced from MYR12,000 (approximately $3,300) to about MYR1,300 ($356) through the G-to-G mechanism."

The reduction in migration costs is important because it has to match the huge sacrifices made by migrant workers serving in other countries so that maximum returns can be obtained from the sacrifices made by all parties involved in the migration process including migrants and their immediate family members. Although the G-to-G mechanism was terminated in 2016 due to the existence of monopolies by syndicates spearheaded by the Malaysian companies (NST Online, 2018), the program should be revived by eliminating the involvement of vested interests.

Second, since the sacrifices made by migrant workers can have various impacts such as psychological, emotional, social and financial, the acceptance and appreciation given by the people in the host country can help improve the well-being of migrant workers. Psychological, emotional, social and financial impacts can lead to negative outcomes among migrant workers. In the period 2008/09 to 2014/15, the highest reported deaths due to suicide among Nepalese migrant workers were in Malaysia (144 cases) compared to other countries such as Saudi Arabia (60 cases), Qatar (54 cases), United Arab Emirates (26 cases), Kuwait (18 cases), Oman (4 cases) and Bahrain (3 cases) (see Government of Nepal, 2016). As such, awareness need to be built among the local community about the rights and contributions of migrant workers to the economy of the host country so that appreciation can be increased. Singapore, for example, celebrated migrant workers on November 26, 2017 with the theme "Caring for our Foreign Workers, Appreciation Dinner for our Partners" organized by the Ministry of Manpower Singapore. This is in line with the International Migrants Day 2012 launched by the ILO (see ILO, 2016) as follows:

"On International Migrants Day 2012, the ILO launched the Migration

167

Works campaign to promote a positive image of migrants that more closely corresponds to their actual contribution and highlights the benefits that migration can bring, both to Malaysia and countries of origin. Working in close partnership with other UN agencies and civil society organizations to develop the strategy, a theme of mutual benefit was chosen for the campaign: 'Working Together, Walking Together: Migration Works for Us All."

The sacrifices made by South Asian migrant workers by being overwhelmed with grief as a result of separation can cause their lives to be stressful and affect their emotional, psychological and mental well-being. Malaysian authorities therefore need to ensure that the personal welfare and mental health of migrant workers are given sufficient attention by recognizing and appreciating their contribution to the Malaysian economy.

Conclusion

Contribution of this study can be seen from the categorization of various sacrifices into five dimensions which can facilitate our understanding on migration and remittances discourses as this phenomenon was loosely captured in previous researches (see Tonder & Soontiens, 2014 ; Schwenken & Eberhardt, 2008 ; Garabiles et al., 2017; Appleyard, 2001; de Haas, 2014 ; Hall et al., 2019; Loganathan et al., 2019 ; Xiao, 2014). Five main dimensions of sacrifices made by South Asian migrant workers working in the agriculture and plantation sectors in Malaysia include financial sacrifice, sacrifice of family relationship, sacrifice of daily consumption, sacrifice of the comfort of life and sacrifice of social relations. These sacrifices are made to ensure that their family members in home country will have a better life in the future than their present condition. As almost all informants in this study came from families with lower socio-economic status, they are willing to sacrifice various aspects of their lives to ensure that their family members will be able to experience a better life through the sacrifices made. Most of the South Asian migrant workers remit their money for various purposes such as settling debt incurred during migration, wedding needs of family members, educational needs of their children or for health care expenses of their elderly family members. The money remitted to the home country is the motivating factor for these migrant workers to continue to make sacrifices as they embrace the fact that the sacrifices made are only temporary in nature. The sacrifices made by these migrant workers often goes "unseen". To reiterate, this study has collected qualitative data and proved that sacrifice is an important aspect that underlies migration (embedding sacrifice in migration) and therefore suggests the incorporation of various elements of sacrifice in migration research and proposes the sacrifice perspective to migration which can form the foundation to "sacrifice theory of migration".

References

Appleyard, R. T. (2001). *The Human Rights of Migrants*. Geneva: IOM/OIM.

Bodvarsson, O. B., & Van den Berg, H. (2013). *The Economics of Immigration*. New York: Springer.

Braun, V., & Clarke, V. (2006). Using thematic analysis in psychology. *Qualitative Research in Psychology*, 3, 77–101.

Braun V., Clarke V., Hayfield N., & Terry G. (2019). Thematic Analysis. In P. Liamputtong (Ed.), *Handbook of Research Methods in Health Social Sciences*. Singapore : Springer.

de Haas, H. (2014). Migration Theory Quo Vadis? *IMI Working Papers Series*. No. 100. DEMIG project paper 24.

Garabiles, M. R., Ofreneo, M. A. P., & Hall B. J. (2017). Towards a model of resilience for transnational families of Filipina domestic workers. *PLoS ONE 12*(8).

Government of Nepal (2016). *Labour Migration for Employment. A Status Report for Nepal: 2014/2015*. Kathmandu: Ministry of Labour and Employment.

Hall, B. J., Garabiles. M. R. & Latkin, C. A.(2019). Work life, relationship, and policy determinants of health and well-being among Filipino domestic Workers in China: a qualitative study. *BMC Public Health, 19* (229), 1–14.

ILO (2016). *Review of labour migration policy in Malaysia*. Geneva: ILO.

ILO (2014). *Towards a fair deal for migrant workers in the global economy Sixth item on the agenda*. International Labour Conference, 92nd Session, 2004 Report VI. Geneva: ILO.

ILO (2010). *International labour migration: A rights-based approach*. Geneva: ILO.

Loganathan, T., Rui, D., Ng, C. W., & Pocock, N. S. (2019). Breaking down the barriers: Understanding migrant workers' access to healthcare in Malaysia. *PLoS ONE, 14*(7), 1–24.

Nijkamp, P., & Voskuilen, M. (1996), International migration: a comprehensive framework for a survey of the literature. *European Spatial Research and Policy, 3*(1), 5–28.

NST Online (2018). *Daily exposes how previous administration created `monopoly' in recruitment of Bangladeshi workers*. https://www.nst.com.my/news/nation/2018/11/427302/daily-exposes-how-previous-administration-created-monopoly-recruitment

Nurhazani, M.S. & Nur Syafiqah, A.G. (2016). A Conceptual Framework on Issues and Challenges of International Migrant Labors in Malaysia. *Australian Journal of Basic and Applied Sciences, 10*(11), 16–23.

Philam Life BalikBayani Program (n.d.). *Make Sacrifices Count*. https://www.philamlife.com/

Piyasiri, W. (2016). *Review of the government-to-government mechanism for the employment of Bangladeshi workers in the Malaysian plantation sector*. Geneva: ILO.

Ravenstein, E. G. (1885). The Laws of Migration. *Journal of the Statistical Society of London, 48*(2), 167–235.

Schwenken, H. & Eberhardt, P. (2008). Gender Knowledge in Economic Migration Theories and in Migration Practices 1. University of Kassel, GARNET Working Paper No: 58/08 August 2008.

Subramaniam, T., Mohd Ariff, M. R., & Arunasalam, P. (2011). Employment Aspects of Indian Foreign Workers in Manufacturing Sector in Malaysia. *Man and Society Journal*, 21, 76–96.

Timmerman, C., Heyse, P., & Van Mol, C. (2010). *Conceptual and theoretical framework*. Project Paper 1. Antwerp: University of Antwerp, Imagining Europe from the Outside (EUMAGINE).

Tonder, C. L. van & Soontiens, W. (2014). Migrant Acculturation and the Workplace. Procedia – Social and Behavioral Sciences, 143, 1041–1047.

United Nations (2013). High-level Dialogue on International Migration and Development. Making migration work: an eight-point agenda for action. Report of the Secretary-General (A/68/190), 3- 4 October, United Nations New York.

Wahab, A. (2020). *Migrant Workers and Covid-19 Outbreak in Malaysia*. IKMAS Working Paper 3/2020. Institute of Malaysian and International Studies (IKMAS), Universiti Kebangsaan Malaysia (National University of Malaysia).

Xiao, L. (2014). The Experiences Of Left-Behind Children In Rural China A Qualitative

Study. A thesis submitted for the degree of Doctor of Philosophy University of Bath, Department of Social and Policy Sciences.

www.ingramcontent.com/pod-product-compliance
Lightning Source LLC
Chambersburg PA
CBHW071103280326
41928CB00051B/2799